Martin Popoff

First published in Canada, 2018
Wymer Publishing
Bedford, England www.wymerpublishing.co.uk
Tel: 01234 326691
Wymer Publishing is a trading name of Wymer (UK) Ltd

This edition published 2020.

ISBN: 978-1-912782-31-4

A catalogue record for this book is available from the British Library.

Typesetting, layout and design by Eduardo Rodriguez.

Table Of Contents

Introduction

I remember first hearing Black Sabbath and loving it, though finding it a mess. This would have been about 1971 when I was eight, and that mess was the first album, a record that sounded old and not in a good way. Quickly it was onto *Paranoid* and me an' the buds were certifiable metalheads, with the most immediate headbang for pups that age being scary monster song "Iron Man," which also had a riff dumb enough for us to absorb.

The first Sabbath album I ever bought was *Vol 4*, and decades later, I realize how smart we were ignoring the guff about the two mellow tracks, realizing this was heavier than the debut, and about as heavy as *Paranoid*. This was also the heaviest band we knew, our older brothers' and older cousins' Zeppelin, Iron Butterfly, Steppenwolf and CCR (!) records paling in comparison. Significantly, Sabbath was our band, a band of a new generation of kids, and not the domain of our elders. No real reason, except for the fact that my friends and I were getting these albums first, and not them.

I recall that we loved that Oz looked our age, and that the other guys had these big handlebar moustaches, just like our favourite hockey players, Derek Sanderson and Rick MacLeish and maybe some of our favourite Sabres like Rene Robert, Rick Martin and Danny Gare (from Nelson, BC, just up the road from our hometown, Trail). I dunno… maybe none of them had them, but they would have invariably looked cooler if they had.

Anyway, *Vol 4* was the first to call my own, then *Master of Reality* blew our minds, although I don't think I had one to call my own for a while—this was one I had to borrow or hear on my friends' parents' stereos. *Sabbath Bloody Sabbath* I recall as almost too scary—we're talking mainly the album cover here—with the music sounding uneasy in a different way, not exactly always heavy, kind of druggy, a concept we didn't get at all, and sort of hot and hazy.

Sabotage was more of the same, and for some reason, we (the "we" I often lapse into is myself and metalhead-in-crime and best friend Forrest Toop) talked a buddy into buying it first. We must have had something else to spend our dollars on that day. Anyway, Geoff Cahoon came home with it and we thought Sabbath had made another weird record. It took us a while to get into it. "Supertzar" was classical, "Am I Going Insane" was comical and throughout there were mellow bits the guys were trying to hide on us (but oh, we found them out). Bear in mind we were only 12. Kiss' *Alive!* was more our speed (and yes, we were Kiss veterans by this point—*Hotter than Hell* was the first bought as an anticipated new release). But Sabbath? There was sort of this wall built between us and understanding.

Oddly, my favourite *Sabotage* memory is racing back home on my bike for lunch, hoping intensely as a 12-year-old metalhead in the '70s does, that the new issue of Circus magazine had arrived. It did, and it was red, and there on the cover was an egregiously cool shot of Oz in a brown jacket looking all Western. This was the best Circus cover ever, better than anything even a Kiss shot could conjure. Inside was a *Sabotage* feature, but groovier was the ad for the album, featuring a bunch of guys in suits perusing a train wreck, sorta 1940s or so. Turns out this had nothing to do with the album art and I was over the moon—my favourite ad ever.

Technical Ecstasy was initially a grave disappointment, but I soon grew to love it. The cover art mesmerized me and the music depressed me. *Never Say Die…* I fondly remember staring out our picture window waiting for my buddy who lived across the street to return from an orthodontist trip to our record buying mecca, Spokane, WA, two hours directly south of us in scary America. His instructions were to locate and buy me *Never Say Die* and The Saints' *Eternally Yours*, a simple mission, I thought. He was successful on both counts, and *Eternally Yours* was the slightly better album, a pleasant surprise because it improved on *(I'm) Stranded*. But *Never Say Die*? I don't remember being too pleased with it. In fact I recall struggling to hear what was going on on the record, through the noise of it. We were pretty sure it was heavier than the last one, but this would take a mathematical comparison to verify its status on our Byzantine heaviness scale (don't ask).

I do remember thoroughly digging the cover art, as well as the higher gloss put on US copies of albums versus our Canadian issues, along with the less angled way the plant folded and glued them together. Years later I still have my original copy and now it's signed by all four guys. I have a bunch of stuff signed by all of them, but this is my prized music collectible, simply because the way the autographs are arranged is nothing short of beautiful.

We'll save our sepia-toned reminiscing about Sabbath in the '80s and beyond for another time (and maybe a second book), but, as you can see, Sabbath had been getting absorbed into my circuitry for a long time, and here we are about to talk about it, in detail, albeit the '70s only.

As the more tuned-in of you might know, this book is an early-years version of my 2005 book *Black Sabbath - Doom Let Loose: An Illustrated History*. However, the period covered by *Sabotage!: Black Sabbath in the Seventies*, has been addressed with new vigor, with much reconsidering and rewriting done of what was in the original book and then a good 30%, 40% more material added from many more interviews.

But back to my methodology, in the spirit of an appreciation, what I've done is focus primarily on the music, as I've done with previous books, going record by record, song by song, touring touched upon as well. I suppose the main reason I do these books at all is to get a bunch of the known facts down in one place, along with my opinions—because I really, really want to convince you to buy Black Sabbath albums—so I can purge them from my trivia-cluttered head.

And in terms of my trademark if you will, the format you see here is one I've used in all my "biographies" thus far, and I see no reason to change it. I've always felt that what we can all experience together, and have experienced together, is the actual albums, less so the shows, even less so the makers of the music and their private lives. Additionally, I've always felt that a judicious analysis of the albums at hand, if done right, makes you want to revisit those records, hopefully with renewed appreciation given the things learned about them. You've spent this money, those records are sitting there. Why not get more use out of them, enjoy them more, and in the process, mathematically and quantifiably make yourself happier?

And what would make me happy right now is firing off a couple of lists… no reason, other than I love lists, and, like I said, I want to turn you onto all things Sabbatherian. We'll keep this simple and traditional; first, my 25 favourite Black Sabbath songs of all time. Ready, set… "Killing Yourself to Live," "A National Acrobat," "The Writ," "After Forever," "Spiral Architect," "Swinging the Chain," "Megalomania," "Hole in the Sky," "Sabbra Cadabra," "Symptom of the Universe," "Lord of This World," "Die Young," "Shock Waves," "Trashed," "Hot Line," "Hard Life to Love," "Back Street Kids," "The Thrill of It All," "Born to Lose," "Dirty Women," "Country Girl," "Into the Void," "Danger Zone," "Gypsy" and "Neon Knights."

And next, the Sabbath stones ranked best to not so hot: *Sabotage, Sabbath Bloody Sabbath, Master of Reality, Technical Ecstasy, Never Say Die, Heaven and Hell, Born Again, Mob Rules, Vol 4, Paranoid, The Devil You Know, The Eternal Idol, Dehumanizer, Black Sabbath, 13, Seventh Star, Tyr, Cross Purposes, Forbidden* and in the pooch spot, *Headless Cross*, even though for some reason that one did well in Germany.

That was fun… in any event, enjoy the book, hope you learn something, and thanks for letting me wistfully reminisce for a bit. Email me at martinp@inforamp.net if you wanna say hi. Next stop, Birmingham.

Martin Popoff, July 20, 2018

Prologue

Before Black Sabbath

"We're all heathens, thank God"

They were basically punks. And just like the iconic punks of (not even) a decade later, Black Sabbath, the four moptops that would become the first and greatest institution in heavy metal, had no clue as to the history they were about to make.

In the late '60s, aims were much simpler and blessed with an innocence. For the boys of Black Sabbath, the blues provided only a cursory blueprint while The Beatles and their backwater Liverpool experience offered the enticing taste of exhilarating escape. Almost as an afterthought, walls of power chords pushed forth in a wave of doom, creating out of nowhere, an opportunity to be scary.

So yes, a period of futzing about, of loitering, followed by a random, fateful sonic earth-shattering… each of these hapless happenstances would underscore the sorry fact that these four were, alas, punks railing against their soot-obscured lot, looking for a way out through volume and the crude delivery thereof.

Yet down more dire straits than the punks who at least had an arty, art school, socio-political sense of their own importance, incredibly, Black Sabbath would make record upon record before they could even look back with any sort of filmy recognition that yes, they had invented a new, doomy kind of music emphatically partitioned to the left hand path as heavy metal.

But as it began, this was just a case of four guys knocking about under the iron-dusky, smoke-cloaked skies of Birmingham's drab Satanic mills. In fact, Anthony Frank Iommi (yes, an Italian), William Thomas

Ward, John Michael Osbourne and Terence Michael Butler, were, for all intents and purposes, the same age, born within a year-and-a-half of each other from 1948 through '49, and each had hailed from the dreadfully conformist Birmingham suburb of Aston. Aston was the industrial seed of this very industrial town, Birmingham also possessing the distinction of having the daylights bombed out of it by the Germans in World War II.

In 1965, rock 'n' roll was goosing Britain in a big way. America had waned in its ascendance, and jolly ol' England was birthing bands like mushrooms. Birmingham participated unremarkably but competently, through The Move and The Moody Blues, even if in the early days, it was London that shined the way. The Midlands would, of course, bounce back with contributions from Traffic, Denny Laine, the well-traveled Clem Clempson, two locals by the names of John Bonham and Robert Plant, and then later on, Judas Priest, who, in more of a simplistic, primarily-coloured fashion, would assume Sabbath's heavy metal mantle in a more commercial time and space.

Working jobs after each, to a man, left school at the age of 15, music was nonetheless an immediate draw. Prophetically, ears tweaked at the louder ilk. "Oh definitely, yeah," muses Bill Ward, the man that would become Black Sabbath's drummer. "There are some major, major people that have to be credited. Ozzy brought this point up a long time ago. Dave Davies, those first chords in 'You Really Got Me,' to me that was just like, 'Man!' It was just so incredibly heavy. And it was a good point that Oz brought up there. Cream I think were incredibly influential. They were such an outstanding band, so they were influential in the sense of saying this road is okay to go down as well. The Who with 'Substitute.' Lyrically I thought The Who were amazing. I mean, The Who are just a fantastic band, but I love what was going on lyrically as well because they were going into places that were almost taboo. The Who didn't play safe at all; they didn't play nice. And just listening to the power of some of the blues singers from the United States—Howling Wolf, just listening to him growl, and Muddy Waters—those all had that kind of 'Yes!' feeling to them."

The Ozzy of which Bill speaks would find work at the car factory his mum worked in, as well as biding time in plumbing, tool-and-die, the mortuary, and famously, an abattoir, where, apocryphally covered in offal, he made extinct upwards of 250 animals a day. He lasted nary two months. Ozzy's family nestled somewhere between working class and dirt poor. Six children, two jobs, small row house… stories of going shoeless proliferated.

In 1966, a six-week stay at the local prison would punctuate his failure at yet another career, that of breaking and entering—it was in jail that Ozzy would get his signature O-Z-Z-Y tattoo across his fingers. "Grand larceny," mused Oz in 1976. "I was in Winston Green for two months. Once I stole a telly and I was balanced on top of this wall, one of them walls with glass along the top, and I fell off; this 24-inch telly was sitting on top of my chest and I was screaming, get me out, get me out!' I had nothing to do inside; You did about two hours work a day and the rest of the time you're locked in your cell. That's why I did my tattoos, with a sewing needle and a tin of grey polish."

"I used to do some crazy things," noted Ozzy, describing his prison experience five years before the above reminiscence. "I was quite yappy, really. When I was 18, I nicked some stuff, a load of woman's clothing. I was going around selling stockings in the pubs; 18 years old, they caught me and I went to prison. That's where I got all tattooed." Of his famous knee-straddled smiley face tattoos, Ozzy said they were "to cheer me up when I looked down. I did it all to pass the time in prison with a needle and India ink."

Asked in 1975, to describe his body paintings, Ozzy went with "just a few signs and symbols. One's a dagger, one's the number three. I did most of them. It's just something I did when I got bored or pissed off. It's something to pass the time. You get a tin of grey polish, not ink, and melt the polish and inject yourself with a fuckin' needle." Ozzy mentions another cool tattoo he saw in the slammer. "I've seen this one of a hunt with a fox's tale disappearing up a guy's ass and 500 horses chasing him. My grandfather had a tattoo that went from the top of his head and ended at the bottom of his foot. It was a snake going all around his head and around his body to his foot. Its head went around and down between his eyes." In the same chat, when asked what put him in jail, stealing women's clothes turned into "I did a few stupid things like busted a copper in his teeth and a few other things. I was like anybody else."

On a whole different career track, Terrence "Geezer" Butler would establish himself as a numbers guy (helpful in later years), working admin at an Aston factory, while guitarist Tony Iommi, from a comfortably middle class background (his family ran a general store), would become a sheet metal worker, soon to receive the crush and cut to two of his fingertips that would become the tantamount heavy metal handicap turned right 'round. With Bill Ward ensconced in the field of coal delivery, a soiled, smudged and sweated picture is painted of an impossibly, comically heavy metal apprenticeship—nay, enslavement. Is it any wonder that doom was born?

"Birmingham was very rough when we were growing up," recalls Tony. "There were gangs, and it was very hard to move away from that. Music was our way out but it was something that we really wanted to do as well. We were all in gangs but we didn't want to be in gangs—we wanted to be in bands."

"When I had my accident, all my hopes had gone down the drain," adds Tony, fleshing out the tale of his machine shop mishap, in which he severed off the tips of two fingers of his fretting hand. "I really wanted to play and I couldn't. I got really depressed for a period. Finally, somebody brought me a Django Reinhardt record. That really inspired me to start playing again. I went to several hospitals and they told me that they couldn't do anything. They told me that I should basically give up. I just couldn't accept that. I thought there has to be a way. I went home and I made myself a set of thimbles. I made them out of a Fairy Liquid bottle. I melted it down into a ball and then I sat there with a hot solvent on and made a hole in it so it would fit over my finger. I filed it down so it looked like the shape of the finger. I needed something to grip the strings, so I came up with leather to stick on there. It was very crude but it enabled me to be able to play. You couldn't trill the strings or anything but it was a start. I still use the same type of thing now."

"You see, I can't use right-handed instruments now," explained Tony to Steven Rosen in 1974, "because I snipped the ends of my fingers off, and on a Les Paul you've got to get right up to the end of the guitar on a reversed right-handed instrument to hit the strings. Not many people know about that (the accident). It happened years ago when I was doing electric welding. One day, I had to cut this sheet metal before I welded. Somebody else used to do it, but I had to do it this day because he didn't come into work. And it was a faulty switch or something. Thhhht! I pulled it out, and it just gripped the ends and pulled them off."

And so with respect to the guitar... "I had to start all over again, which was kind of a drag. I have to wear things now because the ends are so tender. It's helped me a little bit because now I use my little finger a lot. But I'd get annoyed and pick the guitar up and throw it and smash it. At first, I don't think people realized how hard it was to learn to play like that. It involved a lot of determination and a lot of hard work and practice. I've had to adopt a totally different way of playing because of these fingers. I mean it's much easier when the flesh is there as it should be. Instead of, say pulling a note, I have to sort of push it up to get a vibrato. These tips are a bit clumsy, and they slow me down and get in the way. I even have to wear leather on them to grip the strings. But it's just something I'll have to try and overcome."

"He was working in a place that had a guillotine," is Geezer's recollection of the tale. "He used to cut things, and his hand got stuck in the machine and the guillotine came down and chopped the ends of his two fingers off. The bones stick out. That's why he has to wear those thimbles. And that's why he got into Django Reinhardt. He used to play a lot of Django's stuff. After he had the accident with his fingers, he didn't think he'd be able to play, and then I think his mother bought these Django Reinhardt records. Of course, Django had only three fingers. It sort of inspired him and encouraged him to carry on."

"Birmingham had a massive hammering during World War II," continues Geezer, on the significance of environment as it pertains to the Black Sabbath story. "I was born in '49 so there were still a lot of bombed-out buildings around. The place on the corner where I grew up was completely demolished by bombs in the war. So where we lived, it was very, very working class. A lot of immigration there. My mom was from an Irish family; the people next door to me were from India and people across the road were from Africa, so it was very, very mixed racially and culturally. And it's a lot of street fighting, because of all the different ethnicities. There was a lot of white against black and Irish against English and all that kind of stuff, so it was quite rough in a way, and very working class.

Adds Bill, "All I can remember in my early youth—16, 17, 18 years old—is that I was generally pissed off. I just had an attitude. Music was the most important thing. We'd run home from wherever we had to work from, wherever we'd been that day, and get the drums and find enough petrol money or gas money and try to get to as many gigs as possible and play. I needed to have that escape. I love music, I love playing, and I'm so influenced by the British bands, from the Shadows onwards. From the Ventures in America—I love the Ventures. So playing was the outlet, playing was the way to go. I think it had a huge impact on Sabbath because of the lifestyle that we were leading."

"We come from a very proud yet very direct-speaking city or community, which was Aston. There were lots of choices there. You could go into the factories or you could go to prison or you could be a gangster—there were lots of choices. And I chose to play music. And so there's been four choices over there, really. And I certainly didn't want to go to college. Birmingham had a dismal… I like it but I think a lot of people would say that even today Birmingham's profile is dismal. Rain-swept and factories and belching smoke. It's a very industrial place. People play hard and they work hard. So when they finish work in the factories covered in oil and grease and what have you, they want a drink. They like to be entertained with good, solid music. It didn't surprise me at all that Aston and Birmingham were not the first cities, but one of the first cities, to really embrace what would be the undertones of heavy metal in the late '60s and 1970s."

"We thought it was cool," muses local booker and jazz enthusiast Jim Simpson, soon to play a key role in the Sabbath story as the band's manager. "We didn't think it was tough at all. But looking back, I wouldn't particularly want to live through that again. No, it wasn't particularly bad. It wasn't that long after the war, if you think about it. It's 20 years after the war had finished and these things tend to have an effect. It took a long time to dissipate. There was work around, a lot of manual work, and people didn't seem to be out of work. Nobody seemed particularly broke but nobody seemed particularly rich either. As long as you've got enough to pay your groceries at the end of the week…"

"It was getting by nicely, but the music dominated. I can't tell you how many gigs a week there were within five miles. It was probably 300 to 400 gigs a week you could go and see. A pub like the Crown on Hill Street, who I later got involved with, would put on six shows a week. And you've got 20 pubs with six shows a week. And they weren't just in the city center. All the suburbs had pubs that would put on live music, and the great thing about it was if a band was okay, they'd go out and start doing 20 shows, 30 shows a month, and they'd get to be pretty good. If a band's pretty good to start with, they can get to be brilliant in that time, because there's nothing that makes a band improve like gigging, going out there and play. You can rehearse all you like. You get there and play to people and see how they react to it, that's how a band evolves; that's how a band improves."

"But yes, I lived in the Black Country," continues Jim, "the real Black Country where the real industry is. It's in Birmingham as well, but the Black Country was very industry-dominated. Yeah, it was industrial, but people going out to work in the morning didn't seem to be a bad thing. But at night when you came back from a gig at three or four in the morning and you look across the Black Country, go down the hill, look right across the… pan around the Black Country, you can see the glow of dots everywhere like stars in the sky—those are furnaces. All the factories working. You could see the glow of all these furnaces right across the Black Country. It was very dramatic."

Back to the music, as the '60s blossomed, often chaotically and into factions, mods and rockers gave way to the British blues boom and psychedelia. The blues, in the hands of big British egos, eventually revealed a certain bloat, followed by a reaction against it. The predictability at the heart of the blues, something that had once been an endearing and comforting asset, now began to bore club-goers. Psychedelia went the way of enlightened idealism and became progressive or art rock. Or it didn't. A ragtag, grumbling, cynical, disconnected mob of mean mindset not predisposed to Jon Anderson's sunny flower power sentiments went dark—picking up the newspaper was enough to confirm such fatalism as justified, even comforting, bonding, hell-in-a-handcarting. Psychedelia formed an uneasy alliance with bad-assed American garage rock and a predilection for misfit menace to become not so much heavy metal, but simply the redheaded stepchild of psychedelia—the nasty end of a gray and getting grayer scale.

But, being the punks they were, Black Sabbath were unremarkably, boringly oblivious to this sea change, their collective biles churning to a different set of homeward and world-worn circumstances. Like other punks, they formed bands indicative of random fandoms. Tony, now ex- of The Rocking Chevrolets, The In Crowd, The Birds and the Bees and The Rest (which also featured Bill), joined a pre-existing Cumbria act called Mythology.

Ozzy's personal assistant in later years David Tangye (more of an introduction later), puts some clarity to the pre-Sabbath years. "We wanted to put the record straight on a lot of things, the confluence of it, the really early Sabbath stuff, how they started, like for example the band Mythology. It had been totally distorted in other publications. And it wasn't fair on guys like Neil Marshall, who started Mythology. He really worked hard to get that band going. And Tony actually came to that band. It was an accredited band before he got there, you know what I mean? A lot of people have said, 'Well, Tony did this and Tony did that,' but he basically came up to Cumberland to work and that's how it was. But they didn't have managers in those days. There were no itineraries. I mean, I even remember touring around and you would go into the town you're supposed to be playing, looking for the posters showing you where you're supposed to be playing (laughs). Because you had no idea."

Asked if the roots of heavy metal were evident within Mythology, Iommi figures, "Certainly not in The Rest, but in Mythology there was, yes. It was more guitar-oriented blues. I'd be doing lots of solo guitar work in those days. So that was the start of it, really. But blues played a major part; that was my main influence, blues and jazz. I love to hear good blues players."

Backing up, Bill had this to say about The Rest: "Basically we were just playing basic cover songs, but the cover songs we would play, we thought that they were a little bit out of the norm, a little bit unusual, if you like."

In February of 1968, Mythology would also absorb Bill into the band. A sobering pot bust effectively ended the bluesy band's trajectory and a dejected Tony and Bill shuffled back to Birmingham, where a psych band called Rare Breed featured Geezer o'er on the fat strings. After that band's singer left, Rare Breed answered an ad in a music store announcing cryptically "Ozzy Zig needs a gig. Own PA system." Yes, the ad indicated that this Ozzy already had a PA system, and yes, that usually becomes the clincher in such negotiations.

But the hook-up never happened, and Rare Breed became fully extinct. The ad still posted in the store, Tony was next to answer, who, along with Bill, pulled up in his blue van to Ozzy's door in Aston (Ozzy's dad thought it was the cops), privately hoping it wasn't the same Ozzy that Tony used to terrorize back in high school. It was, but they got around that, in the process, Ozzy introducing Bill and Tony to Geezer, who would join up with the new and fragile trio.

"There's a long history because they were at school together when they were kids," laughs Geezer, 30 years later, on Ozzy's and Tony's odd relationship. "Tony always intimidated Ozzy at school together when they were kids (laughs), and there's always been a history of that throughout the band. And when things happen in childhood, you always think about it. You never quite blow it out of your system. So Ozzy's always had this thing about Tony intimidating him. In recent years, they've had a good talk and resolved everything. For now anyway. But yes, it was the old school thing. They hated each other when they were in school. Tony used to beat up Ozzy at school, and it was just a continuation of that, really. It wasn't really on the surface, it was underneath. And when push came to shove, all the old tensions would come out."

Ozzy seems to have blocked it out of his mind, denying that it ever happened, but adding that Tony was a fighter, a kid who could take care of himself. He stayed out of his way, but also was quite stricken by Tony showing up at school and playing Shadows songs on his red guitar.

It has been said that tensions between Tony and Oz never fully faded, Ozzy being a bit of an odd wheel, due to being the only non-musician of the four, Tony in particular putting him down. As well, Tony was known to crave the limelight (Geezer had been described as a bit of a peacock as well), and any front man, especially one with Ozzy's yearning desire to get crowds on his side, is always a threat to the prominence of a band's guitarist.

Geezer had been a guitarist up to this point, but by switching the strings on his Fender Telecaster to bass strings (and then graduating to a three-stringed bass!), a bobbing, weaving legend was born. "When I was in the Rare Breed with Ozzy I was playing rhythm guitar," confirms Butler. "It wasn't until we met Tony that I'd gone off the idea of playing rhythm guitar. At that point I wanted to be a bass player. When we met up with Tony, he didn't want any other guitarist in the band, so it was perfect. I could switch to bass.

But with one guitarist, the bassist has to think about rhythm guitar anyway. "Yes, I think you learn how to fill out the sound and the rhythm section, which is what rhythm guitarists do. They fill out the rhythm section. If there is no rhythm guitar then the bass player has to do that, and that is sort of what I did."

"We only did a few gigs, locally, in Birmingham," adds Geezer, on the subject of Rare Breed. "That is how we got together. Ozzy lived literally two streets away from me and I used to see him around. He went to the same school as Tony Iommi. We lived so close together that we would see each other in the streets. I heard that he was looking for a band in the music shop. I didn't even know it was him. I went to his house and it was Ozzy. He was a skinhead at the time. I thought, 'This isn't going to work out.' Skinheads at that time were into soul music and reggae. He liked Robert Johnson and blues so we got together and formed the Rare Breed. When that finished we were looking for a drummer and we went around to Tony's house to see if he knew of any drummers and Bill Ward was there. Bill said he would join the band if Tony would come along and that is the way we got together."

Ozzy, as advertised, came with a PA system (Triumph amp, mic and two column speakers). Hitting the road, already under the protective wing of Geoff "Luke" Lucas, the band gigged as a brassy, proggy, jazzy, meandering beast known as the Polka Tulk Blues Band, the name derived from that of a Pakistani clothing store. The fresh act's August 1968 show was one of two (the guys have also suggested six, and even nine) featuring the band as a six-piece, the two strap-ons being a sax player and a second guitarist for slide and rhythm work.

"The number one inspiration for me as a bass player is Jack Bruce," notes Geezer, further on his conversion from six strings to four. "I didn't even consider ever playing the bass guitar until I went to see Cream. I used to see Cream whenever they came to Birmingham. Up until then, I was playing rhythm guitar. I saw Jack Bruce, what he could do with a bass, and it just gave new meaning to the whole instrument. And I just swapped me rhythm guitar for a bass guitar."

Years later, Geezer looked back on that same defining moment. "Up until then, bass players used to just stand there and use the pick, be in the background; you would never notice them. And then when I went to see Cream, it was like so different to anybody else I had ever seen. It was like, God, I can't believe you can do that with the bass. I'd never seen anybody play that way before, and use the fingers before, and just his whole presence on stage. It was amazing to me."

"When we all got together the one thing that we did like was the heavier kinds of bands," continues Butler. "We all loved Hendrix and we all loved Cream. John Mayall and Clapton and that kind of thing. And all my friends liked soul music and pop and stuff, but the rest of the guys that became Sabbath, I related to them because we all liked the same kind of music, which is hard to find, really, back then. And we were all from literally one street away from each other. So it was four guys that all lived within a couple minute's walk from each other all liking the same kind of music, so that when we got together and started writing together, it sort of naturally came out heavy."

"I was brought up strictly Irish Catholic," adds Geezer, on a wider transition, mapping the road from religion to rock. "I was sort of a religious maniac when I was a kid. I used to collect crucifixes and pictures and medals and everything, and I wanted to become a priest. I used to sing in the school choir. I just literally loved God. I was just fascinated by the whole thing. I used to read about it and go to every class I could concerning religion. And that developed into sort of wanting to know more about other religions and other spirituality and more about the occult and everything else."

"So yeah, I used to collect crucifixes and statues of Mary and all that kind of thing, and in the end, I just got sick of going to Mass every Sunday, surrounded by a lot of drunks and idiots taking the piss out of me hair (laughs). And so I just didn't want to go there anymore. It was terrible; I was one of the few people with long hair back then, and all these Irish guys used to take the piss out of me, something rotten. And in the end, I just couldn't stand it and I didn't go to Mass anymore. And eventually, when The Beatles started getting into all the transcendentalism, there were a lot of magazines and assorted publications about the different religions, including Satanism, white magic and black magic and everything, and I just got interested in the whole spiritual thing. And I suppose it rubbed off in me lyric writing with Sabbath."

"And being brought up very strict Roman Catholic, there was a lot of bad feeling between Catholics and Protestants where I lived. So we were always scrapping and fighting over religion and stuff. You're just brought up to think that Catholics are the true religion and all that. So it just got me interested in religion which got me interested in Satan and all that kind of thing, and just religion in general."

"And when I first heard blues music, Robert Johnson and stuff like that, his lyrics were about the Devil and his whole image was about selling his soul to the Devil and it really intrigued me. And so a lot of the music that I was listening to was blues music, and on the pop side of it, when the Beatles came along they sort of merged a lot of blues into their music as well. And now they're from Liverpool, which is like 90 miles from Birmingham and they all had working class accents like I had. That was unheard of until then. And that got me interested in the whole being a musician kind of thing. They've opened the way for people like me. You don't have to grow up and leave school at 15, go straight into a factory until you're 65 like my dad did. So it gave me the inspiration, the whole thing, to get involved in music."

"My personal attitude was I hated it," says Bill Ward on the subject of religion. "I didn't like it. And my attitudes haven't changed that much over the years. Today, I've been taught to see where religious men can be right, but for the most part it really screwed me up, if anything. So I really didn't have a lot of credibility for it."

But Bill wasn't raised in a religious household. "No, not at all. We're all heathens, thank God. But we had to go to Sunday school, and I sang in the school choir. The church that I lived next to, literally, was over a thousand years old. It's called Aston Church in the parish of Aston. And

I lived about a one-minute walk from the church, so growing up, having a reasonable voice, they put me in the church choir. That's what all the local boys had to do. So I sang in the church choir at the Aston parish church for about four years. And for me that was a great learning experience because it suited me well when I got into my first rock 'n' roll band, so it was fine."

"But I cared not for it," continues Bill. "It created too much guilt. I don't believe in a fire and brimstone God. That's bloody rubbish. If you don't do this and you don't do that you're going to burn in Hell. What a pile of shit as far as I'm concerned. It's absolute rubbish. I believe in life and love. And that showed up a number of times in Black Sabbath. Even in 'Children of the Grave.' But yeah, because we were born in the parish of Aston, we belonged to the church whether you liked it or not, yes; and forced religion, it scared me. I had nightmares about it. I had nightmares about some guy who was going to… if I masturbated I was going to be punished forever in my life. It was like Jesus… sorry, Jesus, but you know. I'm talking about before I was ten."

"I would characterize it as a dark time in my life because I felt very depressed as a kid, period," reflects Bill. "I didn't like school, I didn't get along particularly well in school or anything like that. The most enlightening part of the '60s for me was the music. It was brilliant. It was almost like, okay, we know this is part of the crap, guys, the way things are politically, but I didn't believe anybody anyway. We were brought up not to trust politicians or words or anything like that. So you had whatever was going on in the country and new factories were being built. All the houses that were communities once in the city of Birmingham, they're all being knocked down finally, 15 years after the war and what have you. There's a lot of re-modeling. Again, the only enlightening thing I could see was music. It's almost like the amount of music that was received matched the amount of chaotic things. It was almost like an equal match. But music saved the day, there's no question in my mind."

"When I first saw The Beatles, I was probably like 13 or something at the time, 12 or 13, when the Beatles came out," continues Geezer, further on his personal version of the apocryphal moment cited by so many musicians of his generation. "And that sort of took over from where religion left off. It was like reality. You know, you could touch it. It was like four people from exactly the same background as where I was from, being able to rule the world. It gave everybody that was from the working classes in England some hope. So that almost took over from religion, and became religion in itself. I saw them in Birmingham, but as soon as I heard 'Love Me Do,' the first single on the radio, I was just completely taken over by it. It was our generation, back in the early '60s. Like Elvis, and everything else, turned on me brothers and the older people's generation, like the rock 'n' roll stuff. Then when The Beatles came along, it was a whole new thing, especially if you're from England. Because it gave you... we realized English musicians could have their own sound."

"As I said, up until then my brothers had Elvis and rock 'n' roll and all that. My sisters had Cliff Richards and all these English copycats of American rock 'n' roll, and I was of the generation, I was sort of too young for Elvis, and then suddenly the Beatles came around. They were from England, sounded like the way I talk, and it's working class blokes from Liverpool, who weren't from London, who weren't from America, and just the songs were so incredible. Just like nothing else I ever heard. And when you hear something that's different and you absolutely love it, it just becomes part of your life. And John Lennon wouldn't be going, 'Oh, it's so nice to be in your country' or anything. He's like, 'We're bigger than Jesus.' And a lot of people didn't like it. I thought it was brilliant. Just somebody to be outspoken and say what's on their mind instead of what they're supposed to say to the press. They were the first ones, or he was anyway. And so my brother had bought me a guitar. And I just started learning the rhythm parts, all the John Lennon parts, because John Lennon was my big hero back then. So I sat about learning all the Beatles songs on the guitar and that's what started me in music. I used to wear Beatles boots and Beatles suits and have my hair like the Beatles."

"I mean, the Beatles started the whole thing. And then the Rolling Stones came along and it was like, 'Oh god, cut their hair;' they were the bad boys. They got arrested in gas stations for drugs and pissing up the gas pumps. Instead of all this goody goody clean image, it was like the badder you got, the better. And it started this whole our generation, sort of fighting back against what we had to grow up with in the '50s, I suppose. Because the '50s in England wasn't a nice place to be. It was gray and nobody had any money and everything was rationed. So you used to be starving to death because there's barely any food around. So it was a whole rebellion against that."

The Beatles are still big in Geezer's life, 35 years later. "Yeah, I collect Beatles memorabilia. It's not a really big collection, but I loved the Beatles when I was a kid, so a lot of it is nostalgia. The collection I had back then got thrown out, as usual. So when I see something I used to have when I was a kid, I buy it. I still got all me old vinyl stuff. I'd managed to keep all that from when I was a little kid, onwards. I've still got the very first album I ever bought, by Dizzy Gillespie. I think I bought that when I was about 11. But the other first few albums… it had to be the Beatles."

Scotching the idea of a six-piece, the Polka Tulk Blues Band became Polka Tulk, then the Earth Blues Band and then Earth, playing their first gigs by September of '68. A remarkable wrinkle in Black Sabbath history occurs next, with Tony leaving the band for Jethro Tull, the happenstance caught on camera for the Rock 'n' Roll Circus TV performance, an event headlined by the Rolling Stones, for members of that band's fan club, other acts along including John Lennon, The Who and Cream. While Tony can be seen somberly trying to fit in (strumming, prophetically, a doomy sort of blues), he had, in fact, already quit the band and had asked to re-join, only to be told by Ian Anderson that he had already been replaced, and that the TV gig would be his last for the quickly rising Jethro Tull.

Recalls Tull vocalist and flautist Ian Anderson, "Well, at the time, our first guitar player, Mick Abrahams fell out of favour with the rest of us for not showing up (laughs), basically, as well as being a bit of a limiting factor for us. Not that it was his fault, but he just couldn't fly and didn't want to travel abroad. He just wanted to play three nights a week and stay at home with his mum a lot."

"So that wasn't going to work out and we were looking for somebody else and amongst three or four people that we… I don't like to use the word auditioned, because that's not really fair to them. It wasn't as mercenary as that. But we got together with two or three people including the guitar player, David O'List, from a very good group called The Nice, which featured Keith Emerson, and played at The Marquee. They were contemporaries of ours, and when they split up Keith went off to put together Emerson, Lake and Palmer. So there was this guy, an interesting but quirky guitar player, another young guy who went on to be quite successful, and Tony Iommi."

"Tony was a guy that we had seen play with his band, and we valued Tony's approach to music. He was a single line kind of guy. He wasn't too hot on being able to play chords and perhaps some of the more subtle harmonies. It wasn't his thing. He was, even then, you could see that he was about a different kind of musical approach, partly governed by physical realities—he had some injuries to his hand."

"And I don't think it was going to be a workable arrangement for Tony within Jethro Tull, because the stuff I was writing was the music that became the *Stand Up* album. There was a big variety of musical style in there, jazzy things, classical-sounding things, folky things, bluesy things and some riffy things. But I think it would have been stretching Tony's stylistic interest more than would have been credible. So it wasn't going to work out. But he did kindly come into the frame a few weeks later to help us out when we were asked to do the Rolling Stones Rock 'n' Roll Circus. Tony came and mimed the guitar part. I think I was the only one singing live on that, or playing live. The other guys were on Memorex."

The strange Tull tie-in came with a silver lining, says Geezer. "The big chance with us happened when Tony was invited to join Jethro Tull. Up until then we were a strictly 12-bar blues band playing other people's music. And we did a gig with Jethro Tull; I can't remember where it was. Somewhere in Birmingham, I think it was. And half way through the gig Ian Anderson came out and he just stood in front of Tony and he was just watching Tony all night long, and we thought oh no, he's going to steal Tony. And then at the end of the night he came into our dressing room, and he said to Tony, 'Can I have a word with you?' And we thought, oh no, this is it."

"So next thing we know, Tony's going down to London. And it just didn't work out. He didn't like it, Tony. He wanted to come back and be with us. He thought it was a bit too regimented with Jethro Tull. And so we couldn't believe it that Tony would give up this incredible opportunity. He'd been offered a steady wage every week and we were like poverty-stricken at the time. And he came back and said, look, if we work like those guys then we can do it. We've got to write our own stuff. And the first song we gave a try writing was 'Wicked World.' We jammed around, seeing what we could come up with, and we came up with the song 'Wicked World.' And that put us on… we thought, this is good, we can do it. We'll have a go at another one, because we had a gig coming up the week after."

"When they asked me if I was interested in joining, I talked to the other guys and told them," explains Tony on his brief side trip. "They told me that I should go for it. We were just starting out at the time and we hadn't gotten anything going. I actually joined but I changed my mind. I wanted to come back and get the band going again. I learned quite a lot from Ian, I must say. I learned that you have got to work at it; you have to rehearse. When I came back and I got the band back together, I made sure that everybody was up early in the morning and rehearsing. I used to go and pick them up. I was the only one at the time that could drive. I used to have to drive the bloody van and get them up at quarter of nine every morning; which was, believe me, early for us then. I said to them, 'This is how we've got to do it because this is how Jethro Tull did it.' They had a schedule and they knew that they were going to work from this time 'til that time. I tried that with our band and we got into doing it. It worked. Instead of just strolling in at any hour, it made it more like we were saying, 'Let's do it!'"

Also rankling Tony about the Jethro Tull situation was his impression that the band didn't feel very much like a gang, Ian eating his lunch at that table, the other three eating at this one, as well as the sentiment drummed into him by the band's manager that he was so lucky to be part of this hallowed act.

By late December of '68, Earth were again gigging around Birmingham and Cumbria. January 3, 1969 saw the band's first gig in London, with Ozzy establishing what would become the band's trademark penchant for wearing crucifixes—only this first time, what Ozzy had around his scrawny neck was an X-shaped tap from a kitchen sink.

"When we were Earth," notes Geezer, "we were doing lots of blues stuff, from Howlin' Wolf, Muddy Waters, John Lee Hooker, and even some soul stuff—we actually used to do some Sam & Dave and Wilson Pickett stuff. And a lot of the English blues like the Cream, John Mayall; some jazz as well."

After a period of mentorship by Alvin Lee and Ten Years After, the band found management with Jim Simpson, who would be instrumental in launching the band toward fame and modest, fleeting fortune. Explains Geezer, on the significance of Simpson, "Well, first of all, he had Henry's Blues House, in the middle of Birmingham, and he used to encourage local bands to come up and play before the main act. You'd have people like Duster Bennett, I think Ritchie Havens, people like that. And you always gave the chance to the local bands to go up first before the main act, and we went up and tried out for it, and he really liked us and says, 'Yeah, you can go on tonight.' And we went on and the crowd went nuts. They loved us. So he wanted us on every week then. So we'd go on every week, and then eventually he asked us if we had management or anything, which we didn't, and he became our manager. He says I can get you more gigs and everything, and so he did."

As Jim has alluded to, the Birmingham music scene was thriving—very much like Detroit at the time, America's version of a workin' hard, playin' hard town driven by heavy industry and equally heavy rockin' bands.

"Yeah, there was a lot of soul clubs around at the time," reflects Geezer. "And then there was this place called the Penthouse and it was in Birmingham. It was like a café on one level, second level was dancing, soul music and stuff, and the top level was where rock bands were. And I used to see Robert Plant with the Band of Joy back then. Bonham was on drums. And Jethro Tull used to play there a lot, when they were the John Evan Smash or something. So you used to have all these like future incredible massive bands playing before they were anybody, really. Every Saturday night I'd go up there and it used to go on all night until eight o'clock in the morning. So we'd be like popping black bombers and all kinds of stuff, and watching these great bands."

"Then there was this other place called the Metro or something, used to be an old railway tunnel, and that had blues bands on… Free, Keef Hartley, Aynsley Dunbar, Fleetwood Mac, Chicken Shack, all these great blues bands. And then the ultimate club, Mother's, opened in Birmingham. And I was always going up there. The Who played there, the Kinks, all these really top bands. And then Zeppelin played there. Eventually Sabbath played there. I mean, normally you'd see these pop bands on the TV and they're awful playing live because half of them hadn't recorded. They were just picked by the record company to represent session musicians live. And you'd see them live and they're awful. And then you'd go and see these incredible bands that nobody's ever heard of, and you think, God, I want to do that and grow my hair and do everything else like that."

Bill Ward, for his part, has fond memories of Spencer Davis Group as well as The Move, the latter for their hard-hitting sound, something they shared in common with local drummer John Bonham, who in turn inspired Bill to play with more power.

"Well, to me John was a pioneer," says Ward. "There was no other like him. Before that, me personally, I'd listened to a lot of different drummers. Of course Ginger Baker, Mitch Mitchell, a lot of people, but I met John I think when I was 15 or 16 years old, and we were playing in gigs like the Wharf Ombersley, which is in Worcester. He was in the Crawling King Snakes. I was in a band called The Rest with Tony, and we crossed paths many, many times."

"An example of his drum sound: we were both playing an all-nighter gig at a little club in Birmingham, the back end of Birmingham. So rough down there, fights every few yards. Just getting your drum kit upstairs into the club was a masterful process. Any commando would have been proud of us just trying to get the instruments into the club. But this club was renowned for fights. And anyway, I was playing that gig that night and so was Bonham. And we were setting up early evening. None of the punters were in there. And he asked me, he said, 'Bill, just stand in the middle of the room.' The room was only about as big as this room, and night time when you're playing, all the sweat runs off the room and you might need to go in there with a pair of wading boots, really, rather than pumps to play your drums."

"He sat behind his drum and he started kicking it, and he's light of foot. One would think he plays really heavy on the pedal, and he's nothing like that at all. He's really light and he's got his balance and he's got the triplets. And I'm talking about… we were probably 16 years old, and he said, 'Let me know if you feel it in your gut.' And so he hit the bass drum a few times and I felt like a huge man had just come up and punched me in the gut. And I was about 15 feet out from his bass drum. And I said, 'I can feel it, John. I can feel that really loud and clear.'"

"And that's how he tested the volume back then, or the tuning of his bass drum. He wanted to know if you could feel it in the gut. And I said I can positively feel it in the gut. And that was one huge learning lesson, and not only for me. I was watching this person who loved to play loud and why he loved to play loud, I don't know. But I know that I, eventually, loved to play loud as well. It was a question of having to because drummers back then didn't have microphones. We didn't have any P.A. Nobody put a microphone on the bass drum, so we had to kick. Jim Marshall was inventing all these new amplifiers and I'm going up against Iommi, who's like splashing out chords and playing a lot louder. Drummers had to learn new ways of playing hard and getting their point across without using microphones. And it wasn't an easy task. Playing loud you can mis-strike often, so we had to learn how to play hard and strike every time. So it's not only accuracy at high volume, but there were lots of skills that had to be learned. And Bonham was a craftsman."

As for the value of playing loud, Bill says that, "For the sake of our conversation right now, I'll just call it primal scream. So it's the same as having sex; there's a desire to have more and feel more and become more orgasmic—it's the same thing. That's how volume is to me. And I had to play louder because I was trying to reach that place that takes all my anger and takes all my resentment and takes everything I am and deliver it through music. So there's no half-ass thing and there's no being on the stage going, 'Oh, well, we're playing now.' It's not that at all. It's just this thing inside, it's the beast and being in touch with that and letting it roar, letting it come out."

"So to do that, the louder the better. The louder we are, the better we are. But I have to say something, because Black Sabbath, all of us, we were all brought up to understand dynamics. I know Tony and I, the first bands we played in when we were 16 years old, we were playing dynamics. We listened to bands like the Shadows, the Ventures, we listened to all the early rock 'n' roll music, and all that's got dynamics in it. It's very important; if you listen to Jerry Lee Lewis, 'Whole Lot of Shakin,' listen to that cymbal ride and you'll hear it. You'll hear the dynamics. So one of the great things with Sabbath is it could drop in volume to practically nothing and still be solid, and then it could roar back up with immense crescendo, and that's what I love about that band. It's just so dynamic and orchestrational. Terry plays orchestrationally, I play orchestrationally. I'm not a back beat drummer. I wouldn't know where… I know a two-one beat, that's it—I don't know anything else. I just react to Terry's bass playing, Ozzy's voice and Tony's guitar playing."

Continues Bill on the subject of his hometown and Mother's and Henry's Blues House, "They were huge. It's like the Fillmore East and Fillmore West, the same value and same importance. One of the first things I remember about Mother's was seeing Canned Heat pull up with an 18-wheeler truck and unloading all this stuff. And I thought, my God, it won't even fit into the club. And when I saw that, as well as the fact that Canned Heat had a #1 record at the time, you could see that Mother's was a very important club. Cream played there on a number of occasions. I watched Carl Palmer when he was like 15 years old playing with the King Bees there. Sabbath… we played at Mother's when we were not Black Sabbath and we played at Mother's when we were Black Sabbath. It was a blast, man, and it was very prestigious. It was just like the Marquee Club in London."

"And Henry's Blues House… my hat has to go off to the credibility of Jim Simpson who put together Henry's Blues House, which brought over so many of the original American blues artists. We had everybody come through there. Keef Hartley Band; I'm not sure if John Mayall came through, but we had a lot of players come through. Clem Clempson before he joined Humble Pie. It's endless, the amount of people that played at Henry's, including us. And Jim, first of all, his importance is huge as a jazz player, a horn player. So he was totally in a groove as far as really very passionate about music. Blues, jazz, he loved all that stuff. And he bought Henry's Blues House, which was a talking point and a focus point, the center and hub of American blues music and British blues music if you were not in London. So it's like yes, we had the blues in the Midlands courtesy of Jim Simpson."

Recalls Jim, on the genesis of Birmingham's thriving scene, "I came out of the Air Force in '59, came to Birmingham in '61, and even then there was what they call a beat scene. There was a really great local band called the Modernaires. I was playing in jazz bands at the time so we rather looked down on beat bands, except for the Modernaires. We'd travel miles to hear them. And slowly those in the jazz band, we sort of slipped towards this Birmingham style which is harder and bluesier and tougher than most styles. Blues bands started to emerge. I mean, football happened once a week, maybe twice at most. Television had three channels, all of which were pretty boring. So nothing played much of a part in young folks' lives other than—well speaking for myself, really—other than sport and music. I mean to play well you've got to give something to it. I played trumpet for many years and I was on the road for 12 years, and I used to practice six hours a day. Where would a 17- or 16-year old kid today find six hours a day to practice? There was kids who used to that. And bands used to pride themselves on being good."

Moving toward his connection with the Sabbath guys, Jim explains that, "I played trumpet in a band called Locomotive, and we had a hit record, a thing called 'Rudi's in Love,' which was a ska hit, and I found I could no longer manage the band and continue playing, so I stopped playing and went into management. Suddenly I found myself with my evenings free, so I got out and listened to other bands a lot more, because Locomotive was always with the reputation of being a hard-working band. I don't exaggerate, probably 28 or 30 shows a month because on Fridays and Saturdays you'd always do two shows."

"And I heard a guitar player called Dave Clempson, who later on went to be called Clem Clempson with Humble Pie, and he was a great player. He lives in Litchfield, and he was in a blues band, and blues was pretty big during the blues boom. So I decided to get involved with them. So I decided the best way to represent them was to hire a room and present them every Tuesday, in this case. So we had this slogan, 'Tuesday is blues day,' at the place called The Crown in Hill Street. And we'd rented and we'd advertised... it was called Henry's Blues House, which I think was supposed to be—I've read since—the first progressive club in the country, progressive being a music term in those days. I'm not quite sure what it meant, but it was the first progressive club in the country outside of London. It predated Mothers, which was the famous one."

"So I put the band on there, and I was a bit nervous that people wouldn't come, so I dressed it up the first week. We had a lot of publicity, we advertised, got some leaflets, we had the dog symbol Henry's characterized, and we had films on in other rooms. It was really a good Tuesday night out. And three of the first 20 members of our "club" were three members of what eventually became Black Sabbath. So I knew them as members of Henry's Blues House to start with. They were nice kids and we always talked. We talked about blues, of course, because they were in a blues band. Pre-Earth, even."

"And over the months we talked more and eventually they said, could they do the intermission spot at Henry's? It only paid somewhere about five pounds, in those days, which I suppose in today's terms is somewhere around 50 or 60 pounds, which is more than people pay for now because people pay in this country to play. So I booked them to play the intermission. Funny enough they didn't want the five pounds fee. They said, could they have a Henry's Blues House T-shirt each as a fee?"

"And that's how I got involved with them musically. And we talked more over the months and they said would I like to manage them? So I said I'd help them out. At the time I had three or four bands I was involved with. Locomotive, still, of course. We had two bands on EMI Harvest, which were Tea & Symphony and Bakerloo Blues Line, which was Dave Clempson's band, and another band… no that was it, just the three. But when I got involved with the Sabbath guys, they played nicely and the audience liked them. I'd known them for a few months and they seemed like nice kids, nice to get involved with, a band that you could have an effect on, a band you could influence. I've never gone for bands that are already established because I like to be in at the beginning; I like to help shape things."

Moving into the recording realm, Locomotive's Norman Haines would be proffered as a potential writer for Sabbath, penning "When I Came Down," which Sabbath can be heard jamming through competently on an acetate that turned up in the early 2000s.

"I remembered the song once I heard it, but I had totally, completely forgot about it," muses Geezer, on this yet un-marketed early Sabbath session. "Jim kept playing us that sort of thing, because he was a jazz player himself, and his favourite band was Chicago. They had just come out with their first album. He had been a trumpet player, so he loved brass sections. So he kept playing us all these jazz records saying, 'This is what you should be doing.' No thanks."

"Yeah, we just did that the one time," says Bill of the track. "We were trying to get songs to get us a recording contract, so Norman had written up this pretty cool song; he was a good songwriter. But you know, it was plain, right from the get-go, that we really didn't like doing other people's music. We did The Crow's version of 'Evil Woman' and I didn't particularly like that."

"I don't know. We didn't have anybody who taught us that," laughs Bill, asked how Sabbath would transition from the blues to the inventors of heavy metal they would become. "The songs, when they came about, they just sounded right. We just used to show up and play aggressively. I think it was just more the aggression that came out than anything else. We just pretty much turned up the volume. I mean, I didn't have a P.A. back then, for my drums or anything, so there were no microphones. I had to play as loud as I possibly could, and I think that sometimes the guys thought I was playing too loud (laughs), so they turned up. So we all just got louder, really. It wasn't anything that was planned."

"I would think so," offers Tony, agreeing with Geezer's assessment that Simpson was a part of Sabbath's fledgling—and soon to be shed—jazziness. "I mean, he was a trumpet player himself, so he sort of liked what we were doing. Of course, in those days, I used to do these ridiculously long solos because every song was like a 12-bar (laughs). And it'd be like a five-minute guitar solo in there, which was great for me, because it gave me the opportunity to try learn new stuff, new parts."

Gigging regularly up and down England, Earth would soon embark on their first overseas jaunt, to Germany and Hamburg's Star-Club, influential of course due to its association with The Beatles, but also important with respect to Sabbath, for this was the locale at which a selection of the early Black Sabbath classics were written—live. After a second European trip, landing with hijinx in Denmark then over to Hamburg again (as well as Sweden and Belgium), the band returned home enthusiastic and not without a sizeable following and buzz. Hamburg beckoned again, in August of '69 for a three-week stay, amidst premature publicity that the band were recording their debut album—with Gus Dudgeon of Bonzo Dog Band and Locomotive fame, later to improve on that resume through work with David Bowie and Elton John.

The Star-Club stints hardened the band incredibly, also serving as a creative launch pad. Playing upwards of five, maybe even seven, 45-minute sets a night to a mostly indifferent crowd ("six people, and three of them were nutcases, plus a prostitute," quipped Geezer) that treated them as so much wallpaper, Sabbath would bring on stage barely written originals and then finish them off o'er the hours. As well, extended solos would be taken by all (except Oz), sometimes one of the guys blowing it alone for an entire set.

And as Ozzy regales, touring in the early days could turn nasty. Especially in Northern Scotland. "It was one of those horrible little towns, you know the type, three shops and about ten boozers. To get there, we had to drive for hours over these bumpy dirt roads. There were three people in the whole club for our entire first set. It got to be 10:00 and that's the hour when the pubs close, so pretty soon all these farmers started coming in. They're all drunk out of their minds and started shouting things like, 'Play something we can dance to, you cunt!' Some of them had these pennies they would heat over a flame and throw at the stage. There we were trying to play music and they were pelting us with these horrible bloody hot coins that stick your skin when they hit you. Then they started complaining about our volume. They sent up a note: 'Turn down or...' and below that was a large bloodstain." What did you do? "We turned up!" "We had too," added Geezer. "After all, we're only in it for the volume."

On the way o'er the channel, August 9th of 1969, Earth decided to change their name, due to the existence of another "rock and blues at high volume" band called Earth. Another story had our more beloved Earth booked for—and then showing up to—a formal dress gig meant to go to an easy listening band from Plymouth called Earth. In any event, the change wouldn't happen right away, but the guys were fond of a song they already had in their repertoire, a song based on the Boris Karloff movie that goes by the name of *Black Sabbath*. Other reports have the band contemplating the name change due to potential confusion with the bands Rare Earth or Mother Earth. Others have the band calling the name a bad omen because a few of the guys' relatives had recently died in quick succession, this story usually revolving around Geezer and some aunts and uncles, his dabblings with black magic to have had something to do with the high mortality rate surrounding the band and its extended clan.

"I'd never liked the name Earth," says Jim, adding yet another twist to the tale. "I don't think they particularly liked it, but I think they thought it was okay because it wasn't offensive. The turning point came when we found another band called Earth, and that was the cruncher to change the name. And we thrashed around with all sorts of ideas, none of which rang true until Geezer one day put his head around the door over there and said, 'I thought of a name. A good name for us.' He put his head back again. 'Oh yeah? What is it?' He teased us for a while, put his head around the door, back again, 'How about Black Sabbath?' And I think we all said yeah, that sounded right. As I clearly recall it was Geezer who came up with it."

As for the motivation behind the name, Jim figures, "It just sounded nice. Maybe that's a reflection of the low level of the other names we'd been throwing around until then. There was nothing that any of us remotely joined hands on before that. It just sounded right."

Notes Geezer, offering additional subtleties but somewhat clearing the air, "Well, the proper story is, when we were called Earth, I mean, we turned up at this gig one day, and there were like all these older men and women, all dressed up all nicely and everything, suits and dresses and everything on, and then we started playing, and the promoter came up and told us to shut up and play our proper stuff. And we go, 'What proper stuff?' And he said, 'The single that you've got out.' And we go, 'What single?' And there was another band called Earth, and they were like the ultimate pop band, really teeny bopper kind of crap, middle-of-the-road stuff, like The Archies kind of thing. And we were wondering why we were getting so many gigs at the time, and it was because of this other Earth, so we had to change the name."

Back in England, relates Geezer, the boys discussed the idea of a new name with Jim Simpson, who countered with Fred Karno's Army as a more worthy moniker—Joe Leg was also kicked around. Black Sabbath soon stuck, although the band's first professional recordings would still be under the guise of Earth. Gus Dudgeon was, indeed, along for the inaugural session, and the band was to record "The Rebel," accompanied by Norman Haines of Locomotive, also written by Norman, forcefully suggested for the band courtesy of Jim Simpson. Dudgeon was soon replaced by Rodger Bain, and "The Rebel," along with "A Song for Jim" were recorded and then never issued. "A Song for Jim," the very first song Sabbath ever recorded under the new name, was rejected because it was too jazzy—Tony was a huge Joe Pass fan, as any visitor to his home found, Pass being the dinner music of choice. "The Rebel" (the second song Sabbath ever recorded), would also not make it onto the band's first album, having been deemed too commercial. It must be noted that in interviews, Sabbath has been known to call their cover of Crow's "Evil Woman" the first song they ever recorded, although this is likely shorthand for the first song commercially issued, which it was.

Now, as if by magic, the invention of heavy metal comes about through the very process of naming the band Black Sabbath, in conspiracy with the writing of the songs "Wicked World" and "Black Sabbath."

"We scratched around a lot trying to find a style," recalls Jim, recounting this fascinating process. "We liked a different direction because the country was inundated with blues bands. And they all sounded the same, they all looked the same, they all smelled the same, they all wore the same denim jackets and the guitarists played 60-minute long solos and stood in their boots in great misery while they did it. And we were all anxious to get out of that, because by that time we devoted some time and effort to it and we all believed that the band—all five of us—was going somewhere, so we had to do something different."

"My background is jazz and blues, so I was guilty of playing a lot of jazz things to them, which didn't really influence their style in any way, although you can clearly hear jazz influences in early Sabbath. The way Bill Ward rides the high-hat is just like Kansas City Jo Jones with the Basie band. And I used to play Ozzy a lot of Jimmy Rushing. Jimmy's got that same style of voice as Ozzy that comes from deep down in his stomach somewhere and it's a big, open-throated roar. And also Ozzy actually recorded a song of Jimmy Rushing's in the early days called 'Evenin'.' Never released but those little influences matter, although they didn't influence the main style."

And then it is said. "I sort of think it just came with that one song, 'Black Sabbath.' I always felt that song delivered it, and looking back I can't see things that lead towards that. That was just sort of carved out of nothing, I think. The band just came up with it. You can't say it was developed into this or developed into that. There were lots of little influences around, but that sort of huge step into what is generally referred to as metal, now as it is, seems to come from nowhere. It just seemed to come from the band and that one song to start with. And that set the day, from that point on. It set the direction to go in, and we all saw it. We all saw it—as soon as it happened, we said this is it, we've got it. This is where we're going."

The aforementioned "When I Came Down" became the third song Sabbath ever recorded and it too was never issued. The one-only

7" acetate of that track (handed to a mate and helper of Tony's in 1969, after he had given Tony a ride home from the pub) is backed with an early version of "The Wizard," making that likely the fourth track Black Sabbath ever recorded. Of note, a radically different, and lighter, version of "When I Came Down" would emerge on an incredibly rare album credited to the Norman Haines Band, consisting of material from Haines' post-Locomotive band Sacrifice recorded in 1970. On this record, the track is re-named "When I Come Down." Also of note, very brief snippets of both "A Song for Jim" and "The Rebel" can be heard on the *Black Sabbath Story Volume One* video. These audio recordings haven't been released first and foremost because Tony is famously disinclined to issue Black Sabbath rarities, although Tony has also said, with respect to these two tracks, he doesn't know where the original recordings are anyway.

"They ended up on the video," offered Tony, offhandedly. "No, we wouldn't release anything we weren't proud of. I've got stuff at home, 24 multi-tracks donkey's years old. There are some tracks we did with Gillan that have never been released. I don't think there's really any point. You release the stuff you think at the time is the best for that album. It would probably have collectors value. I've never really given it a thought, quite honestly. I'm not going to start releasing stuff just to make money out of it."

An early capture of the band punk rocking their way through "Blue Suede Shoes" live, now widely available, rounds out the very early days oddities. "'Blue Suede Shoes' is something we'd done to test the camera shots when we played Germany, The Beat Club," says Tony. "We just wanted to check the sound and camera shots, so we just played 'Blue Suede Shoes' for a laugh, and it ends up out... and it's there forever now! So you've really got to be careful what you do. It was just one of those things we did, just joking around, as we always did. Christ, if they'd taped some of the stuff we did… my God! Shadows numbers..."

After informing a crowd a few nights previous of the band's impending name change, Black Sabbath would play their first gig under the new dark moniker on August 30, 1969, in Worcestershire—to seal the deal, faithful roadie Luke had spelled it out in black electrical tape on Bill's bass drum head.

Album 1

Black Sabbath

"God could be Satan"

Before Black Sabbath got down to the business of shocking the rock world with their self-titled debut, they had to write—as we've mentioned, sometimes right there on stage—the songs that would stud that sledge. Through the band's incarnation as Earth and into the early days surrounding their aborted single session, the guys set about gradually replacing their long list of protracted blues covers with originals, one by one. Eventually, joining "Wicked World" and "Black Sabbath" would be "The Wizard," "N.I.B.," "Behind the Wall of Sleep" and even second record classics such as "Fairies Wear Boots," "Rat Salad" and "War Pigs." These would form from clumps of clay, organically, at sound checks and in the van, all before the debut record would come to pass.

"We'd played the majority of them at gigs, yeah," remembers Tony, of the songs that would make the debut Black Sabbath record, tracked October 16th of 1969, issued on a spooky Friday the 13th the following February, and not until June 1st in the US. "So we were more or less very familiar with them by the time we went into the studio. We were playing Europe quite a lot, actually. In Hamburg, at The Star-Club, we actually broke the Beatles record, which we were thrilled about. So yeah, I think the first one was done in about eight hours, because at the time, for us, it was just like doing a gig. We'd walk in, get the gear set up and play (laughs). We would just play through the songs and Ozzy would sing in a little box and that was it. You would do an overdub, one guitar overdub, and that was it, you're out, finished."

As opposed to later albums, where Tony would perform his magic right in the control room, the sessions for the self-titled album indeed had the band set up in the same room as their amps, playing as if it was just another live show. Tony had also quipped that "you couldn't do your guitars in the control room back then even if you wanted to, because the control rooms were so tiny."

"A lot of people think the bass player is supposed to be more melodic, like Paul McCartney, playing all these nice things to give everything more depth," said Geezer, on the early establishment of his heavy, guitar-ish sound. "But I couldn't do it that way so I just followed along with Tony's riffs. In addition, when we used to go into the studio, they'd say I couldn't have this much distortion on my bass, because bass players don't do that. But that's me; that's my sound. We used to have battles with producers and engineers about distortion and what bass is supposed to sound like. It was always an argument on every album."

"In the studio they would always try to separate the guitar and bass sound," agrees Tony. "They get into the control room and listen to our tracks separately and complain that Geezer's bass sounded so distorted. They didn't understand that what we had together was the sound we wanted. You just can't start listening to the parts individually, because together they created our sound."

"Nobody gives an unknown group a lot of money to make an album with," said Ozzy, on the record's whirlwind session, which took place at a four-track facility off of London's Tottenham Court Road. The band was said to have been turned down by 14 record labels before respected progressive rock label Vertigo picked the band up. Vertigo had been conceived by Phonogram, who had seen EMI's Harvest label skillfully tap into the zeitgeist of pioneering British rock and folk. It was a mini boom for boutique labels, and a lot of good signing got done. But if commercial success for Vertigo acts was patchy at best, the last laugh comes in the fact that the label's many records by baby bands are now highly collectible among discerning hard progressive rock aficionados.

Backing up a bit, Geezer and Tony help lay the administrative groundwork for the enabling of the first album. First Geezer: "We'd been put down by everybody, from our parents, onward. They said we'd never do anything with our lives. Because I was going to college and everything before that, and they thought I was going to be the one to end up training in a good job, accountancy. It was like a good professional job to be in. There were seven kids in my family, and I was the only one that sort of did well at school and went on to college. And when I left to form this band, they went nuts. Everybody thought, 'Well, it's just a pipedream. He can't possibly do anything with it. There's no way you can ever have it as a career.' And then when we finally wrote a whole album's worth of stuff, and tried to get a record deal, the record companies just wouldn't let us into the building. They'd tell us to piss off and go away and write proper music. Everybody hated us! In the end, we went through this independent person that was like a broker for record deals. He saw something in us, and he signed us up. I think he was like a professional A&R person. He liked what we were doing and he sold us to a record company. And when we finally got into a studio, that was like the greatest thing that we could possibly do. Because we were showing everybody that we could do it. I think that was one of the best memories."

"This chap Jim Simpson was our contact and he ran his blues club," explains Tony. "We used to play there once a week or once every couple of weeks. He got a few people down to listen to us, and a lot of them weren't interested. But Tony Hall was one of the ones that was interested. All he was really interested in was making an album. And we were like, 'Oh, that's great!' We didn't know anything more than that. And Tony Hall was willing to sign us for an album."

"We auditioned for lots and lots of record companies but nobody would have us," adds Geezer. "I mean, in the end, we'd go with anybody, to get the record done. And Vertigo… we didn't really have anything to do with it. They just gave us £1000 to go and record the album. We kept about 100 quid each, and the rest of it went on the studio. Vertigo was like the new progressive label, because there were a lot of bands coming out that they couldn't classify as pop or whatever, so there were quite a few new labels. Like Harvest was created by EMI, Vertigo was Philips, and it was quite prestigious to get on that label at the time."

"I don't think they really have those kinds of people now," adds Geezer, when asked about Tony Hall. "He was like an A&R man, but the A&R people had a lot more power back then, and he was like a broker between different record companies and publishing companies. And you would go to him and he would say, 'Well, I think you should go with this.' He was more like a manager really, what managers do now."

So yes, Tony Hall was involved, but there was also the band's new manager Jim Simpson and quite critically, Vertigo Records chief Olav Wyper. But Sabbath's ascendance turned out to be a trip against all odds, according to Jim.

"People just didn't get it," says Simpson. "This metal thing, at first audio glimpse, sounds very simple. Oh, anyone can do that. It's all very open and it's not that difficult; well it's very complex. People who didn't listen properly didn't get it, and they didn't understand the impact and the heaviness of it. For us, what we all aspired to in those days was to be heavy. In the early days we perceived… the early rivals we had… mine was Led Zeppelin. And our advertising strap line reflecting the desire to be heavy. It said, 'Black Sabbath make Led Zeppelin sound like a kindergarten house band.' And we used that."

"I mean, if you were beamed to this earth from Venus in those days and suddenly landed in Henry's Blues House in front of Ozzy and Sabbath, you knew you were witnessing something very, very special. Oh gosh, I don't like… me and poetry don't mix, but it had a magnificence about it. It didn't so much strut as it was stamped over everything. It had an arrogance, a self-belief, a confidence. It made you feel good. I was very proud to be behind a band like that, especially when people didn't like them at the beginning. We just felt it was five against the world. We'd all work hard at doing our respective things and I'd go to London… we did a demo in Birmingham, which is not very different than the first album. Exactly the same tracks without the sound effects, which enhance them wonderfully. But musically it was very, very similar."

"And I went to 14 record companies. I must have talked to 20 or 30 to get 14 appointments. The band were working six nights a week and were working in and around London. They had always been a bit slow on things such as this, but in the middle to the north it was doing well. In Germany we were doing well. Working in Holland and Belgium, Germany, Switzerland, Midlands to the north, but not actually in London. But I took the day sheet and the newspaper the band had and this recording to 16—was it 16?—14 straight record companies, and they all turned me down, one after the other. And I'd come back and we still… we didn't feel defeated. We just knew they hadn't got it. So we had to do something else. So eventually we borrowed money and eventually we recorded with money lent to us by David Platz of Essex Music, and recorded the album which was eventually released as *Black Sabbath*. The exact finished album with all the sound effects on it. Rodger Bain produced it at Regent Sound Studios, and I took that around to the same companies, and the same companies turned it down."

"If you were scared of making a wrong decision about music and if you're sitting there in your posh, purple office with your white suit on and you're championed as being an important A&R man at CBS Records—as they were—you want to hear something safe. You want to go to the boss and say, "Listen, I've got something that sounds just like that Rolling—what are they called?—Stones. Yeah, something like that. I've got two bands that sound just like them and they smell the same, too.' Then they feel safe. But something new, they're scared of it."

Which brings us to Olav Wyper, who would distinguish himself as the engine behind the esteemed Vertigo Records.

"Right, so okay, one of the people I went to was the head of A&R at CBS, both times. A man called Olav Wyper. He turned it down twice. Then he was headhunted by Philips Records, in Stanhope Place, who had just set up their own underground label, whatever underground meant. EMI set up an underground label called Harvest, and they were having some success. And just like I said, more bandwagon-jumping—if EMI have Harvest, then we at Philips have to have an underground and Prior has to have one and CBS, RCA, we've all got to have our underground labels because other people are doing it and they might steal our business margins."

"So Philips set up this thing called Vertigo, and they headhunted Olav to head up that division. VO1, 2, and 3 were released and they released their LPs in sets of three. And the first tranche I think was Juicy Lucy, Manfred Mann Chapter Three, and Hiseman's Colosseum, *Valentyne Suite*. Those were VOs 1, 2, and 3. VOs 4, 5 and 6 were readied, and I can't remember what they were, but VO6, whoever was supposed to deliver that, was late delivering the product. Well, because Olav had to have his third album, he called up and said, 'Jim, about the album you played me.' I said, 'At CBS?' He said, 'Yeah, I think we can do something about this here.' I said, 'Great, I'll get on the train. Tomorrow, shall I come around?' 'No, you don't need to come. We'll send you the contract.'"

"I said, 'Well you didn't even listen to it. You heard the beginning of the first track, beginning of the second track and said no it's not for us. It's a whole album that's 38 minutes and you only heard about two.' I mean think about it, I think it's a strong record. So I said, 'Well we need to negotiate terms.' He said, 'No, I'll tell you what we can do. I'll give you a £500 pound advance.' And I'd been turned down by 14 companies. For me half of me wanted to grab his arm and the other half wanted to negotiate. But he was intransigent, and I realized why later. He needed a piece of product to fill that VO6 slot. That was why he took Sabbath."

"And the week it went on the charts, as I promised him, it sold. We did 5200 records the first week. We went straight on one of the charts. There were two main charts in those days. One was Record Retailer and it's now become Music Week, and one was Music Business Weekly, who later merged to become Music Week. And we went on Music Business Weekly charts, straight in, I think #24, #25. And a total of 5000 records."

"Olav phoned me and said, 'Well done, Jim. Congratulations.' I said, 'Yes, great isn't it?' We were all excited that what we said had come true. He said, 'How'd you do it?' I said, 'Well, like I told you there's a following out there.' Because kids on gigs had been asking for records for months. In those days setting your own record label… it wasn't as easy as it is now. It was, actually, but we didn't realize it was as easy. He said, 'Well how'd you get on the charts?' I said, 'What do you mean?' He said, 'How'd you get on the charts? You bought it on, right?' I said, 'No. First of all I haven't got money to buy it.' I never did, never had, before or since. Second, I wouldn't know how to. 'Well we've sold over 5000 records. How'd you do that?' I said because kids have gone out and bought it. And he's convinced to this day, probably, that we bought it on the charts."

"It all has to do with the Vertigo label," begins Wyper, telling his side of the story. "I was at CBS for many years, and in 1967 I went to their annual convention in Las Vegas—wonderful place to have a convention—and the A&R people had been working on developing a whole load of new acts. Yes we had Dylan, yes, we had Simon & Garfunkel, we had all those sorts of people, but we didn't have the newer contemporary acts that they felt the label needed, particularly in the American market. So they created—well they didn't create, they found—all these new acts, and these were revealed at the international convention that they had in '67. And it was very interesting because it wasn't the kind of repertoire we were familiar with in the UK—Blood, Sweat & Tears, Taj Mahal, Spirit, Leonard Cohen, Laura Nyro, all those kind of people—and I was mightily impressed with them."

"So I then decided we'd release them in England in the autumn of '67, which we did, and we sold zilch. Nobody was interested whatsoever. There was very little radio play that we could get anyway. There was only Peel who was playing anything at all that was contemporary, and we just couldn't get it off the ground. I come from a marketing background, so I used to think about well how the hell can we do this? And then I had an idea, which was that we put together a sampler album, but we put on the sampler album as the headlines, we put Simon & Garfunkel, we put Bob

Dylan, we put the Byrds, because everybody knew those. Nobody knew the other things."

"So we put a selection of tracks by all of these new acts on that thing, and we called it *The Rock Machine Turns You On*. And we put it out at just under a pound and we sold zillions. As a result of that, people got into these other acts. Because we figured if you liked Dylan, if you liked The Byrds, if you liked Simon & Garfunkel, the odds are you're going to like this kind of music as well, but we can't get it exposed any other way unless you hear it. And the only way to hear it was to have a record you could play. So we did that, and all of a sudden we got all of those acts off and we started bringing them over to England to do dates."

"When I got to Philips in '69, Philips was a completely creatively more abundant company. Yeah, they had a few big acts, but they didn't sell huge volumes of records and there was no depth. I mean there was Dusty Springfield and she did very well, and there was Walker Brothers and they did very well, but there was nothing new. They'd been around for a while. There was nothing new, and I wanted something to rejuvenate the company. The two labels were Fontana and Philips, and they were so far down people's recognition factor. People weren't used to buying hit singles on those labels, except in sort of rare instances. And I wanted to do something else, but the key to it, going back to what we'd done at CBS, was finding the right kind of artists, and what I wanted to do was to create a new label."

"So at the end of every day we used to gather in my office and sit and talk and have a bottle of wine or two, and out of one of those this whole idea developed. Then it was a question of where do we get the acts from? Because we needed to do it quickly. The only act that was on Philips that had any credentials in the right area was Colosseum, who'd had one album out, *Those Who Are About to Die Salute You*. They were managed by Gerry Bron and produced by Gerry Bron, so my first port of call was Gerry Bron to say, 'Are you getting the new album ready?' 'Yes we are.' 'How would you feel about it not coming out on Philips but coming out on a new label called Vertigo? And there'll be lots of promotion, lots of advertising, the whole company's going to be behind it. What do you think?' And he said, 'I think that sounds very good; I'd like to be a part of that.'"

"So we had our first act," continues Olav. 'The second act was another ex-Gerry Bron act, which was Manfred Mann. Manfred had left the Manfreds and wanted to do… his background in South Africa was in jazz music, and he wanted to go back to sort of progressive jazz. And I went to see him and he played me some stuff and I said right, you'll be on our first release. The third one was Juicy Lucy. Not brilliant, but okay. So we launched in the autumn. From the idea crystallizing in my office, three months later we'd launched the label in November '68."

"But we needed more acts all the time to feed into this, because what I wanted to do, initially, was put out three albums at a time to make a big statement. And we also had up our sleeves a sampler like we had with *Rock Machine*, which we did a year later. But I had to go to Birmingham for a meeting, and I got to Birmingham much earlier in the evening than I had intended. I checked into the hotel, had a meal, and then I thought it's only a half past nine. What the hell am I going to do? And I went to the front desk and said, 'Is there any music going on?' 'Oh yes,' they said, 'there's a classical concert at the Queen's…' I was meaning rock 'n' roll, and the guy said, 'Haven't a clue.' But there was a young guy in the back there who was a bellboy or something who said, 'If you're interested in that kind of music, if you walk the back way from the hotel towards the train station, there's a pub on the corner there. They have music every night upstairs.' 'Oh, okay, fine.'"

"So off I went. And I climbed up the stairs and could hear music—live music—playing. And a man I now know to be Jim Simpson was on the door taking the money, and I saw him do a double-take as he saw me, because I'd been in the papers and whatnot, and he did a double take and I thought oh, I've been nobbled. I went in. There was a band playing and the place was about a third full. And everybody was at the back of the room that were there. And there was a bar down one side. And there was a hub-bub of noise. Nobody was paying a blind bit of attention to this band. Then they finished and they took the stuff off and a new band was setting up."

"And all of a sudden the doors behind me opened, and I won't say hundreds, but certainly a large volume of people came into the room. And the people who'd been at the back all moved down the front. So I thought, oh this is interesting. Because when I signed bands or artists, I was as interested in the public's reaction as my own thoughts about it, because if they connect with the audience you've got a chance of actually doing something. If they don't connect, you could be wasting your time. And clearly there was a huge connection before they even started playing."

"And they come out and there's huge applause, and the room by now is full and I'm down towards the front because I thought this was going to be the right place to be. And whoa, on they came, and it was Black Sabbath. And they were absolutely amazing—they just tore the place up.

And what I was surprised about was Tony Iommi is a brilliant guitarist, absolutely fabulous guitarist, and I was surprised being… my first thoughts were it's a heavy metal band. But in fact, as they went on, I realized they were much more than that, because a lot of the lyrics were not only intelligent but they dealt with some difficult subjects. And musically they were terrific. Absolutely terrific. And of course they built up a huge atmosphere."

"Then there was an interval," continues Olav, "and at the interval I went out to the front and there was Jim. And I said, 'I guess you look after the band?' 'Yes, I look after the band.' 'Are you promoting the gig as well?' 'Yeah, in order to get them work I have to promote the gig.' So I said, 'I think they're very good. Could we perhaps have a chat afterwards?' And he said yes. And then he said, 'You're Olav Wyper from Philips, aren't you?' And I said yes. And he said, 'Well yeah, I'd like to meet you.' So I went back in, the band completed the second set, which was also brilliant. By now more people had arrived and we're all sort of pushed together down the front. So after the gig, next door to this pub was a Chinese restaurant, and I took them, all of them, out to dinner at this Chinese restaurant, and talked them into coming with us on Vertigo. And they were aware of Vertigo because the first releases had been out. And I wanted them to be on the next release, which indeed they were with the first album."

Asked about the magic he heard that day, Olav admits that "the sound was not a sound that I was that familiar with, to be honest. Because they seemed to have worked out, either instinctively or deliberately—I never asked the question, to be fair—the relationship between bass, drums and guitar. Because Bill would lay down a very, very solid rhythm, and it was placed loudly at the forefront of the mix, the very basic mix with the very almost amateur gear they had out front. And he and Geezer, the two of them, laid down a fantastic rhythm which was very constant and very loud and then Tony just soared above it. And there were lots of jazz influences in his playing, for sure. And the combination of those two things gave it a sound that I thought was quite unique. And then of course you had Ozzy's vocals, and the combination of all three of those elements was absolutely fantastic."

As for Geezer's memories concerning the signing of Sabbath, well, further contradictions with the stories from Jim and Olav arise.

"We went to seven record companies before we got a record deal. They just didn't get it. We literally used to have to play in their offices or we'd have to go down to London at like nine o'clock in the morning to where *they* wanted to go, the record companies. And I always remember this one record company. We were in Carlisle, which is the northern-most part of England, and we had to do a gig and then drive all night to play this audition at a pub at 11 o'clock in London. So none of us had slept. Tony used to do the driving in those days because we couldn't afford a driver. And we lugged all our gear in. We were all absolutely exhausted. And the guy came from the record company and had this horrible attitude about him, but we're all going this is our big chance. And we started playing, and he just literally walked out. After about half-way through the second song. Just walked out. And that's the way they treated us. They really didn't get it, or they didn't want to get it."

"With Vertigo we had to go and record three cover songs before they'd even listen to us," continues Geezer, "because they heard some band from Birmingham writing their own stuff. 'Well let's hear something else.' We want to hear them play something that we know. So we did these... somebody else's songs. I think one of them was 'Evil Woman' that went on the first album. And two or three other cover versions. And for some reason they were interested, and then we got this A&R guy called Tony Hall, and he really liked us, and he finally got Vertigo to sign us. I mean they gave us enough money for two days in the studio and that was it."

"But we were really glad to be on any label. EMI had a label called Harvest; I think ELP were on it or something like that. Because people didn't really know how to classify us, so it was kind of a miscellaneous thing. If they couldn't sum you up as blues or rock or whatever, they'd put you on this other label. So that's how we ended up on Vertigo."

Bill Ward said Vertigo signed the band "because that's the only label that would have us. It's one of those jobs. It's like the Beatles story, again. Parlophone was the only label that would pick the Beatles up. And yeah, we'd shopped to a lot of different labels, but it was like no way. Because a lot of record companies are going to look for safety first. Everybody's going to be a little shy of taking on a risqué band. I'm not saying that's the blanket statement for all record companies either, but back then, nobody was interested in Black Sabbath's music, and I think we got a deal through a deal through a deal through a deal. And I think Philips were a little bit blind-sided. I don't know if they could see this train coming, but it got us on a record. We were barely grasping who we were, so it wasn't important for the press to grasp who we were or the record company. God, they had no chance. We were barely going, 'Hmm, we're doing something here, aren't we?'"

Further on the Vertigo signing, Bill says that "both Jim Simpson and Tony Hall Enterprises—Tony Hall was representing us and trying to shop us too—Vertigo were really the last people that we could try. It was rather like a Beatle-esque story when Decca turned the Beatles down and they ended up on this silly label called Parlophone, and basically all the label had done at the time was with George Martin and did silly comedy acts and that. So the Beatles went into Parlophone, but at least they were on vinyl, and when they were on vinyl of course then that's all it took with the Beatles. I think we were kind of like where the hell are we going to put this band? And we got to get them something. We got to get them on the air some way. So I think we ended up on Vertigo. I don't know if they wanted us or not. I don't remember meeting anybody from Vertigo, to be honest, but put us on vinyl and that's all we needed. Put us in a record shop and we'll do the rest. All the mainstream labels, we had no chance. I mean just out of appearance alone, we put off most people, let alone listen to our music. I mean have you ever seen any early pictures of The Pretty Things? We had real long hair and were real haggard. Really quite different people."

"We had trouble fitting in, but what we had was we had us and we had our music and we had our initial hardcore fans. So we had that. But I think Vertigo was a label that really didn't understand us at all. *We* didn't understand us, so I don't expect the record company to. We were just starting to like… oh wow, you played that? What did you just play, Bill? What was that lyric? So it was kind of like that. We were learning about us as well, so I wouldn't have any expectation at all that Vertigo knew what was going on."

As alluded to by Geezer, the first spot of product to come out of Sabbath was a single, pairing Crow cover "Evil Woman" with Sabbath original "Wicked World." Issued on another Philips imprint, Fontana, according to Wyper, the single was rush-released to create some underground interest.

Come time to create visuals to go with the band's recently conjured penchant for black witchery, Vertigo Records came up with cover art that featured a grainy photo of a green-tinted "witch" in front of an old English house. Open the original gatefold vinyl, and you have the album's credits and a short spooky tale housed within an upside-down cross.

"Certainly, the upside down cross was not our idea," notes Tony. "When we saw the album cover, that was in there, but I suppose what it was, was that they were asked to do an album cover, and it went with the name of the band and they put this image together and did the album cover from that, whoever designed it. And they came up with that idea. From then on of course, we had all sorts of things happen over the years. Because playing under the name of Black Sabbath, you can imagine the sort of people we attracted."

Original—and now quite rare—UK issues of *Black Sabbath* had the gatefold art black with white type. Later issues were white with black type. North American issues were housed in standard, non-gate sleeve and didn't include this artwork in any form.

The mysterious lady on the cover soon revealed herself. "Yeah, it was a gig in, I believe, Lincolnshire in England," says Geezer, "and this girl came up to us, dressed just like the cover. And she was allegedly that person. Whether it's true or not, there's no way of proving it."

"We didn't know her at the time," affirms Tony. "We did, of course, meet her afterwards down the line. She showed up at a show and said, 'I was the lady on the front of the album.' And we went, 'Oh!' (laughs). But no, we didn't see her at the time."

"I just found out, again, from the internet," adds Geezer, on the locale of the infamous cover shoot. "Someone had gone there and got a photograph taken there, and I was actually going to use that as the album cover for my new album (this interview took place during the press for Geezer's '05 solo album *Ohmwork*). I was going to go to that exact place and have the band stand in front of it, that mill. And it's a place in Oxfordshire, not far from where I live in England." In fact, the structure is the Mapledurham Watermill, located on the River Thames.

Ozzy's kitchen tap necklace, and then the inner gatefold's surprise crucifix, were early examples of what would become Sabbath's penchant for crosses. Indeed, Ozzy's handy father Jack wound end up making about a hundred of them for the band, and from thereon in, you always saw shots of the Sabbath guys, crucifixes around their necks, prime stated purpose being to stave off evil, which the band frankly and overtly attracted through their actions, their early lyrics and their ominous new invention, heavy metal.

"We couldn't afford to buy any, so Ozzy's dad made them," affirms Geezer. "I mean, we really took it seriously at the time. They were aluminum. Our old manager bought us solid gold ones eventually. I think that was in payment for the album we had out at the time (laughs)."

"Ozzy's pop, who was a toolmaker, forged the first ones," said Bill on the subject in a mid-'70s interview, muddling the subject of the metals. "They were made of iron and very heavy. They were made to protect us against the evil spirits, against the Satanists. It was so strange. Satanists were calling us to complain about our using Black Sabbath as a name. At Christmas, Pat Meehan, our manager, is getting us crosses in platinum! The rest have been either in gold or in aluminum. Can you believe it, platinum!"

"Sometimes we've felt that God could be Satan," preached Rev. Ward in the same interview. "What I mean is we are living in an evil world. Therefore Satan could be God. But let's leave it at that, please. I have a concept of God that isn't just Christ, but is a God for everybody. That's why we all wear crucifixes. God is neither good nor evil. There's some of the devil, or Abraxas, in God. That's why Black Sabbath can be into God, why we can worship him and wear these crucifixes. If he was supposed to be only good, we couldn't believe in him."

"We thought to ourselves, we need to get a new angle," says Ozzy, looking back 30 years later. "There was all this flower power and wishful thinking, that the world was so great. If you were in the sunshine with flowers in your hair, smoking pot, that was great, but the world isn't all sunny. And we thought, 'Isn't it amazing that people pay to get the shit scared out of them?' So we just decided to do an opposite angle to all the flower power stuff. Because that's really more Satanic; if there is a Satan, he isn't going to have fire coming out of his ass and horns on his head and a fucking forked tongue. He's going to be just like you and me. He's going to be cunning and baffling—if you actually believe in that kind of thing. I think Heaven and Hell are on this earth. You can make anything you want out of it. But more people have died in the name of God than anything and as far as I'm concerned, any kind of violence achieves nothing."

"Well, it's actually all down to a designer called Keith McMillan," explains Olav, on the cover art fashioned for *Black Sabbath*. "I don't know whether you've come across Keith. I met Keith when I was at CBS and I produced the very first pop promo in England that was shown on Top of the Pops for Fleetwood Mac's *Albatross*, in fact. We made it in black and white; that's how long ago it was. And there was a young guy who was the focus puller on that shoot, and we got talking and I said, 'What are you doing? You're a not a focus puller; that's not your job is it?' He said, 'No, I'm a student at the Royal College of Art. I'm a photographer, in fact, but I know somebody who's involved in the shoot professionally and if ever you need a focus puller or anybody to carry cameras or boxes, I'm your man at the weekends.' And we'd made this on a weekend."

"And he said to me, 'My final exhibition, my sort of pass-out exhibition, is in a couple weeks. Would you like to come?' And I said yeah, sure, and he gave me a ticket and I turned up. And I was completely bowled over by these photographs. Some were in black and white, some were in colour, but the thing about each image was it told a complete story. You could just look at it and you knew it wasn't just a picture of this. If it's two people, you knew the relationship between the people, you knew the background was important."

"So when we started Vertigo I got him in and said I'd like you to have a go on some of these sleeves. He ended up doing most of them, in fact. And because his imagery was so accurate, I didn't want to give him any ideas. I'd give him a white label pressing and say come back to me with ideas. And very rarely did I ever not like his ideas. Usually they were absolutely spot-on. And he'd listen to the music, he'd go and see the band, he'd go and talk to them, he'd meet them, then he'd come back to me with a mock-up of what the sleeve might be. And it might be partly drawn, it might be with some… if he'd been able to take some photographs of the band, they'd be Polaroids and they'd just sort of be pasted in."

"And I had said all the albums will be gatefold; most of them, in fact, will be three-fold, which they were because we wanted to make a statement. It was very important with Vertigo that it presented a sort of musical lifestyle. So if you were into this kind of music, any act on that label would appeal to you. And we advertised the label as a label, and we obviously promoted the bands on it, but we promoted the label as a concept as fondly as we did the acts. I'd always been very interested in kinetic art, optical art. And in a previous life when I'd been in PR, I'd set up for Peter Stuyvesant, the thing called the Peter Stuyvesant Art Foundation, and we had exhibitions and gave bursaries to new artists."

"One of those new artists that I insisted was in that was a lady called Bridget Riley, who's one of the leading artists of that kind of thing in the world. And I was a huge fan of hers and used to talk to her and things, and discovered how a still image, when you looked at it, could make it move in your head. And so I wanted a kinetic design and I wanted it on just one side of the label. And so that when it rotated it did something, it said something. I wanted it to be different. I wanted it to stand out from all the other labels. It was very rare to get a gatefold sleeve, and a three-fold sleeve? Completely unknown. We broke new ground doing that. And what I wanted was the buyer of the record to have an experience that was visual as well as aural, that would make him want to go on and collect more of it."

More specifically on the famed Vertigo swirl logo, Olav explains that, "record labels didn't have designs on them. They just had the information on them. And the way that the Vertigo design came around was I… we'd been playing around. Philips, at the time, was the only record company that had an art department. Everybody else had all the art done, the sleeves designed, ads designed outside. For some reason Philips still had it all done inside the company. And I set them challenges to come up with ideas. I wanted this thing, as it revolved, I wanted it to say something to the person who put it on and was watching it go around."

"And I was stuck in a traffic jam on the way home one night, and the inside of my car had fogged up. It was winter, the heater was on and it was raining, and it had fogged up. And I was looking out of the window, and there was a shop. It had a bit of an art display in the front and I wanted to see it and I couldn't. And I started doing that (moves his finger in a swirl), making a bigger circle, and as I got to the biggest circle and could see what it was, suddenly it occurred to me—that's what the record label had to do. And when I went in the office, Margaret Glover, who was the best of the young artists, I said to Margaret, 'Look, I've got an idea. I don't know how to work it, but this is the basic idea. I want it to do that, but not just draw you in by taking you there—it has to work against itself.' And she came up with that design. And I had a huge fight with Philips in Holland, who didn't want it to be a label other than Philips—and I offered to resign and take my entire team with me. So they gave in. And I also insisted that I had the label on one side and all the information relating to what was on it on the reverse side. Soon as I left they changed that."

And hence the iconic Vertigo swirl logo was born.

But to get to seeing it on a Black Sabbath record, first you had to crack the cellophane while the green witch looked on… "Yes," says Olav, "and that cover art opened a whole opportunity and world for them. And it all came out of Keith's head. Keith was brilliant at what he did, and very rarely did I ever say I'm not sure about that. Because his instinct for it was absolutely right. It created a mood, the whole thing about the occult. And the sort of whisperings about, 'Oh, listen, they're an occult band. I wonder what they believe in,' had started in the press. And that sleeve helped that whole idea."

'One thing about Olav," reflects Jim, "he knew about packaging and marketing. The photographer was called Keef something, and I was in the same boat as the band. I was badgering to discuss the artwork and he said, 'No, trust me, I've got a guy to do it.' And I think Keef did most of the other Vertigo stuff, and it was the house style. And we were all very skeptical until we saw it. And then we all… it hit us immediately. It was exactly right. It was exactly how we would have imagined it had we the ability to imagine. It was great. I guess you might say we had final approval, but I doubt even that. Remember, he had this schedule to fill. He had VO6, firstly without any recordings, secondly without any artwork. He got it done and done quickly, so he and Keef got their heads together and they did a brilliant job. Had we disliked it, my feeling is we would have had a head-on collision with him. But we didn't—we liked it. And they're quite right when they say we had little to do. We didn't even discuss the photo session. We saw the finished photo session."

As for the upside-down cross, Simpson says, "It was all part of the package. That was Keef, the photographer and the designer. They delivered the whole thing. And I have to say, we didn't go through it with a fine tooth comb and say, 'Hmm, that cross is upside-down.' We saw it as an entity, and as an entity we felt it worked. And obviously we were bowled over by the image on the gatefold sleeve. That was a stunner. For me personally, I guess I didn't even notice the cross was upside-down, particularly. I just saw what was a nice piece of design. I didn't think of the imagery and the fact that it might upset people by being upside-down, I just thought it looked like a nice image."

"I don't know the story of how the cover came together," muses Bill. "It was something that was presented to us, and being our usual morbid selves, which is pretty much where we were at, just grumpy, angry, rebellious young men… it always reminds me of that movie *Rebel Without a Cause*? Where he says, 'What are you rebelling against?' And he says, 'Whaddaya got?' So that was kind of part of our whole frame of mind. So when we saw that album cover, I think we were all instantaneously attracted to it. I just saw something that was really morbid. It goes great on a rainy day with a bowl of soup or something."

"The inside cover, none of us liked it—didn't like it at all. Because it had an inverted cross in it. Because I think there was some wise guys or some people who had either deliberately put that together as a ploy, as an advertising promotional ploy, or who had seriously misgauged us as a band. And so there was no collaboration between art and artist at that point. I don't even know who was responsible for it, but I guess somebody thought it would be a good idea to have that, and that was something that we were representing somehow."

"But that wasn't us, not at all. I saw our band as a really solid, hardcore rock band that was hard and interactive with the audience. I saw us as almost punk-ish. There were many times when we would interact with the audience, somewhat violently sometimes. If you've seen The Who throwing their stuff around, well there were other bands that did that, including Black Sabbath. There were many times when our interaction was pretty rough around the edges, and it was all balls-out, it was real. So I saw us like that and I was very passionate about who we were, or who I thought we were, and I saw us as this outrageous, loud, and really dirty band."

And the upside-down cross was a bridge too far.

"Yes, I mean we were all interested in things that were unusual, the same way as a lot of 18-, 19-year-old men would want to look into different things. All of us had an awareness of things supernatural; we all liked horror movies. We all liked, to one degree or another, classical music and the violence in classical music. So we had common interests, we had common ground. It didn't surprise me. We all had a common interest when Tony went to what I call dark notes. What are commonly called the tri-tones. When he went to those dark notes, for a drummer it's just like Heaven, or what I conceive as Heaven, because it's just so beautiful to play to. It's huge, it's enormous, and there's so much energy inside it. So for a drummer it's the perfect romance."

"But yeah, upside-down cross, I thought it was a bad taste call. I don't think any of us liked it. And not just that, we were a band that did everything together. If we all walked to the right then we all walked to the right. Nobody walked to the left. We had this very weird coming together as a unit. And Ozzy's father had given us the crosses, which were the original Sabbath crosses. And there's nothing upside-down about those crosses, and he'd given us those because he believed they were in a higher power and he believed the crosses might help us in our many journeys. He was just concerned about us being able to—this is Ozzy's father, Jack—and Jack was concerned about making sure we were all safe and sound. So what he did, he gave us all… I think there were five originally made, one for our road manager as well. So Satanic rock, I think that's part our element today, but it wasn't a part of Sabbath's… I mean, we went and covered many topics, but in the literal sense of being Satanic, no."

"We weren't allowed to see anything like that," recalls Geezer, on the packaging for the first album. "We saw that I think the night before the album came out. Literally when it was in the shops. Like oh, by the way, here's your copy. I always remember going over to the manager's house and he had like an album each for us. And we're like, 'Oh, what's this?' And he said, 'Your new album.' But no. we saw the sleeve. We were going, 'Oh, this is good.' Then we opened it and we saw the upside-down cross and all went absolutely mental. Because I just didn't want to be associated with anything like that, upside-down crosses and all that. Having been brought up Catholic and everything, I just kept thinking my mom and dad are going to go nuts at me when they see that. But that was it. That's as far as it went. Well, we can't change it now. It's in the shops tomorrow."

"When I look back on it now I love that front cover," continues Butler. "It's great. And because you think you're going to sell about ten copies and that's it, you don't think of image and all that kind of stuff—you just want people to hear your music. And I just thought by having the upside-down cross, it would just put a lot of people off. I mean this was 1969, well 1970, so there's a lot of things going on. Religious wars in Ireland and being blown up in England, Vietnam going on and everything, I just thought it was a bit too heavy."

The occult imagery of the *Black Sabbath* packaging quickly resulted in Sabbath being confused with a much more overtly Satanic band plying their trade in 1970. "Yes," says Geezer, "there was another band called Black Widow at the time, and they were doing all these fake sacrifices onstage and trying to invoke Satan, and we just thought it was really hokey and silly. So we didn't want any kind of association with that thing. So to us it looked like the record company were trying to push that image on us and it would be… I mean there was one song on the album, 'N.I.B.,' which is like putting that whole… it was about Satan falling in love, which was just like a humorous kind of put-down of all these people that thought they were into black magic and everything. But I think because of the imagery a lot of people—and obviously the name—people just thought it was all about black magic without listening to the lyrics."

At the production helm of Black Sabbath's self-titled debut album (at the behest of Tony Hall and his Tony Hall Enterprises) was a chap called Rodger Bain, who wasn't so much there to produce the band but rather get them down on vinyl quickly and efficiently with a minimum of fuss and as much audio fidelity as he could wring out of a couple days' sessions. Rodger had seen the guys play at Henry's Blues House, famously saying that they had "the biggest balls in Britain." The stated aim for the work they were to do together, according to manager Jim Simpson, was to out-heavy Led Zeppelin's recently issued and much vaunted *II* record.

"He brought two days recording," chuckles label boss Wyper, on the subject of Rodger, "which, for the record company, of course, was a complete joy, financially. But he also brought liveness, because it was recorded live. It wasn't recorded the way most records were, where you tended to do the rhythm track then you did the solos and all the rest of it, and you did the vocals after that. You may have done a guide vocal, but then you'd go in and do the vocal again. It was all live, basically, and what they captured on that first album, without a lot of production technique, was the rawness of the band onstage. And that was a very important element for the fan base they'd built up. As the albums went on—and certainly *Paranoid* was part of that—they were more produced."

"It was a new thing for Rodger as well," muses Tony Iommi, "because we were sort of his first project, I think. And because we were very green through the whole thing, we didn't know any different from who was going to come from the record company or what. We didn't know who was who. So they just sent Rodger Bain along to sort of work with us, really, to produce this album. So it was sort of his test as well, really, for the record company. But he was very good, good for us in those days, because we knew absolutely nothing. I mean, by today's standards, he probably wouldn't know a lot, but he did at that point, certainly a lot more than we knew as far as the production side of it went. He seemed to work a lot with the engineer we had at that time. I think it was Tom Allom, who was very helpful as well. So it worked as a little team, to come up with ideas, like on 'Black Sabbath' with the bell and the rain. But he didn't have much input musically, because all that was basically done. But the little effects and sounds were down to them."

Assisting Rodger was a young Tom Allom, who would go on to great things as long-time producer with Judas Priest. "I stumbled into it," laughs Allom. "I got a job as a recording engineer in a little recording studio in London. The other engineer there knew me from a time where I did a holiday job at a studio that he had started out at. He knew me and he knew that I was interested in tape recording and he said, 'Do you want to have a crack at it?' I said, 'I'll have a go at it.' It was a console that had 12 ins and four outs. We had to persuade the boss to get a second four-track machine. It was soon after that when we did the first Black Sabbath album."

"We did that with them using two four-tracks," continues Tom. "They were not in sync; we were bouncing from one to the other. It wasn't anywhere near as difficult to learn the ropes as it would be today in a full-fledged studio. At the same time, you had to learn to work with what you had. You had to do an awful lot outside of what you had on the console. We really didn't have any outboard equipment. It was really quite elementary."

Allom was completely green at the job. "I was. I started in the fall of 1968, so I had only been there for a year, if that. It was baptism by fire. I had no idea who Black Sabbath was when they came in. But we captured a new sound and Rodger Bain, who was the producer, has to take credit for that. He really did understand the way it should sound. I had never seen the band live. Rodger was a very intuitive producer and he never got anywhere enough credit for what he did. There was just something about it. I can't say that we did this or we did that—it just happened. The first album was done in four days. It was two sessions, from 10:00 AM to 10:00 PM. Can you imagine getting Black Sabbath up at 10:00 AM? Those two sessions were for the recording. Then, there were two sessions from 10:00 AM to 6:00 PM for the mixing. After those four sessions, it was done, finished and in the can. I think the whole record cost £500 pounds, including the photo of that lady in front of the mill. They did quite a good return on that £500."

And that £500, of course, includes the bell and the rain. Opening Black Sabbath's debut record was the band's earthquaking namesake track, an excruciatingly slow, yet inexorably advancing mud wall of doom. Relentless rain and metronomic tubular bells accompany the band as they play the devil's music, scaring the bejesus out of an unsuspecting rock public ill-attuned to such overt tales of Satan. All the while Tony crouches behind a simple, lightly strummed riff that is the soundtrack to Chinese water torture, a riff that explodes in metal glory periodically, and then as the action heats up, caves way to a thrilling, staccato, even more metallic squall of post-flower power profanity.

The band knew they had something, as Bill explains, just not quite sure what. "When we did the song 'Black Sabbath,' I think we knew we were definitely onto something different. Just by the audience reaction at the pubs we were playing at at the time. We loved the heavier stuff. We were all into Hendrix and Cream and Zeppelin. I don't know. The one thing that appealed to us was taking that sound and, not consciously making it heavier than everybody else, but I don't know… it just fitted our feeling at the time."

"Well, certainly Cream, I liked, but I more so liked John Mayall's Blues Breakers, to be honest," says Tony, again underscoring the band's almost imperceptible graduation from heavy blues to the heavy metal that suffocates the track. "That was more the bands we sort of all liked. And when Clapton joined Cream of course, I wasn't too keen on that. I did like them, but not as much as John Mayall's Blues Breakers. So that was our early blues influence."

"The Shadows," laughs Tony, yet another time, trying to articulate the influences that improbably had taken rock 'n' roll from the American black experience to "Black Sabbath." "All different sorts of things. I don't know what makes you come up with that sort of music. The music just formed the way it did. Our roots were the blues, John Mayall, Cream. And we never termed ourselves as heavy metal anyway. It's always been just 'rock' or 'heavy rock.'"

How about more specifically, the minor keys, the doom, the diabolus in musica illustrated by the "Black Sabbath" riff? "Nothing I can think of. We just sort of liked it. It just sounded heavy and ominous, and we just liked that type of approach. It just materialized from the stuff we were doing at that time, which was all blues. We were just dabbling around and said, 'Oh I like that sound,' and it just formed the basis for all those songs. I mean, 'Wicked World' was the first song we wrote, then 'Black Sabbath.'"

"On the first album, we never had any input," once said Iommi. "Only from the standpoint of what we were giving them. That was how we played, and that's how they taped us. Our sound was based on the guitar. The initial riff I'd come up with would set the scene for the song. And I sort of had more influence than anybody else, probably because I'd been with Jethro Tull. They looked at me like, 'Oh well, he left them and come back with us, so we gotta listen to him.'"

"The 'Black Sabbath' lyrics, Ozzy came up with them," notes Geezer, who would proceed to write almost all of the Sabbath lyrics through all of the records from the ensuing Ozzy era. "He just like wrote them on the spot. We didn't even write them down. It was like, that was the first thing out of his mouth. He knew I was into the occult and things like that, so we used to talk about it. I told him about some weird things that were happening to me, and I think that stuck in his mind. And when we did the song 'Black Sabbath,' it had a doomy riff anyway, so he just came out with those lyrics, as a warning to me about Satanism. It was about how you had to be aware of what happens to yourself when you get mixed up in black magic."

"My lyric writing came about because no one else in the band could do it," continues Geezer. "Ozzy did some lyrics. I think he did like two sets of lyrics on the first album. 'Black Sabbath,' like I said, he just like ad-libbed those lyrics, but then when it came down to coming up with something else, he was stuck (laughs). Tony couldn't do lyrics, Bill couldn't do them, so it was left to me. So I sort of got the knack for them. But 'Black Sabbath' was another bass riff. We knew it was different then because it was a different approach. I don't think bass players wrote stuff before like that. At the time Paul McCartney was the most famous, but the Beatles didn't write riffs on bass. So I think we sort of set a precedent for the way we were writing from then on. Everything was sort of bass riffs. Even when Tony wrote them on guitar, it was like how the bass would be."

"I remember playing 'Mars,' Gustav Holst (hums the riff), on the bass when we were doing those… when we were rehearsing. And I'm not sure if it did, but it seemed to influence Tony to go (hums more of the riff), the same sort of tritonic thing. And it was just done in a flash. Like, Tony came up with the riff, Ozzy started singing the lyrics; it really did write itself by the end of one morning. And we just thought this is really weird, different. Let's just give it a try on the next gig. And we did the gig and we thought, should we play it or not? And we played it right at the end, 'Black Sabbath,' and the crowd just went absolutely mental. And they're saying, 'Play that again, play that again.' So we played it again. Played it three times. And we just realized that we had something that nobody else had, which just spurred us on to keep writing."

"I mean we played this place maybe three or four times and they all knew exactly what to expect from us because we were playing the usual 12-bars. And then we threw in 'Wicked World' and finished with 'Black Sabbath.' And until then people were just at the bar drinking, completely ignoring us. And the whole place just stopped dead, like what the hell is this?! And it was just such an incredible feeling."

And at the very nexus, heavy metal was born. Or to put a finer point on it, it was born in the writing, but had now been foisted upon an unsuspecting public. Geezer demurs at the assessment. "You'd have to ask the other people. I don't understand it myself. With me it probably started with The Kinks. 'You Really Got Me' was probably the first really heavy song I heard. Or The Who, 'Anyway Anyhow Anywhere.' But 'Black Sabbath,' that had the total slowed-down everything and the weird timing, and different lyrics that weren't about falling in love or breaking up with your baby. So I think people cite it from that, I suppose. And heavy metal means lots of things now. It went from being derogatory to being encompassing. So many bands, so many different kinds of metal out, you have to be a metallurgist to figure out what it is."

Bill confirms Gustav Holst's particularly foreboding "Mars, the Bringer of War" as an influence on "Black Sabbath." "Those notes that Tony picked, Geezer was trying to pluck the notes to 'Mars' and the very next day Tony showed up and just changed one note. I'm not saying Tony took that riff from Holst or took it from Geezer, even, but I know there's a story about that that Geezer tells. But when Tony played it, it's the way he played it. He lengthened the notes and he held them out. In that sense, I think that's completely orchestration. I think an orchestra could get behind that and sound incredibly powerful."

As for the fast part, which one might frame as an early metal gallop, Ward says, "What's really neat about the latter half is that whenever I'm missing some of the feelings or the memories of the late '60s, and where I was in my life, and where I was with the fellas, that was a great example. It's a great example of the almost renaissance feel there was in that era. It's still popular today—it hasn't gone anywhere, its longevity is forever. But it really helps me in my own personal… sometimes I miss things, obviously, and I miss those times. And when I listen to Tony playing that, it reminds me of a time. There are some other bands as well that remind me very much of the atmosphere of that era, of the early '70s and late '60s."

"But I liked the idea of when we would put something together and it crunched and it was balls-out and it sounded brilliant—that would make my day. That was it for me. And that other people were attracted to it and scared by it. I've always tried to be detached from that and let them find what they need to find in it. I'm saying that because I don't believe that we were deliberate; I think that's what I'd like to say about that. I never remember being in rehearsals with the guys where Tony or any of us would turn around and say, 'Yeah, that's not quite right; that's not quite scary enough.' Where we were thinking about our audience and saying, 'Now let's put this in instead; that's more scary.' I never heard any deliberate writing like that. The writing was influenced by the four of us. Actually by the five of us—there's the other elements we haven't talked about yet. But it seemed very natural to me, very matter-of-fact. Some hard work was involved too. We didn't just sit around and a song would suddenly show up. I know all of us worked hard to make each song. But it seemed very natural and not contrived—the music would come to us."

"Again, it's reaching that primal place inside," continues Bill, a born drummer in that he often circles back to this concept. "When I went on stage every night playing drums—which I still do—I have to reach a place inside. If I don't accomplish that place inside at that gig, then I don't feel I had a good gig. I have to meet that place where I can be almost primal, find the bottom of myself. It's almost orgasmic, I guess, this place I have to find every single night, and it's great because when all the band's playing and feeling the rush and the power, it's like yeah, a great place to be. So the sound of that song was very attractive to a lot of people, and they were going there and we would go there. But it was a different place now. Everyone had heard The Who, everyone was listening to Zeppelin, but now it was going somewhere else and it was very loud when it was going there. That attracted an immense... millions of people."

"And it was scary too. If it repels people, it's because they don't want to talk about the subjects, they don't want to hear it. That's why people play safe music. When you're writing on different subjects that are not necessarily subjects that everyone wants to talk about or everyone wants to hear, then the ears turn down. Most people want to live in a cotton ball and feel safe, get their meal at six o'clock at night and maybe get laid on the weekend and that's it. And for some people, that's okay, that's enough, there's nothing wrong with that. Whereas other people don't necessarily have that desire for that. They're crazy for loud and strange music."

"Black Sabbath" includes a third verse which was rarely used (one can experience it on Ozzy rarities/hits package *The Ozzman Cometh*). Fleshing out the short tale of an ill-meaning witch, Satan by her side, this bit of text adds a nasty image of a child watching its mother in flames, the narrator then added to the bonfire as well.

Comments Ozzy, nearly 30 years after the fact, "My greatest hits album, I wasn't too keen with putting the Sabbath basement tapes on it. It isn't really my career and isn't the best Ozzy hits. These songs weren't hits. See, every record company's got to have a different angle though, and there's the interview and the one new song, so I guess it's a good idea because number one, they're fresh, because they were before we even made a record. And I don't know where they're actually from, I really don't. But I know they were before the first album, because when we used to do 'Black Sabbath' before we recorded it; there was an extra verse and the verse is on there. And the lyrics, I didn't know what the fuck I was on about. We'd do a lot of writing on the way to the gig, or the morning of. We'd have the melody line and that's it."

The fact that any rock band was writing about Satan was a hair-raising rarity. In fact, during the decade following the issuance of *Black Sabbath*, only a handful of bands would dare follow. Monument, Coven, Bram Stoker, Pentagram, Black Widow, perhaps Alice Cooper here and there… there was next to nothing. Before Sabbath, you had Arthur Brown, maybe even Screaming Jay Hawkins, and certainly avowed magick man Graham Bond, who was to die mysteriously, hit by a subway in 1974. But the sum total is paltry, and none of it matched malevolent word with the stomach-churning volume and electricity of committed, undisputed heavy metal quite the way Sabbath did.

Leicester's Black Widow bears special mention on a number of counts. One was that the similarity of the band's name to Black Sabbath almost caused the Sabs to change their name for yet another time. Also, Black Widow were the real Satanic deal, or at least more enthusiastically showy about it than Sabbath was. Their 1970 United Artists debut *Sacrifice* included titles such as "Come to the Sabbat," "In Ancient Days," "Conjuration" and "Attack of the Demon," and live, the band did feature Satanic rituals as part of their act, resulting, not surprisingly, in all sorts of press. The two bands would be constantly confused for a couple of years in this regard and in others—a famous mainstream *Black Sabbath* record review denigrating the singer on the album, Kip Trevor, who was, of course, none other than Black Widow's lead singer and not Black Sabbath's. Musically there was no getting the two confused. Black Widow was a jazzy light progressive act with flutes, who over three records became vaguely louder but still very much prog. Sabbath, on the other hand, started hard and just got impossibly harder.

As Geezer has said, there certainly was a level of interest in the dark arts, culminating in Butler painting his apartment black! "Yeah, that was when I was into the ol' black magic stuff," affirms Geezer. "I'd left home, and I'd always wanted, like most teenagers, to have a garish-coloured room, so I decided to paint my room totally black and have all inverted crosses over the place—totally into the black magic thing. I think the ceilings were orange (laughs). It was like a Halloween museum. Plus I had some posters, psychedelic stuff. I used to read on the subject a lot as well, and I used to read a lot of fiction. Plus I was into things like *The Hobbit*, *Lord of the Rings*, all of that, back then, which was really popular in the late '60s."

Geezer explains, 35 years after the event, that a line soon had to be drawn in the sand. "Ozzy had brought me this really old black magic book, and it was all in Latin and Greek or whatever. And somebody had sent it to him, and he knew that I was interested in reading all that stuff. He brought me this book 'round, and I was looking through it, and I hid it in the cupboard where I was living. Because I just got a weird feeling from it. And the next day, I went to get it out of the cupboard, to re-read it, and it had disappeared. Completely gone into thin air. And then, I was lying in bed one night and I just felt this presence, and I woke up and I saw this black shape, just standing at the bottom of me bed staring at me, and it just totally freaked me out. And I told Ozzy about it, and that was when I went off black magic (laughs). This was like 1969. I took it as a warning to get out of it while I can."

And Geezer never saw that book again. "Never. Totally disappeared. And it was only me in the house at the time."

The above telling of this tale differs slightly from the apocryphal black cat story told by Sabbath fans, in which Geezer is actually in the act of looking at the book (described as 400 years old and handwritten). He then is startled by a black cat, turns back to the book, and it is gone.

"Oh yeah, Geezer's done all sorts of bloody things," laughs Tony. "We did actually live this sort of life at first. We were very interested in the other side of life, particularly Geezer and myself. We used to go and watch the horror movies and all sorts of stuff together, and really talk a lot about the other side of life. To the point where… it got to stage in the band where we were frightened to say anything, because things were happening when we were saying them. We thought, oh, let's not say anything about this. So it became sort of a bad penny. But that, it wasn't my apartment, it was his. He would do stuff like that, you know. Have all his candles burning. Black walls. He would live the part. That's the sort of thing he would do (laughs). We used to go around the black magic shops as well, when you can find one, of course. So there was a lot of interest, as far as that was concerned. Not a lot of practice, but interest."

"In those days, we didn't hang with Jimmy Page," clarifies Tony, when asked if he or Geezer ever went so far as to commiserate with the noted occultist over such matters. "It was more Robert and John we hung out with. Because Jimmy… you never saw Jimmy that often at all."

Speaking to Hit Parader, Tony talked about the band's penchant for the dark side, as well as expounding on other mysterious happenings concerning Geezer. "Things we've written about in the past have just been things that have happened, but people don't mention, really, things that are happening in the world. Satanism and a good bit about drugs and the bomb and things like that. Geezer's had dreams. This particular instance he had a dream that I was stuck in a lift and couldn't get out and all this kind of stuff, and right next day, I got stuck in a lift and couldn't get out. Which was really weird, because the night before he had this dream and he told me about it and the darn thing happened the next day. Just like that. It's happened a few times. He's got this thing. He can dream of things and they'll happen. Even in the early days with the things we got into on the first album, there was something pushing us into doing those sorts of things. It just sort of came out like it was meant to come out."

Geezer says he's had these dreams "from when I was a little child. I don't know if there's anything in the fact that I was born on the 17th day of the seventh month, 1949, 49 being seven sevens. I was the seventh child of a seventh child. And I always had a sort of… dreams that would come true. Sometimes I'd see ghosts and just get premonitions of things that would come true."

"A lot of people, when we first went over to the States, realized how different the band was," continues Tony, on Sabbath's sense of mystery. "It was like a new thing for them, because we were writing about things that were actually happening that people didn't really write about. Satanism and one thing and another. People really got into it. We were trying to throw things up to people so that they'd realize what was going on."

Back to the music, the second track on Black Sabbath's self-titled and genre-defining debut is jumpy, progressive proto-metal classic "The Wizard." Opening with harmonica, the song then goes into rule-breaking jam mode before settling into a pounding, metallic Bill Ward showcase of a verse, evocative of Keith Moon and his pioneering, rarely copied "lead" drumming technique.

"I really liked 'The Wizard,'" reminisces Bill. "That was a real sod to figure out. There are a lot of movements, just like 'Symptom of the Universe.' So doing that live, way back when—because we don't do either of those songs now unfortunately—but being on stage in the middle of a tour, those songs are really quite… not difficult, but you had to be pretty physical to be able to play both those songs. Especially 'The Wizard,' because it actually doesn't stop for me as a drummer from the beginning to the end. There's no actual time, so I'm actually just pushing it through with all the different rolls and things like that from top to bottom."

"I was reading *Lord of the Rings*, funnily enough at the time," laughs Geezer. "The lyric came from Gandalf and all that." Emphatically, "The Wizard" houses one of those Sabbath lyrics that is good, rather than evil, although all that ominous power chording around it might mask the casual listener as to its benevolence. Bottom line, this is a good wizard, spreading his magic, making the sun shine, making the people sigh happily. Only the demons worry.

It is of note that musically, Blue Öyster Cult would famously rip off—or send up, so to speak—"The Wizard" for their semi-hit and crowd favourite "Cities on Flame with Rock and Roll," Buck Dharma barely disguising the riff. Columbia had been jealous that they had lost out when Sabbath went with Warner Bros. stateside, and overtly bellowed that they had wanted their own, all-American version of Black Sabbath. Blue Öyster Cult had been a psych band that had gone through as many crazy name changes as the Sabs, eventually arriving at one last weird moniker, but with a sound that indeed, approximated a version of the thundering one owned by Black Sabbath. BÖC would begin a period of commercial success following 1976's *Agents of Fortune*, a stadium-level run which would last through the early '80s. The two bands collided for the bickering bad blood Black and Blue Tour which darkened much of the second half of 1980, with Sabbath out presenting their *Heaven and Hell* wares, the Cultsters wielding *Cultosaurus Erectus*.

Blue Öyster Cult drummer Al Bouchard cops to the nicking. "Patti Smith was loft-sitting for Johnny Winter. I don't know if she had anything going on with him or just taking care of his loft. Anyways, she was there, and that was the first time I met her. And I think that was the first time for all of us, and we rehearsed there in Johnny Winter's loft. And that first day, we wrote 'Cities on Flame with Rock and Roll.' That was our first attempt at imitating Black Sabbath. And of course we stole the lick from 'The Wizard;' it's well-documented. We stole the first part from 'The Wizard' and the second part from '21st Century Schizoid Man.' So, two of our favourite licks."

But yes, returning to the originators, next up on the Sabs' self-titled came a tangle of music that is partitioned differently depending on what version of the record one owns. Essentially the two full tracks are "Behind the Wall of Sleep" and "N.I.B.." The original European issue of the album lists just those two tracks. The original North American issue calls the vaguely psychedelic 32-second wash of music preceding "Behind the Wall of Sleep," "Wasp," and calls the funky, iconoclastic, highly memorable 41-second bass solo from Geezer that precedes "N.I.B.," "Bassically." This particular pressing grabs all four titles and assigns them a timing of 9:44 and also bands them as one track. The European version bands them as two tracks, assigning 3:40 and 5:58 respectively. Apparently all of this tomfoolery has to do with higher royalties being paid if you could get ten "songs" on an album.

"Behind the Wall of Sleep" is an unheralded, under-rated Sabbath track, Ozzy crooning in that strange low register he quickly left behind after the first record. Lyrically, the song is a cryptic, poetic, almost proto-environmental tale of death and dying.

"N.I.B.," often erroneously said to stand for nativity in black, gets its title in a less sinister manner. "'N.I.B.' is kind of a famous song," begins Bill. "That's the one we threw together in Switzerland in 1968, and actually 'N.I.B.' is named after me. The guys nicknamed me Nibby. I mean, Tony still calls me Nib to this day. It came out of a session, a time when we were doing a lot of opium (laughs). And we were all high and everything and for some reason through the hallucinogenics of it all, Geezer and Ozzy thought I looked like the top of a pen, you know? A pen nib. And they totally got lost behind the idea of that, cracking up. And it just stuck. And that's been it for the last 30-odd years. But I think it's just a real good hard rock song. I like Ozzy's lines. The 'oh yeah's showed up. That was kind of the stamp of approval on that one."

Still the nativity in black thing makes sense: this is probably Geezer's most patently evil lyric. "'N.I.B.' was supposed to be a humorous song about Satan falling in love with a woman. Because at the time, there were all these corny old films about the guys saying we'll give you the stars and the moon, like to your girlfriend. Whereas Satan could actually do that (laughs)." Humourous perhaps, but most definitely seductive and convincingly written.

"It was totally spontaneous in the studio," adds Geezer, on "Bassically," the aforementioned intro to "N.I.B.," "because I had just gotten the wah-wah pedal, and I was just playing about with it, and the producer at the time really liked it. And 'N.I.B.' was one of my riffs, so he just said, 'Do your bass solo and then go into the song.'"

Side two of the original vinyl begins two different ways, depending on which version of the record one purchased. European issues featured a cover of Crow's "Evil Woman."

Addressed earlier, but again, why a cover? "Why? Because that's what we thought we had to do," relates Bill. "Because we're really naive, I mean, even to this day. I think that's what we thought we had to do, but as soon as we did it, everybody was just so uncomfortable. I mean all of us were just going, 'Ugh, this feels horrible.' It was like going to the dentist or something. So we knew—we knew we had done the wrong thing."

Nonetheless, the track works. In this considerably heavied-up form, it makes sense for the leaden band at hand, both through its purposeful rumble and its, well, evil woman theme. Of note, an alternate version of "Evil Woman" can be heard on the expanded CD issue of *Black Sabbath*; here one finds pervasive flute-playing by Tony, and an Aerosmith-like horn arrangement. On both versions, the chorus is a little melodic, and even a little obvious given how the vocal melody follows the chord progression, but the overall melody is, all things considered, pretty dark. "Evil Woman" was released as a single on January 9th of 1970. The album, as mentioned, came out a few weeks later, selling 5000 copies in its first week and hanging around the UK charts for 13 weeks at onset (peaking at #8), and 42 weeks over various time periods. The album would eventually go platinum in the US, representing sales of over one million copies.

North American pressings of the album included Sabbath original "Wicked World," which was used as the b-side to the above-mentioned "Evil Woman" single, thereby, spanning the pond, killing two crows with one stone. As regards "Wicked World," once past a spirited but jazzy and dated intro, a characteristically doomy verse infects and spreads. Ozzy's vocal is back in low register mode, nearly to the point of sounding like the work of someone else, someone wiser. It is of note that similar to Steven Tyler on the first Aerosmith album but on no later records, Ozzy was singing this way to emulate the vocals of old blues legends. One might also surmise that there's an element of merely wanting to sound grown-up as well. And in Ozzy's case, certainly one would also have to bake into the cake a palpable lack of confidence and surety as to his singing abilities—a voice low register and with richness lent gravitas, an element young John would crave like a crutch at this juncture.

Says Bill of Tony and his jazz influences, "The first thing he ever wrote is 'Wicked World,' so I put the high hat down and he's on the top and it's totally jazz. So our very first song, you can really hear a lot of the jazz influences. You can hear it in 'Fairies Wear Boots' too; when you're doing those kinds of chops, it's swing, and the band can swing real well."

"Certainly 'Wicked World' was a 'make it up as you go along,' definitely the solo part," explains Tony. "It was very much a jam, so that would vary from time to time, night to night. So when we actually did record the album, it was actually longer than it is on the record, because I sort of went on a bit (laughs). And I wanted to do it again, but it was like, 'Oh, no, no, there's no time,' and that's the way it was in those days. You had a run at it, but it was such a long number for them and for that time, if you do it again, that's another ten or 15 minutes. 'No, no, that's enough' (laughs)."

Lyrically, Geezer is on his way to establishing himself as cynical documenter of the world's many plights. In a very short space, he speaks of war, disease, and finally a single mother trying to earn a living.

"I think there are quite a few," reflects Geezer, on themes in his lyrical canon. "That song was influenced by Vietnam. Elsewhere, I think science fiction played a big part, things like 'Iron Man.' So science fiction and fantasy and the supernatural, and a lot of politics as well. The one thing we didn't want to do was normal love songs, because everybody in the world was doing them. And our whole band was against all that anyway, everybody talking about splitting up with their girlfriend and stuff. But the reason we got together and made our music in the first place was because nobody else was doing it. So I just wrote about things that were interesting to me at the time. If I'd read a particularly good book, I'd condense that down to a song."

Closing the album is another tangle of tracks with jams. European versions cite "Sleeping Village" and "The Warning," an Aynsley Dunbar's Retaliation cover, as separate tracks, the former at 3:50, the latter at 10:30. North American copies list "A Bit of Finger," "Sleeping Village" and "Warning" (not "The Warning") as one track at 14:32.

In any event, what you get is an extended blur of jamming, albeit somewhat structured and well recorded. "The Warning" is a depressing love-gone-wrong song lyrically, but an appropriate enough doomy blues for the fit of the album as a whole. Still, the blues is something Sabbath had outgrown, the ensuing catalogue having little to do with the genre. Affirms Geezer, "We started out as a blues band and many of the songs on the first album were quite blues-based. But there were never any songs where we were thinking about another band or their style. Our biggest influence was Led Zeppelin though."

Asked about "The Warning," Geezer shudders. "That was all the record company. I mean, we weren't even allowed at the mix of the record. We were only in the studio for two days making the album. We weren't allowed to have any say whatsoever. And in fact when they put the cassette out, they chopped one of the songs up into three parts, the song called 'Warning.' The solo was like… the first part of it finished on Side A and the solo to that song was like the third song on Side B. It was nuts. We didn't have any say in it whatsoever."

"The Warning" quickly collapses into additional bouts of psychedelia and even boogie rock (think pre-Schenker UFO), before mercifully drawing to a close with a reprise of, or a return to, "The Warning," culminating in the song's powerful chorus clang. All told though, it's not the most inspired or purposeful pile of music from the Sabs. And, given its nearly full-side girth, it's a large part of why the first Black Sabbath album is arguably the dodgiest—and unarguably the most meandering—of any record the band would ever make.

Confronted with *Black Sabbath* at the time, the legendary Lester Bangs, writing for Rolling Stone, was not that impressed, indicating that, "Across the tracks in the industrial side of Cream country lie unskilled laborers like Black Sabbath, which was hyped as a rockin' ritual celebration of the Satanic mass or some such claptrap, something like England's answer to Coven. The whole album is a shuck—despite the wooden Claptonisms from the master's tiredest Cream days. They even have discordant jams with bass and guitar reeling like velocitized speedfreaks all over each other's musical perimeters yet never quite finding synch—just like Cream! But worse."

"That's what Rolling Stone thought," counters Olav Wyper, who kept his own personal copy of that review. "But they were wrong because the public will buy what they want to buy. A film comes out and it gets terrible reviews and people all over the world go to see it because the word of mouth is good. Also there's something strange about the concept of a critic reviewing something like popularist records. Because it's not made for them. They're too sophisticated in their musical tastes. The public isn't, necessarily, although they could be educated. I mean, if the people that were in that club hadn't moved down the front and suddenly loads of people came in and within half an hour you couldn't move, you were all standing up there like sardines, if that hadn't happened, I'm not sure, to be perfectly honest, that I would have signed them at that time. I might have gone back to see them because they were different, but if the difference that I saw didn't communicate to the audience, then maybe not. The audience is right. I don't buy records—they're the ones that buy records."

Lester's review—through the obvious impossibility of the language to quite comprehend what was going on—proves that there was this emphatic invention of heavy metal taking place, a breath of hot black air that wasn't there before. "Black Sabbath," "The Wizard," "N.I.B.," "Wicked World"… this was about as much as Led Zeppelin had accomplished toward the heavy metal cause through double the work—not that they were trying, noses upturned. Purposely attempting something they wanted to create or not (!), Led Zeppelin had turned in the seminal "Communication Breakdown," along with "Whole Lotta Love," "Heartbreaker" and "Livin' Lovin' Maid," through *Led Zeppelin* and *II*, issue March 1969 and October 1969 respectively. Less convincingly, proto-metal behemoths "Dazed and Confused," "Good Times Bad Times" and "How Many More Times" were also committed to vinyl (and all three from the debut), but nobody had quite put the package together the way Sabbath had.

It is of no concern, because Black Sabbath's second album, *Paranoid*, also issued in 1970, would summarily bury and make moot the above comparative, and whilst bringing on another one we will not ignore, that of the band's positioning against the likes of Deep Purple, with their *In Rock* album, and Uriah Heep, who bring to the party a little something called *Very 'Eavy, Very 'Umble*.

Purple had their own label deal happening, but Heep would join Sabbath as a Vertigo signing.

"When Gerry Bron agreed to put Colosseum with us, I gave him a production deal," recalls Olav. "I want so many acts a year from you and I get first choice on all the acts. And he rang me up. I've been friends with him for more years than I care to think. In fact he now lives in our old house in London and we go and stay with them in our old house—it's really strange. But Gerry rang me up and he said, 'Look, there's this band called Uriah Heep and I'm going to manage them. I've seen them, I'm going to manage them. I'd like to record them, I think. I think you might enjoy it—can we go and see them?' So he took me to see the band."

"And they were a different kind of band to Sabbath, clearly. They were exciting to watch, the singer was fantastic, completely different vocal style from Ozzy and the audience liked it. I think I first saw them at Dingwall's in Camden Town. I think it was Dingwall's, which was right next door to where Gerry Bron had his office, which was why it was Dingwall's. And they were fantastic. They were more open as people than Sabbath were. And I felt they would be more accessible to the fans, and indeed they were."

Notes Geezer on Uriah Heep and Deep Purple, "I thought they were quite good. In the early days I liked Deep Purple *In Rock* and that stuff, and the first Uriah Heep album. It was very heavy. That was good. Because they weren't trying… they were doing it their way. They weren't trying to blatantly copy us, kind of thing. They were more keyboard-based as well. So they were doing it in a totally different way, so it was good to listen to. And they were all good musicians, good singers."

"Lyrically I found them just a little bit light," adds Bill on Heep. "Good band, nice people, but I just wasn't attracted to them that much in the sense that it seemed a little light."

Album 2

Paranoid

"I could feel in them that the Iron Curtain was still an issue"

There wasn't really so much of a pronounced tour for Black Sabbath's debut album, nor, for that matter, for its resounding, head-pounding follow-up *Paranoid* (re: the title, Tony had said vaguely that there was a lot of paranoia going around…). Earth dates blended into those for Sabbath proper and recording the self-titled record was no more than a sidetrack amongst pub gigs. After the second day of that, the band soldiered on with business, the record was released, and on they went.

Indeed, the songs of the set were as much selections that would show up on record #2 anyway. The band had played sporadically through 1969, then intensified the pace in early 1970, playing every corner of the UK imaginable through March, April and May of that year. Early June saw more of the same, with mid-month marking the making of *Paranoid* ("in a couple days, three days," says Tony), followed by a handful of German dates. All in the month of June. The album was recorded at Regent Sound, also studio of choice for the debut, Rodger Bain again at the production helm, black magic lyrics dropped from the itinerary due to all the press hassles the first record 'round.

Says label head Olav Wyper concerning the band's occult leanings, "It made them different, because how many other bands had that reputation? They didn't. Now whether it was accident or whether it was design, goodness knows, but it worked and it was something to jump on and take advantage of."

And Wyper was pleased with the sales of *Black Sabbath*. The future looked promising for Vertigo's heaviest band. "Yes, it did brilliantly in

England, it did brilliantly in Germany. One of the problems that we had at Philips when I took it over was that we didn't have a good American outlet. Because the outlet for our records in America was Mercury Records, and at the time, at the very beginning time when I joined, they didn't even own 100% of Mercury; they owned half of Mercury. So they would say to Mercury, 'This is a new act we're developing,' and Mercury would say, 'Pfft, we don't like it' and therefore it wouldn't come out. Because what needs to happen is that Philips would then sign these bands for the world, couldn't get a release in America so it didn't get released. And they didn't have a management in Holland to whom we all reported. They didn't have a management in Holland who took the view that if we can't get it out with them, let's see if we can get it out with another company. It just didn't come out. What I did was—until they bought the rest of Mercury and Mercury saw the error of their ways—I would do deals with the management and say, 'We don't want America. You can have America. I'll point you in the direction of people you ought to talk to in America, but it's not going to come out on Vertigo in America. In America it'll come out with whichever label we can help you into a deal with, and we want an outright royalty.' Which I think was something like 5% from memory."

And so *Black Sabbath*… "did well because it was on Warners, and Warners completely took them up. It did very well. It's not that often that a band from one country, particularly a European country, sold that well. Because we were more used to it coming the other way—it's a hit in America and it will be a hit in at least northern European territories. We weren't terribly used to something from northern Europe going the other way, and oh, it's a big hit in America. I think if you'd been into the American acts that CBS had at that time, you were more open for new areas. And not only was it good, it had a terrific image. There was all this business about what do they do, how to they behave, are they a cult, what's happening? Everything just came together and fitted in like a jigsaw puzzle perfectly and very quickly. Kids got off on it. Ozzy had a unique voice, or has a unique voice, certainly a different kind of voice to anybody else at that time. The band was not a big band. There were three musicians but they made a bloody great big fat sound, which wasn't entirely manufactured in the studio. Because they had a live sound that was huge."

"But the critics didn't like Black Sabbath at all," continues Olav. "Both albums got panned in America. I'm tempted to say that part of that was proprietary. It's not an American band, therefore it's not that good. There was a complete difference between the way the American companies operated versus English companies. I worked for, eventually, two of the American companies. I worked for CBS and I also ran RCA in London after Philips. And everything that was released in America was expected to be released in England and in the rest of Europe. Everything that was released in England was not expected to be released in America. And you'd go to international meetings and you'd be told this is the best thing since sliced bread, and you would think it's not going to work in England and you wouldn't put it out. And then people from international would come down on you like a ton of bricks and say, 'Well why haven't you done this?' 'Well. because we don't think it…' 'Well, it's not up to you to say. It's American so it's gotta be terrific.'"

Says Bill, on the subject of what the first record had done for the band, "We got more gigs, and that's what we loved to do. We loved playing gigs. We lived to play. So we had a little bit of a foothold. We had the possibility of making another album, which was really huge back then. Especially when you're 21, 22. So yeah, it brought us a lot. And it gave us our first experience in sound technique in the studio. Even if it was only for a couple days, we were relatively quick learners. So it established a number of things and it put us in the right places like the Marquee club in London and Henry's Blues House. We could go further north. We were going to Glasgow. We could definitely go to Europe. We spent time in Germany where they love hard rock. It's crazy."

"The press hated us and the fans absolutely loved us," chuckles Butler. "Because to the fans, they'd built us up from scratch. We used to play a lot of the same gigs around England because there were only so many places that you could play. None of us had any money. I mean the fans, we used to stay at their houses. They used to put us up for the night and stuff. So the fans loved us because we were one of them. We did a gig and then we'd go out for a drink with a lot of them. So we got on great with the fans because they sort of made us and we reciprocated the feeling. Press hated us because we hadn't gone down to London. And in those days—and it probably still is—if you weren't living in London, then you were a nobody. You couldn't possibly make it in the business. And we'd only played in London two or three times, and all the press was based there and now they're going, 'Who's this lot from Birmingham? Crap and rubbish. You'll never hear of this band again."

And as for the first album, "We didn't think it'd ever do anything," remembers Geezer Butler. "Recording the album was just something we did on the way to Denmark."

"They were quite negative," agrees Bill with regard to the press. "Yeah, they were quite negative. English press didn't like us at all. They'd call it morbid tripe and they would slag the people who listen to it. Same old story, man, headbangers. This is for the hordes and masses who can't get a job. Basically very condescending statements, very un-intellectual statements, very completely un-experienced statements. Very un-knowledgable."

Paranoid was to be the album that set Sabbath up for life (well, at least with respect to an identity, a convenient label). Fans would show up in droves and the critics would begin what became an endless debate over the evils of heavy metal, touching down hither and thither on the sorry, scroungy, depressive state of the band's fans and whether Tony could play guitar or not. Also in question would be the band's bulldozing lack of dynamics or subtlety and whether all those spooky lyrics were merely designed to shock and sell versus having any sort of poetic or social value. Most quaintly, rock critics would wring their hands over the idea that Sabbath had created some sort of new thing called downer rock, and what the appetite for such a thing said about the state of America's kids.

Paranoid was recorded June 16th to the 21st, with the band working once again at Regent Sound. "On the second album, we did the tracks in the same little four-track studio and then we took the tapes to Island Studios and transferred them all up to eight-track," notes engineer Tom Allom, Island being the legendary Basing Street studio built by Chris Blackwell in an old church. "When I got confronted with the original four-track tapes for the Classic Album series, I heard what was on the four-tracks compared to the final mixes, and remembered that we didn't do much in the way of overdubs. It was still very much the basic tracks that formed the album. We did the tracks the same sort of way. I would not think the whole thing took more than ten days. *Master of Reality* was the third one that I did. They wrote that in the studio and that kind of dragged on and took a massive month (laughs). That one was a test, as they were not really prepared like they were for the first album. They recorded, essentially, all of the tracks on the first album beforehand. I had done the demos when they were Earth and then they came back about six months later. When I did the demos, I was really new to the job."

"Rodger Bain and I got along well," continues Allom. "It is neat to be involved in something that so many people think was such an important part of music. It really gives you a good feeling. What they were doing together was incredible, actually. They were a three-piece band and they were almost a jazz band, really. Bill was not playing a straight beat. The other thing that blows me away when I think about it, is how young they were. They were 20 years old. It is amazing. I was only 21 or 22. To have developed that unique style by that tender ago is incredible. It didn't seem that way to me then. It did take me by surprise because I had never heard music like that because, then, nobody had. I find it more impressive now than I did then."

Pre-production writing sessions for *Paranoid* took place at Rockfield Studios in Wales. "The band were cranked up as if they were on stage," recalls Bain, speaking with Russell H. Tice (an alias!). "The building we were in was a fairly old barn. The whole of the roof actually did move. I can remember Ozzy saying, 'Why don't we record here?' 'Cause the atmosphere of the place and the people were so great. The biggest chunk of time was spent in the rehearsing and routining stage, the object being that when you go in to record you're not sort of experimenting in the studio. What you're doing when you go into the studio is transferring it into a recorded version."

Added Allom, in the same article, "It was a good-sounding studio; we always got good results in that room. It was an absolute shithole, but it worked. The console was some custom-built thing; just a piece of old dross. Terrible thing—it didn't even have any midrange. We had to get it modified to get some midrange. We had two one-inch four-track Studers. We did have a Pultec. We had some Neumann mics; I think we had a couple of 67s. We finally acquired an old M49. We had a couple of old AKGs, whatever the forerunner of the 414 was. We had some old 64s, the pencil mics. I recorded Bill Ward's drums stereo using those pencil mics. Very few people recorded drums stereo back then. I thought it might be a good idea."

"The bass was recorded with a split lead," says Bain. "One was direct, the other was off the cabinet. It was loud. Mic placement was probably one of the key ingredients. Having a successful album under our belts would have given the luxury of spending more time." As regard's Tony's guitar solos, "It was double-tracking if not triple-tracking," says Rodger. "It would be a close mic and an ambient mic that would be way off. But it was the combination that gave it that punch and gave it the size of the sound. I think the secret to that was really 'cause it was straightforward. You know, if you put compressors on something, EQ it over the top, you lose that power; it just weakens the whole sound. The original way we worked was to keep it really raw."

"We were having the greatest time of our lives," muses Bill, "because when we were allowed to go in and do *Paranoid*, we already had things like 'Hand of Doom,' which was severely brilliant as far as I'm concerned. We were now looking at 'War Pigs,' which I just loved; playing 'War Pigs' onstage is so incredible. So we had some great songs. I think we did really well and the credit has to go to our two producers, Rodger Bain and Tom Allom, for dealing with this now very excessive band. By the time we got to *Paranoid* we had new amplifiers, I think we had new drums, a lot of things, and we also had the whole experience of more and more touring. We were playing every night and that was now coming into the studio. And these guys, these poor guys, Tom and Rodger, had to capture that and put it onto a piece of tape. So it's like my God, how do you get this monster walking through the door and capture that and put it down? I think they did a good job. I know that they did their best. When I listen to the recordings and I compare them to the sounds we can achieve these days, of course they're kind of sentimental. But we all listened to them at the time and everybody thought, 'Oh my God.' And so *Paranoid* was a huge experience. We were becoming worldly, and I think that great result set us up for the even more worldly *Master of Reality*."

Geezer has to laugh when he looks at the band's quick rise to the place where *Paranoid* was perched. As Bill has alluded to, as the songs got better, the gear got better.

"When I started off, I couldn't afford a bass. So I had a Fender Telecaster because I used to play rhythm guitar, and I had to tune that down, tune the strings down. And the first gig we did, I borrowed a friend of mine's bass. He had a Hoffman violin bass, and on the way to our first gig I stopped at his house and borrowed his bass, and it only had three strings on it. And I'd never ever played a bass before until the first gig that Sabbath did. But it was just 12 bars, so it was really basic stuff. And then when I finally got my own bass, Fender Precision, I just basically followed what Tony was doing on the bass, just playing his riffs. So it naturally made his riffs heavier. I think that's the way the sound evolved."

With regard to amps, Butler says that, "for about the first year I was using a 4x12 cabinet with only three speakers in it because we couldn't afford four speakers. And a 70-watt Laney guitar amp that I used to use for my rhythm guitar. And then eventually when I could afford it, there was a company in Birmingham, and we got to know the guys that run it and they said we'll do it for you cost price if you use our gear. So

I said great, I can finally afford some stuff. And Tony and myself bought Laney stuff. So I was using a double, two 4x12s and a Laney bass amp. And the trouble was, Ozzy only had a 100-watt PA system, so nobody could hear Ozzy."

"But it just happened so incredibly fast. I mean one moment we're playing these tiny little blues clubs for like five quid a night, and soon the first album charted; I think it came in at #13, the album. We didn't know anything about it. We were in a car going to a gig, and in England they had the album charts on a Saturday afternoon, and we always used to listen to the album charts. And we were listening to the album charts and the bloke said, 'And new at 13 this week we have Black Sabbath.' And we went what? Is there another band called Black Sabbath? And then he played the track off it and it was us. We were all celebrating in the car going to this gig. It just took off from there, really. And when *Paranoid* came out and the single was #2 in the charts, then the crowds just doubled and tripled in size."

The first inklings of the quaking record to come arrived in the form of "Paranoid" as an advance single, the album's mercilessly simple and point-blank heavy title track being issued July 17th of 1970. But once the record proper dropped (on September 18th for UK fans, also the day Jimi Hendrix died, and not until January 1, 1971 in the US), a much more bombastic and overarching composition was chosen to represent Black Sabbath 2.0.

"War Pigs," provisionally named "Walpurgis," had already been a live favourite for the band, and indeed, the lyrics changed completely over time from something much more brutal and witchrafty, to the ugly, aggressive anti-war classic now considered one of Sabbath's top two or three most enduring compositions. Asked about the alternate lyrics, Ozzy says that, "what we'd do is get the melody line, and the lyrics were always the very last thing to be written. I'd get comfortable with the melody line, and Geezer or I would write them in the studio. But other than that, I don't know where they're from."

"That was totally against the Vietnam War at the time," offers Geezer, "about how these rich politicians and rich people in general, they start all the wars for their benefit and get all the poor people to die for them. Which is still happening now."

In fact the album was going to be called *War Pigs*, but the label got cold feet due to the hostility it perceived for the band in the US, given the fractious debate over the merits of the Vietnam War. Adds Tony, "The album cover was designed with the guy with the shield and sword, and it was supposed to have at least some resemblance to *War Pigs*, and then they banned the title in England; they wouldn't allow us to use *War Pigs*. So we had to come up with a title quick, and they said, 'Oh, *Paranoid*.' So, here we go, suddenly we were stuck with a cover that didn't have anything remotely to do with somebody who was paranoid. And that was it; it was called *Paranoid*."

"I just wanted to reflect what we were going through," says Geezer, on his lyrics generally. "I mean this whole Devil worship and all that, that was totally misinterpreted. A lot of the stuff was about war, because we thought we were going to get dragged into the Vietnam War at the time, in England. Plus pollution, poverty, all kinds of things. And just looking at politicians, the way they couldn't understand us, the working class, and how the working class always had to do the work for the government. And the whole thing of where we lived at the time. It's much like living in any inner city area these days. You go out and you don't know if you're going to come back again. There's always getting in fights and stuff like that. So every day you had to watch out for yourself. And the IRA thing; I mean I came from an IRA family anyway, so I'd seen both sides of it. And all those things combined into when we did write music, putting all that heaviness into it, both musically and lyrically."

Geezer's metaphor concerning the generals and how they resembled witches at black masses extends to the idea that while witches conjure Satan, the generals are doing much the same, Satan being a metaphor for war.

"Well, first of all somebody came up with the picture," recalls Bill in further corroboration as to the titling of the record, "and we were like, 'Hmm, okay, all right, not too bad.' But the working title for that album was *War Pigs*. And Warner Bros. didn't want it to be called *War Pigs*, which would make sense at the time. Record companies have to take care of how they look and everything."

"We used to sort of jam around with 'War Pigs,'" offers Tony, on the song's very early origins. "Again, some of the songs were actually put together when we were in Europe. We used to play at these clubs playing seven 45-minute spots a day, and we would get bored, because there would only be a handful of people in them, and we would start making songs up. And 'War Pigs' was one of them, that we started making up. And we might have had 'Fairies,' as well."

Adds Bill, "I think the first memory I have of working on 'War Pigs' is at The Beat Club, Hirschen, which I think was in Zurich, Switzerland. But it was a real horrible place, basically full of prostitutes and some of the johns that used to come in for the prostitutes. But as I recall, we were starting to put those things together at that time, which would be roughly 1968. I would probably think that we would've finished 'Iron Man' and 'War Pigs' at Monmouth. We did all of our early stuff there at Monmouth."

Monmouth of course refers to the location of Rockfield Studios in Wales, where, oddly, the band would never wind up recording an album.

"It's just a reflection of society, real life," says Geezer, repeating a theme Sabbath would often bring up with the press in defense of their more virulent pronouncements. "Everyone has their point of view. I used to write like that. 'War Pigs,' 'Lord of This World,' even 'Paranoid.' It's just an observation of society. I'm not preaching or trying to come up with any answers. But 'War Pigs' is such a strong song. That's why we start concerts with that song. It has absolutely everything in it. It's a great song and it gets you up to play the whole concert. From there it's like, full steam ahead."

"I think you have to be a fan of politics if you live in the world," muses Geezer. "You are subjected to politics and it's always a good subject to write about (laughs)—good for musicians and comedians. Back then, it was more about the Vietnam era. Because we used to get a lot more things on the television in England than anybody ever did in America. They would show like all the propaganda that was going on, on the TV in England. And people didn't know what I was talking about, when I came over here, because they weren't allowed to see that on the TV. And we just thought England was going to be next to be dragged into the Vietnam War. I grew up post-World War II, and the area we lived in in Birmingham was bombed out during the war, and it was still being rebuilt when I was growing up. And I knew a lot of families whose fathers were killed in World War II. My uncle was shot in World War II, so war really affected me. And me brothers had to join the army; one of them had to go fight in Egypt, so it was all very real to me, and it was scary, in a way. And when the Vietnam thing came in, people were saying it was really bad and England was going to join in. So that's why we wrote 'War Pigs.'"

Political tendencies also came from Geezer's father. "Well, he had been brought up in Dublin, when the British were like shooting everyone over there, being Catholic. So he was very much working class, and 'of the workers' and that kind of thing. He didn't like government whatsoever. But on the other hand, there was no work in Ireland, so he actually joined the British army—he was in that for about 20 years. So on one hand, he was for the military, but for the working class as well."

"The political climate was horrible," agrees Bill. "We were kind of like war babies. When I say we, I'm talking about the band. I was born three years after the Second World War, and where I was born, Aston, in the city of Birmingham, the landscape was all bombed out on my street. The factories had been bombed during the war. Growing up as a child, the bombed buildings and burned-out buildings were very much still there. Nobody demolished them from 1945. But I didn't know any different. I thought it was fantastic, all these places to play, factories that were once just flattened by landmines by the Germans. So as kids we would go and play in these areas and it was a lot of fun."

"One of the things that was like a shadow in our house—and I think in most houses in Great Britain—was the Iron Curtain, because there was always that threat. Berlin's only about 300 or 400 miles from Birmingham, so it's not that far to the Iron Curtain, so there was always that. That was huge. There was always this kind of uncomfortable feeling, and I could feel it from my parents as well, in the sense that they'd already been through the Blitz and they'd been through all of the war, just like many other parents in Great Britain. And I could feel in them that the Iron Curtain was still an issue which was never talked about, but it was felt.

As for the Irish Republic Army offensives, "It scared everybody in the city," reflects Bill. "That's what it was like. All the security things we do in America now, since 9/11, that was happening back in England since the '60s. I mean literally, we were so well-trained in the city to take care of the bags and not leave a bag lying around, it's almost inbred in me. If I see something in an airport or a bag sitting anywhere, I'll call a cop or something. It's just that well rehearsed now. Everybody who lived in Birmingham or the Midlands or throughout London or wherever the IRA were attacking, it's terrorism so you're going to feel it. You don't know when it's going to happen. There were very strict security measures. Even to just go shopping. So no, it was crap. It was crap hearing about the amount of people dying, and the IRA were targeting public houses and you'd hear about people and some of the things that happened to them with the bombs. It was horrible."

"War Pigs" is of course intensely catchy due to its verse construction, Tony's slamming, simple sparse chording spanned by nothing more than Ozzy's admonishing, sanctimonious bleat and Bill's timekeeping high-hat. But as the song grinds on, Sabbath prove themselves capable of sophisticated, almost progressive rock maneuvers. Of note, some copies of *Paranoid* list the amorphous blob of instrumental intro to "War Pigs" as "Luke's Wall." Or not. The US original resorts only to the record centrepiece for the designation (no mention on the back sleeve or within the gate), messily going with "War Pigs – 7:55 Luke's Wall."

"There is always war going on somewhere in the world," says Geezer, ruing the song's accursed universality. "You can relate that to any war going on at any time. Unfortunately, wars are always with us. We're just wasting our time; it is out of our hands. Just look what is happening with the Iraq thing, with all the ordinary people dying over that crap. You vote for a person who promises one thing and then turns around and does another. I think politicians are just puppets to the handful of people who rule the world anyway. There is nothing we can do about it, unfortunately. It is always going to be the little people who get sent to war and die for all these rich idiots. Why would anyone care for Iraq when the American health system need money? Why spend all the money that could help fix that problem in Iraq? We have enough poverty in our own countries we need to worry about before going anywhere else."

Black Sabbath's biggest (yet arguably one of the least substantive) song of all time, "Paranoid," followed up the grand gestures of "War Pigs," exclamation mark to a novel, punk proposal after a banquet of prog. Beyond being Sabbath's signature track, "Paranoid" is unquestionably and widely beloved, taking #1 in a worldwide poll conducted for this writer's *The Top 500 Heavy Metal Songs of All Time* book—fully 28 different Black Sabbath songs cracked the Top 500, with the source album notching #6 in the companion albums-based book.

But, as Geezer explains, "Paranoid" is famously known for being an off-the-cuff afterthought. "We'd finished the album and had packed up all our gear and the management said they needed an extra three or four minutes to put on the album. The record is too short otherwise. The record company won't accept this. And we said we didn't have anything and they said, 'Can you write something? Come up with a quick jam?' And Ozzy would literally be singing the lyrics as I wrote them. Tony came up with the riff to 'Paranoid' and I quickly scribbled down the lyrics to Ozzy's thing. The whole thing was written and recorded in two hours. I was looking through the basement the other day and I found all the original lyrics from the *Paranoid* album, and verses from the song 'Paranoid' that weren't used. It might be interesting for people to see the original versions some day. But it's just getting the time to do it. Lyrically, 'War Pigs,' 'Iron Man,' 'Paranoid'… I used to try and give a message of hope or something at the end of each song and now I don't bother. Now I realize I can't change anything!"

Indeed as Butler alludes to, one can experience a glimpse into the band's creative process through a version of "Paranoid" included on the expanded CD reissue, where Ozzy sings a completely alternate and very verbose set of what are essentially place-holder lyrics.

"Well, we needed another song," affirms Bill. "We didn't have one, and it was about 12:30 in the afternoon. We were down at Regent Sound, right there in the heart of London, SoHo. So anyway, we stopped working and we went out to the pub and had a couple pints and a sandwich and stuff, really had no idea what to do for the song. Anyway, as always, we get back into the studio and Tony immediately came up with the main riff you hear in 'Paranoid.' And as we got around our instruments, we started to jam. And we hadn't been jamming for more than five minutes, I wouldn't think, and we started to get pretty much an arrangement. And then we ran down from top to bottom. And it was like oh, okay, here we go, this is fun; this is a fun song. And Oz put a bunch of lyrics straight on it and Geezer put a bunch of lyrics there, and he had a melody and Ozzy had a melody and that was it. I think top to bottom, the whole song took possibly about 25 minutes."

Indeed Geoff Lucas (the Luke of "Luke's Wall") has said that he and Spock Wall had gone to Birmingham to pick up some equipment, away for not much more than a couple hours, and by the time they had gotten back to London, the song was done. At this point, the band had moved to Island Studios for the mix of the album. At that converted church studio, recording took place in the basement crypt and mixing upstairs in the prayer room. As described by journalist Russell Tice, the Island console, featuring in-line compression and equalization, was assembled by Dick Swettenham, the engineer who had helped make Olympic Studios such a cherished recording locale. Tannoy speakers through Lockwood cabinets delivered the results in terms of monitoring.

Tony's weirdly buzzy guitar solo on the track was played straight with the effect added after the fact. "It had a very strong beat, a powerful riff," recalls Rodger Bain. "I remember pressing the talkback and saying words to the effect of, 'That's pretty good. What is that?' And sort of getting disbelief. They said, 'You're joking.' I said, 'No, that's really good; that's a really strong riff.' They said, 'We're just pissing around. We just made it up.' I said, 'Well that's great, let's do it!'"

The "You're joking" quip resonates given that Geezer has said that he was worried that the song was too close to Led Zeppelin's "Communication Breakdown" to be considered for inclusion on the album. Geezer has also said that Ozzy practically read the lyrics fed to him by Geezer, but the evidence of the alternate version on the CD reissue betrays the fact that a considerable amount of reworking and accelerated evolution was going on. In any event, the basic storyline that the song came together quickly can certainly be believed.

Recalls Ozzy, speaking with Russell Tice, "I remember going home with the tapes and I said to my then-wife, 'I think we've written a single.' She said, 'But you don't write singles.' I said, 'I know, but this has been driving me nuts on the train all the way back.'"

Added Warner Bros. head Joe Smith, "We were looking for a single and they were hard to get. There was still resistance in Top 40 radio to playing any single by one of these bands. If somebody's going to take a shot, 'Paranoid' was the record to take a shot with. Also, it was a great title for a single at the time. What astounded us was the sales. Black Sabbath was our most efficient seller. There's a certain curve where the sales end. With Black Sabbath it never ended. It never totally stopped. The fever would be gone, but you'd still be selling 5,000 a week or 10,000 a week, so we never had returns with Black Sabbath. They had six platinum albums in a row; multi-platinum albums. There is a feeling among kids now that they missed something and here's a chance to get it back, and Black Sabbath is one of the very few groups in that genre that's out there playing."

Mused Bill, "I thought 'Paranoid,' in comparison to some of the other songs, like 'Hand of Doom,' was a little bit light, to be honest with you. I thought, 'This is a bit of a pop song.' I didn't really pay a whole lot of attention to it."

"Paranoid" is of a certain then quite modern metal construct that improves upon a formula cast pretty much for the first time through the aforementioned "Communication Breakdown" by Led Zeppelin. One might call it proto-punk, a staccato chugger, its riff, a machine gun riff. Whatever the descriptive, Tony's quick hitting—and palm-muting—of the power chords became a signature metal maneuver good for a couple of songs on most metal albums through the rest of the decade and into the '80s.

Lyrically, the song is deeper than credit is usually given. "I used to suffer a lot with depression," explains Geezer. "I used to go in and out, like, happy one day and down the next. And I was just going through a bad time at the time, so I wrote those lyrics. I just couldn't seem to get through to anyone. That's what the lyrics came from."

"It's not so much of a problem now, because they've come up with some really good things like Prozac and stuff," adds Geezer, on his current state. "But when I was growing up as a kid, I used to get these weird, strange moods, and people thought I was being miserable and standoffish, and I didn't know what the hell was happening to me. And it wasn't until about ten years ago (our chat took place in 2005), when I was going through a really bad depression. I was living in St. Louis at the time and I went to the doctor there, and he says you've got really... you've got depression. And that's when he put me onto Prozac, and after all these years I realize how bad I'd been, once I'd gotten back to sort of almost normal again. I realized that I'd been suffering from it for 20, 30 years."

Geezer recalls that, "It was all right in the '70s. It was all the drugs I was taking (laughs). That sort of made it go away. So it was mainly in the '60s, I had it worse. There was a time when Sabbath first started and I was in Germany, and it just hit me in Germany for some reason; I was in a really bad state and I just didn't know what was going on. You know, nobody talked about it and nobody explained it to you, and I managed to get through that. And in the '70s I wasn't too bad. I think I just had one bout of it. The '80s were okay. And it was mainly the '90s where it came back. The whole lyric, all of the lyrics in 'Paranoid' sort of summed up the way I felt at that time. 'Finished with my woman because she couldn't help me with my mind.'"

In that light, one can find a richness of imagery within the song, imagery that offers insight into the nature of depression, this feeling of alienation, being locked within one's own mental prison. It was all the more grist for a certain, often repeated critical accusation that Sabbath's dire, drunken, often riotous fan base was having their dead-end depressive mood reinforced, articulated, affirmed. Part and parcel of this denigration, through the lyrics, the band was seen as empathetic but irresponsible, dishing the downer rock due to being down themselves, no apologies, this is the real world, welcome to it. And critics were quick to point out that this shared yolk of sullenness was between the band and a fan base who were almost exclusively teenage males—and what could they know about good music?

Supporting such an oscillating view between nihilism and reality, journalist Robin Green gathered some fan reactions back in 1971 for a piece that was to appear in Rolling Stone. Said one follower, "I'm scared of them; they're evil and strange. I like to be scared. I hope they sacrifice something tonight. A human sacrifice would be good. I'd do it myself if I wouldn't go to jail for it." "It's freaky," said another. "It makes you think you're in a graveyard; it makes you feel more alive while you're there." A third added, "We dig Black Sabbath. You can get high on their music without even being stoned."

Green also obtained comment from some of the Warner brass. "Their music is loud; it's painful. I've been driven out of places by the noise. They play to a young crowd, say 14 to 17 years old. But who knows how they hear about them? The word just gets around that this is a group to go see." "It's really incredible," said a second label honcho. "They're not like our other performers and we don't understand their popularity; no one can figure it out. They haven't had that much publicity, but their concerts are sellouts and their albums sell millions. The baby teenyboppers all just boogie up in the balconies and then run out to buy the records, and we love 'em."

Another piece from the same year had onlookers proclaiming various feelings of bafflement. "They're just a greaser band. No one knows how they got started. They're loud and electronic and get an ugly audience—not your Grateful Dead audience, not even your Poco audience—kids on Reds, the Johnny Winter audience."

"They're metallic, like a magnet. I like their words, they're weird, about death and Satanism, but I kind of like it," said one teen fan, another adding, "They have drive. They have a better three-piece sound than any group since Cream. They're not musically inclined, but they're basic and powerful. And they're kind of sadistic."

Geezer replied with, "People feel evil things, but nobody ever sings about what's frightening and evil. I mean the world is a right fucking shambles. Anyway, everybody has sung about all the good things.," to which Bill added, "Most people live on a permanent down, but just aren't aware of it. We're trying to express it for people."

"We like to see people enjoying themselves, and if we come across doomy and evil, it's just the way we feel," was Tony's assessment.

Back on planet *Paranoid*, "Planet Caravan," Black Sabbath's first ballad (although more of a funeral dirge), came next, said soundscape gauzily drifting along in stark contrast to the cold steel of the two tracks previous. "We did that in a rehearsal room in Birmingham," recalls Tony. "It was a time when I had just gotten this flute, and I just started playing this thing on the guitar first, and it was very light sounding, and I didn't think anybody would like it, really. 'No, we like that' and Ozzy started singing and that was it, and it became a song, and I played a flute on it, just to make it a bit different."

"Ozzy's using the famous tremolo from the Hammond organ system," explains Bill. "We put his voice through a tremolo, which is a Hammond reverberation effect and Tony had that weird sound, and Geez just got in somewhere. It was something that I believe was just made up in the studio and totally worked."

"That was about visiting planets, in your own sort of spacecraft, getting away from Earth," says Geezer. "It would be a good idea to do that now with all the hatred in the world. It was just about how there was so much hate in the world, and these people wanted to get away from it, to try find a better world."

Butler has repeatedly championed the diversity of sounds one experiences with Black Sabbath, intimating that an appreciation for a wide spectrum of styles was ingrained in him from the start.

With respect to Birmingham, Geezer says the city gave the world, "Duran Duran, UB40, all kinds of stuff. As they say, Birmingham is a very eclectic society. Such different loads of cultures going on. And I lived next door to a Pakistani family one side and an Indian family the other side, so you'd hear all this tabla music and sitar and stuff and what the hell? But it would be interesting. The stuff they were playing, you couldn't hear it anywhere else. So there's such a lot of different music. You had a Jamaican family across the road that would be playing blue beat, as it was called then back in the '60s, which became reggae. So you'd have all these different sounds, an integration. And as I say, I was from an Irish family so I grew up listening to all the Irish stuff. Wherever they'd come from, they'd be playing their own kind of music. Birmingham, because it was such an industrial city at the time, a lot of men who used to work in the factories were killed in the war. So Birmingham was probably the main city that needed immigration. So there were people coming in from all over the world, really."

"We do that to add a bit of light and shape to the album," says Tony, on the band's balladeering tendency, "Planet Caravan" marking a first to be oft repeated. "I remember when I first started doing quiet stuff, the others were like, 'Well, where's that gonna go?' And I tried to explain, 'Well, it's good to do that, because that makes the heavier tracks sound even heavier.' And it gives a bit of strength to the album. I would always try and do something on an album that was a bit like that. As I say, it was a bit of a jump in the deep end, as far as being questioned, 'Ooh, is that gonna go on the album? Do you think it's a bit too opposite?' But I think it worked to have a few acoustic things in."

If "Paranoid" is Sabbath's "Communication Breakdown," then "Iron Man" is undoubtedly the band's "Smoke on the Water," both tracks living on the big dumb riff no self-respecting guitarist would dare be so audacious, so devoid of self-respect, as to write. Of course, sometimes the simplest ideas are the most timeless, and such has been proven with both of these songs, as is the case with much of the canon of a band like AC/DC.

"I thought it was a really stupid concept," laughs Geezer in his inimitable sardonic style. "The title was from a comic book, *Iron Man*, and was all about this being; it was an ecological theme. We were all very environmental at the time, and it was about this entity that turns into metal and is incapacitated at the end, just lying there. He can't talk at the end of it but he has all this knowledge that can save the earth from catastrophe. I think I'm a natural worrier (laughs). I don't know; I'm not sure. Some people are political, others are totally apolitical. I think me dad was very political, so I was sort of brought up very politically minded."

"I was into English comics but not really American comics," adds Geezer, clarifying who did what on the song. "I think Ozzy just came up with the title 'Iron Man.' When we were writing that song, Ozzy just threw in a line about Iron Man. It was just like a throwaway line for him and I said, 'Let's write about that' and I just made it up. I didn't really know about the comic at the time though. Tony came up with the riff to 'Iron Man.' It was one of the heaviest riffs I had ever heard and I wanted something that reflected the heaviness of the riff."

In a separate interview, Geezer adds still a different slant to the tale. "There was a lot of space exploration being done by NASA at the time. There were a lot of things in the news about pollution and nuclear war at the time as well. It was about a guy who had gone into space exploration and had seen the future of the world. He came back to warn everyone about what was going to happen to the world and he got caught up in an electronic type thing when he was entering the earth's atmosphere and he got turned into iron but his brain was still working. It was really just a science fiction story."

Evocations of both *Frankenstein* and The Who's *Tommy* reside within Geezer's unknowing portrayal of this comic book "Armored Avenger," who, in primary coloured newsprint, was comically unwieldy and slow, a bit of a joke as a superhero.

Says Bill, "I just wanted 'Iron Man' to be really heavy; I know that much, from a drum point of view. So I came up with that slow bass drum thing, and it feels different every time we do it live. That's because I can never get the bass drum the right way. But that's just my internal struggle for the rest of my life to live with."

An amusing feature about the bass drum at the beginning, it starts in the right channel and then migrates to the centre of the mix as if it's huge footsteps. Ozzy's "I am Iron Man" intro is put through the same distortion effect that was used on Tony's guitar on the record's earlier track, "Paranoid."

Notes engineer Tom Allom, "Microphone placements were very important in those days. You couldn't use a lot of heavy EQ, as we didn't have it. You had to get the blend right. I was watching *Iron Man* on network TV a couple of nights ago, the movie, and at the end, the song 'Iron Man' plays. It still sounds pretty cool. The guitar sound is not quite what I would want to do now, as it is quite thin, but it does have a real energy to it. The drums are almost dry as a bone. I remember we only had four mics for the drums. Bill Ward played in this little drum booth in the corner of the studio. They sound so real. They were a fantastically good band; they were so tight."

Famously, "Iron Man" comes up first when critics want to put down Ozzy for a lack of imagination when it comes to vocal melodies. This one plainly follows the riff, but across the catalogue, the accusation is proven to be quite unfair. There are many complex vocal melodies that run counter to Tony's riffs all over the first eight Black Sabbath albums, although, granted, a bunch of the most egregious examples of simplistic vocal melodies are indeed right here on the *Paranoid* album.

Says Butler, citing another area of intransigence, "When Ozzy would come out with his vocal lines, he would just sing anything from off the top of his head. It really didn't make sense what he was singing. For some reason, I got the job of doing most of the lyrics. Ozzy has done quite a few himself. It just gets really hard, you know, to do a whole album of lyrics. Once you know what the subject is then it gets a lot easier. It was particularly hard with Ozzy. He comes up with a vocal line and he never changes the vocal line. You have to fit every syllable to what his vocal line is. If you come out with one syllable too many then he won't sing it. That is the hard part. It's easy—well it's not easy—it's hard enough writing the lyrics, but the really hard part is fitting all of the syllables together."

Side two of the original vinyl opens with "Electric Funeral," a doom-drenched downer rock classic if there ever was one. Geezer is in fine ghoulish form, describing the particularly nasty effects of an atomic blast, the world's utter annihilation to be followed by some sort of supernatural conference on the fact between the forces of good and evil. Comments Geezer on the lyric, "The big Cold War thing was going on at the time and it just seemed like any second it could happen." In fact, this is another one of those under-rated and under-appreciated Geezer lyrics, poetry, or at least impressive imagery, flowing from nearly every line.

"Hand of Doom" follows, Sabbath, or more specifically Geezer and Ozzy, laconically handing out more downers, before Bill and Tony explode with "War Pigs"-like metal mania. And like "War Pigs," the song houses unexpected additional movements. "We wrote that in Wales and I can remember feeling quite ecstatic about the track after it was complete," remembers Bill. "We must have played it five or six times a day; we all liked it that much that we would go back and play it. And I think it's still one of the band's favourite tracks from the early days."

Geezer remarks on the song's graphic anti-drug lyric. "In me former band, before Sabbath, and in the early days of Sabbath, we used to play a lot of American military bases around Europe, and in England. We used to talk to the soldiers who had just come back from Vietnam and stuff, and they used to always talk about the drug use over there. A lot of them were on heroin, and they used to have this stop-off point in England where they had to come off heroin before they could go back to America, because the government didn't want the American media to see the troops were on heroin and all that kind of stuff. And I used to talk to a lot of the soldiers about the drugs, and that's where 'Hand of Doom' came from."

"The lyrics are true to life," said Geezer to Circus magazine back in '81. "The words we write are true, about things that are happening. A lot of bands write about things like love. We write about what's happening in the world. Things that are true but that people don't necessarily like to talk about. I suppose we prick a few consciences in a way." Added Tony: "Raw words to go with raw music. People think about evil all the time, and feel evil things, but rarely do they sing about what's evil."

Tony had told the press at the time that, "'War Pigs' and the drug songs are just our opinions—we're not trying to influence people. We don't know if people will take it all in. One of the biggest problems in the music scene today is the kids that try to read things into songs. They often create things that aren't there. The music of Black Sabbath is simple, basic stuff; the lyrics are plain, laid on with a plate. But with those kids, it's like a big battle with the mind trying to sort things out. We haven't got the power to try and direct people in politics or anything else."

"Because it's happening all around us," says Ozzy, when asked about "Hand of Doom" and the other drug lyrics. "People take drugs just like they breathe air, in one form or another. It's better than boy meets girl, boy loses girl, those kind of lyrics. We like to write about other things happening around us. Like describing someone lying there with a needle in his arm, wondering if he's going to get out of this mess. You can't avoid these things. Geezer wrote those grotesque lyrics to 'Hand of Doom.' They were meant to be shocking like that, about people who take drugs all the time. I take drugs sometimes to get high, to escape reality, but I don't make a habit out of it because I've got responsibilities, to my family, to my band. Something's wrong with people who have to depend on them, and maybe through lyrics like 'Hand of Doom,' we can make some of them realize, 'Hey, that's me they're talking about.' You can't just treat them like pieces of shit; they need to be helped."

"I think it was very much for us a reality," reflects Ward, on the concept of bleakness. "It seemed like the right place to go. It did for me, at least. I know we all had some feelings about the counter-culture or a lot of the peace movements. I'm not saying this to make a statement to discount the wonderful music that came from the peace movements or counter-culture. I think it was full of brilliant ideas. But I think all of us had an attitude to, well, that's all well and good but that's not what's going on right now. I'm sitting here looking at a guy getting his guts beaten up or somebody getting knocked out or all kinds of things. In a very rough city. The realities didn't match. Some of the songs of hope weren't matching what was on the ground, and I think a lot of our music began to take a really good look at what was really on the ground and what we were seeing."

"And to me, music was a life-saving thing. To listen to music and then to walk out of the café with the bright lights and walk into the dismal streets… we still had gas lights then, and the people would be coming around putting the gas lights on. It sounds like something from Jack the Ripper. Going back home as a child with the gas lights was incredibly depressing for me."

"But we had two brilliant lyricists, Ozzy and Geezer, who were able to write those images, paint those images, and bring about that kind of colour in the lyrics that were very grounded, very honest, very realistic. We didn't want to talk about 'her.' I think the only time we talked about her—and I'm talking about, 'If you leave me baby, I'm gonna go crazy'—the only thing we ever did was 'Paranoid:' 'Finished with my woman.' Oh wow, that's going a bit across the edge there."

"I like things like 'Hand of Doom;' we all did," continues Bill, transitioning into the band's experience with the drug culture of the day. "I started using dope when I was 15. I was drinking daily when I was 18 and taking all kinds of speed, whites. We had whites back then when we were kids, and anything that goes up, I used to take it. And obviously to keep myself balanced, I'd take anything that went down as well. So I was already a sack of shit by 18, 19 years old as far as my drug use and my drinking. I was already—as Bon Scott once said—on the highway to Hell. But to me, it was part of the culture; it was perfectly normal. Everybody was doing it; it seemed like the most natural and normal thing to be doing, to be honest. When you're writing songs like 'Sweet Leaf' and when Terry was writing about 'Hand of Doom' and heroin and all those kinds of things, those were commonplace. Quite honestly I stopped using heroin in Hamburg in 1969. I tried it a few times, didn't like it, but I loved speed. So whichever worked out. But yes, I think all of that drug culture in the band had a huge influence; it helped to create whatever it created."

Next up on *Paranoid* was a bit of a respite called "Rat Salad." In effect, this one is a Bill Ward showcase—pair and compare with Led Zeppelin's "Moby Dick"—not as if Bill doesn't get to stretch out in numerous other places on the album, soloing in short bursts as an equal partner in a loud and aggressive power trio.

Asked about the track, Bill explains that, "everybody was a star back then; everybody got their chance, for 30 seconds or a couple of minutes to play solo. I just love the way the concerts were in the late '60s and the early '70s because the bass player had his bass solo etc. That was the art at the time; that was the fashion, in music, to do that. So I got to take my little drum solo and put it on a record. We really didn't know what to do with it lyrically. There were some nice little cuts that Tony and Geezer were doing so we just said fuck it, let's do this. And the title fits things very well because inwardly, Sabbath have a lot of inside comedy, a lot of inside jokes; name-calling is definitely a big thing for us."

Rat was one of Bill's nicknames, Ward acting as the main receptor of most of the name-calling (and practical jokes), some of the other Ward jibes being Nib, Nibby, Stinky and Smelly. "Well, I'd been called Smelly for years and that's like a drop-off from Rat, like a little cul-de-sac. They called me Smelly because I played so fucking hard on stage and the sweat is just unbelievable (laughs). There's lots of unmentionable names. Always the names are abusive and everybody got their own abusive name."

"Rat Salad" is essentially a form of heavy metal jazz, not quite King Crimson, but something deliberately in that wheelhouse from the band, given other spots on the record and the self-titled debut before it.

"My mom and dad, during the war—like a lot of moms and dads in Great Britain—they were influenced by when the GIs brought the records over," says Bill, who calls the influence of jazz on his playing "huge." "So we had a huge record collection of American records, and every Saturday night those records would be played. Well they'd be played any night, really, but Saturday night was a big night and all the records would come out, and me dad would sing to them and me mom would play a bit of piano. I listened to all those songs, all of that era and I loved it. It had that sense of honesty and impact and I loved the dynamics. It's very important for musicians—at least it was important for me—to learn dynamics, and that shows right from our first record, *Black Sabbath*. That's all dynamics, especially the song "Black Sabbath." So Glenn Miller, Count Basie, Gene Krupa, the man. I was terribly influence by their music. I loved it, I listened to it and I still listen to it today."

"Krupa's drumming was just outrageous," continues Bill. "He was free. He just went wherever he wanted to go. It felt like he had no restrictions, nothing that was holding him at all. He just went wherever he wanted. He was like Moon, Mitch Mitchell, all the guys, Ginger Baker. There was nothing holding him back. It's like I'm here, this is what I'm going to play and he just laid it down. He always laid it down in the right place, and tough, and that's what I really enjoyed about him.

He didn't play over the band, he didn't play under the band. He played *with* the band."

"And as drummers, that's one of the first things you have to learn, to play with the band and that's in Sabbath's music. When we would sit down and make a piece of music together, one of the things I would try to create in the image of our sound, I would try to create with drums a lot of atmosphere, and balance the sound, say, with the lyric. Whatever Ozzy would say, I'd try to mimic that with a particular drum fill or drum beat. And it's part of building that with Geezer, with bass, trying to build all that into this enormous wall of sound. It was my desire, always, to support Tony. To be a huge rhythm section, which was Geezer and myself. And I would use a lot of toms to work with certain words to help create a doomy image, if you like. It was like wearing a really well-made suit, so that's how it felt with me. I need to go to the toms. Like on 'Black Sabbath,' Ozzy sang, 'What is this which stands before me?' And I knew where I had to go with the toms. I had a choice that day."

"Rat Salad" is a clear example of this as well, toms everywhere, percussive punctuations, ensemble cooperation with Tony and Geezer. "Yes, see, I'm an orchestrational drummer," says Bill, "which means I don't play beats. But I play atmosphere. And I try to bring mood and I try to be very respectful of what the other three guys are doing. What is Ozzy singing, what is his melody like, what is Tony playing and what is Geezer playing? And I try to weave in and out of them and add support."

Bill is respectful of Tony's jazz leanings as well. "Tony liked Django Reinhardt and so did I; I was a big fan of Django's. And Tony just has that natural feel for jazz. He's been playing it since I first met him, and I think we were 16 when we first met. But I love getting down and jamming with him. Doing a sound check. We liked to cut loose sometimes and just get into some old stuff. And I really like the fact that we both could go there. I wasn't the greatest jazz player on earth, but I liked to play those grooves—it's nice—and I still do to this day. So yeah, I think it was really beneficial. Coming back to 'Black Sabbath,' if I may; all of that is jazz-based drum-wise; it's in swing time. And there's no time, there's no meter. There's no meter in 'Black Sabbath,' the song. It's all on feel and it moves and it changes."

The band's chemistry is palpable on "Rat Salad," with communications lines wide open. "Yes, and there's an energy force that's unseen that seemed to be with us throughout," says Bill. "I think our band got very tight when we were in Europe going through all the Hamburg days and all the Zurich days and all the Copenhagen days. I really think that helped us tremendously tighten up as a unit."

And as the story goes, "Rat Salad" was one of those free-flow tracks that the band could jam at any length, to fill up the multiple sets required of bands playing on the mainland. In essence, the song was assembled during those sets and designed for those sets.

"The extra force that I'm talking about was either our own intuition, because we'd become so tight, or it was something intangible," reflects Ward. "It almost was uncanny—I think I'll stay with the word uncanny for the explanation. Often we would show up at our rehearsals and start to play and it's like we automatically knew what each person was going to play. So it almost gave the impression that the song played itself. Whether that's because we were so tight with our intuition or we just seemed to go at the same time to wherever the next change was… eight bars of that and oh, it's over here now. Especially with Sabbath's music, because Sabbath's music can't be predicted; it's unpredictable; it will change and go somewhere else into a new piece or whatever it will be. So it almost was like there was an energy force that was equal for everyone. And it almost safeguarded us. I could feel it. Magic things happened when we were creating music. Things that were uncanny. And so I've always affectionately called it the fifth member, this energy source."

"Rat Salad" was certainly an example of this as well, with its multiple and almost incongruous parts, something also demonstrated across the likes of "Electric Funeral," "Hand of Doom," War Pigs" and even "Iron Man," even though that song's central riff is so strong, listeners tend to forget about everything else going on.

Closing the record is another swingin' Sabbath classic in "Fairies Wear Boots," with the dreamy, jazzy, psychedelic intro called on some issues of the album, "Jack the Stripper."

"That one, like 'N.I.B.' and some of the really early Sabbath stuff, was done at the Aston Community Center," remembers Bill. "I think the idea came from the thing that was going on at the time between the Mods and the Rockers, which was a big thing back then. And I think originally it might have been aimed towards the skinheads. But again it was Geezer and Ozzy who put the lyric together. And it's very much an early Sabbath feel, a '67, 'early '68 feel in the sense of the jazz and again really no solid sense of time. We kind of just clumped my drums around

Geezer and Tony really (laughs). Every time we do that song I can never play the same thing twice. Every time we go on stage it's always different. So we keep making these different versions of 'Fairies Wear Boots.' It's probably pretty close but every night I never know what I'm going to do. It's usually quite close to what I had played the night before but I'm never quite sure until I'm actually doing it because it's based on wherever I am physically and wherever I am mentally at the moment; I don't base it on any level of criteria. I don't have that. I seem to be lacking in whatever it is you have to have to get it perfect or whatever every night."

Adds Geezer, "'Fairies Wear Boots,' Ozzy wrote that. We got set upon by a gang of skinheads. And skinheads in England used to wear these great big Doc Marten boots. The higher up the leg meant how more hard they were. So skinheads used to have these almost knee-length Doc Marten boots on. So we got attacked by about 24 of them one night and we beat the hell out of them. There were about five of us against 25 or 24 of them. We murdered them, so we call them a bunch of fairies. And Ozzy wrote the lyrics, 'Fairies Wear Boots.'"

The above recounted event is possibly one and the same with the time Sabbath had a bunch of equipment stolen in Newcastle, after which they were set upon by skinheads, with Tony sustaining injury to his right arm, causing the cancellation of a gig the next night. Conversely, it is said that Tony had received a black eye, at which point the crew came to the rescue swinging mic stands.

The prog and illogic of "Fairies Wear Boots" contributed to the idea of Sabbath being very much an album-oriented band rather than an eager participant in singles. Also contributing is the consistent sense of arrangement, digressed upon only for "Planet Caravan."

"Girls buy singles," says manager Jim Simpson. "Guys buy albums. That's how it was. Singles band didn't have the longevity of albums bands. I think the Rolling Stones are a great example of that. Still around after 120 years or whatever it is they've been playing. An album band builds a market. A singles band tend to be fashion-oriented and fashion, by its very definition, if it's fashion today, it's got to be unfashionable tomorrow so something else can take its place. And I think a lot of the bands saw more of a future in selling albums. It was more respectable to become an albums band. And people started making concept albums and making albums that hung together. The original albums were just 12 tracks, 12 singles. The Beatles would take probably six of their 12 as singles, subsequently."

"But an album is more serious," figures Jim. "You've got to give more thought to it. Of anything anyone said about Sabbath in the early days, they couldn't criticize the structure of their albums. *Paranoid* is an integrated album, from track one to the end, it was one piece as it were. And I think music like that tends to last longer. As much as I love a lot of three-minute-and-15-second pieces of music—of which there are many—I think something about English bands, we don't do it so well as the Americans. And a lot of people were producing happy little ditties, weren't they? As an alternative to worrying yourself sick about your kids being slaughtered in Vietnam. So heavy rock wasn't the only style around. But the heavier music, the more solid, serious music, I think reflected a seriousness of the musicians, rather than the environment.

"But there were other styles going on as well. A lot of Jamaican rhythms were breaking through. Now a lot of the reggae stuff, ultimately, was protest music as well. The early Jamaican stuff was pretty light-hearted. We had a hit with a song called 'Rudi's in Love,' which is about as Latin-frothy as you can get. But having said that, that was Locomotive. That band moved into sort of rock things as well. They had a song called 'Mr. Armageddon,' which everybody remembers now as a classic single, but I remember the fact that it hardly sold a record at the time. So audiences weren't necessarily buying the heavier stuff because it was heavy. I don't know, singers are out there singing songs and writing songs that are based on their experiences, and if their experiences include a fear of the war in Vietnam then that will creep into their music. If they want to write something and then go to San Francisco with flowers up your nose, well that's a bit of a light relief which takes people away from worrying about the heavy things."

By the end of 1970, Black Sabbath had the music industry up in arms over their daring, blaring music. But competition was in the wings. Three months before *Paranoid* hit the streets, a newly reconstituted Deep Purple (Ian Gillan and Roger Glover had replaced Rod Evans and Nick Simper respectively) had formulated their shockingly heavy *In Rock* album. In many ways, *In Rock*, with its speed, precision and pyrotechnics made *Paranoid* sound dated. It was the new perfect heavy metal album, and the critics gave it the nod, further positioning Sabbath as the heavy band for shiftless ne'er-do-wells against Deep Purple and/or Led Zeppelin, who were both loud and wild, although haughtily more sophisticated.

But most often, the cage match was set between Sabbath and Zeppelin. Just as the generation before split itself into warring factions of Beatles and Stones fans, high schools across North America defined sociable, smart, literary, possible musician types as the Zeppelin fans, while the jean-jacketed longhairs smoking dope behind the backstop were more likely to have in their possession stolen eight-tracks and cassettes featuring the hopeless anthems of Ozzy, Tony, Geezer and Bill.

"Well, I suppose it automatically became a rivalry," reflects Tony, "because we were both heading for the charts, and we were the only few bands that were like that. There was Deep Purple, Led Zeppelin and Black Sabbath, really. So you couldn't help having sort of a rivalry. I didn't know Ritchie at the time, but I know him now. We knew Zeppelin well, because they were friends of ours in the early days and we were from the same town. So we used to see them a lot, certainly Robert Plant and John Bonham. We were very familiar with what they were doing."

"When they started Zeppelin I remember Bonham saying, 'We've got this band; we're joining with Jimmy Page.' He started telling us about it. And I remember the days from before he joined Zeppelin. He used to play in different bands around Birmingham, and he was always getting fired because he was too loud. So one week he would be with a band. We used to play these alternate weeks; this was before I was with Sabbath and before he was with Zeppelin. Bill and myself had another band. And Bonham was with various bands. So we used to see him every other week playing at this place called The Midland Red Club in Birmingham, and he'd be there one week, and then the week after that, he wouldn't be there. 'What happened?' 'Oh, he was too loud; we fired him.'"

"Some of our fans would like Zeppelin and Purple," continues Tony, "then there was the other side who just liked what we did, or their own fans. So I think we all had our individual things, then we had a joint thing where some bled onto the other. We were classed as more of the heavier, doomier, downer rock sort of band—and working class; Purple were more rock, jolly rock if you like (laughs)."

"Yes, well, I liked what was going on, but I saw Deep Purple as a pop band," muses Bill. "Again, no disregard to the fellas or anything but I could hear the pop lyrics in the sense that there was that sort of mainline through it. We were singing about shooting heroin and 'Hand of Doom,' 'Children of the Grave.' We were inside a lot of hardcore issues. And I mean, I love Purple; I saw them as a real solid rock unit but I didn't get the rest of it. And it was the same with Zeppelin, and I love Zeppelin and I totally admire John Bonham as a percussionist. But Robert's lyrics were kind of like love lyrics. And that's not a put-down.

But Ozzy was screeching his balls off singing, 'What is this that stands before me?' And we were serious about it. It was a very serious band as well as a happy band. But those lyrics meant all the world to us. They did to me and they still do. That line still means a lot to me every day (laughs). So I could hear some really good rock units forming, but I always felt we were the odd band out. We'd come in under the gun all the time (laughs) and I just loved it."

"I know for myself, I knew we were doing something different because everybody hated us," continues Bill. "We were thrown out of most places. I felt very alone, along with Tony, Ozzy and Geezer, which created tremendous unison by the way. That was one of our strengths. I felt like it was us against the world, and as a teenager of course, one can feel that way a lot. I knew deep down inside that we were into something that was not a part of anything else I'd been hearing. It was odd; I felt like an oddball. In hindsight I guess one could look back and go, oh my God, we did that and we did this and that got created and fashion came from this, and so much came from hard rock which then turned into metal. But it was different. It was raw. When Led Zeppelin's first album came out, one of the things I was particularly fascinated about was the smoothness of the album. And ours, when I compared it, was so raw and almost punk-ish, gritty—there's mistakes all over it and I just love it."

Adds Geezer dismissively, "I liked Deep Purple *In Rock*, but I don't really like anything else that they've done. We didn't really like Deep Purple, to be honest (laughs). That wasn't one I'd really listened to, although I think I had the album eventually."

Released that same month was Uriah Heep's aforementioned *Very 'Eavy Very 'Umble*, or just *Uriah Heep* stateside. Savaged in the press as a mere Deep Purple clone, their record nonetheless was roughly as heavy and riffy as *Paranoid*, perhaps even more accomplished and efficient, although granted, neither album was a match for *In Rock*. "We didn't even recognize it then," notes Geezer on Heep. "We didn't even think of them as a legitimate band."

So yes, one could argue that *Paranoid* was inferior in terms of craft to both of the above records, obviously with more validity concerning *In Rock*. Indeed *Paranoid* contains many echoes of the debut record's morose bluesiness, its jammy qualities, its competent yet raw and somewhat chilly recording values. There's a bleakness to *Paranoid*, even a sort of mean-spiritedness, that puts it second to last in this writer's opinion with respect to rankings of the Ozzy-era albums.

Part of that summation surely must come from the fact that in terms of airplay, it is the band's Led Zeppelin's untitled fourth—if one is to be sick and tired of any Black Sabbath songs, the list of those songs will very likely include "Paranoid," "War Pigs," "Iron Man" and "Fairies Wear Boots," a happenstance not helped when any given Sabbath show through any era is likely to include most or all of these in its tired, predictable set list.

Sabbath's friendship with Led Zeppelin eventually spawned the rumour of the Black Zeppelin Tapes. It begins with a conversation between a book publisher (one of this writer's) and an un-named ex-manager for the band, in which the publisher points to a box in the corner of the office marked Black Zeppelin Tapes. An explanation ensues that at one point, Black Sabbath and Led Zeppelin were rehearsing just down the street from each other, and that, for a lark, they decided to switch singers for a bit of fun. The results, apparently, were caught on tape.

"No, we never ever did that," counters Ozzy. "No, what happened on one occasion, when they had Swan Song and we were floating between management and record companies, they came and tried to get us to sign to Swan Song, and we had a jam session in the studio, but we never recorded it, as far as I know."

But did Robert Plant ever sing with Black Sabbath?

"I believe so, but I don't think it was ever recorded. It might have been recorded, I don't know. Jimmy Page wasn't there. It was John Paul Jones, John Bonham, Robert Plant and us guys."

Adds Geezer, "The only time that we jammed, the whole band together, was when we were doing *Sabbath Bloody Sabbath*. They came down to the studio to see us. We'd grown up with Planty and Bonham. Bonham was Tony's best man at his wedding. Like, I'd been around to Planty's house and jammed with him, but the only time the two whole bands got together was when we were doing *Sabbath Bloody Sabbath*. They came down to the studio to see us and we just had a jam, for some reason. That was the only time the two bands actually got together. I think we just did some blues stuff; we both started out being blues bands."

As for the existence of tapes, "There's not supposed to be," laughs Geezer. "But I'm sure somebody's got one somewhere. No, it wasn't recorded. Led Zeppelin did come over and we had a big jam session together. I can't even remember what we played. We were probably all stoned out of our minds (laughs). Our manager recorded everything we ever did live, but not that. That's how *Live at Last* happened, which came out after we had left."

"But that was another big influence on us, Zeppelin," adds Geezer, demonstrating his regard for the band, which—don't forget—had three records out before *Paranoid*, two before *Black Sabbath*. "Especially since we knew Robert Plant and John Bonham from Birmingham. That was probably our biggest influence because they completely took it to another level. So we thought at the time we just wanted to be like Zeppelin. It was a musical thing for us. And with us and Zeppelin, and then Deep Purple came out, this whole sort of hard rock, heavy rock thing took off. It seemed to be everybody was trying to get heavier and hard or whatever."

"But Zeppelin was just a combination of everything that we loved," reflects Butler. "It was the blues, loads of guitars, great bass playing, incredible drummer. Just like the best singer around, a combination of all the things that each one of us wanted to be. Page is a great guitarist, such great musicians, and we'd all seen them in clubs around Birmingham as well. Plant used to be my favourite singer, and then when he got the job with Zeppelin and we heard him on the Zeppelin album, it was great. It's like one of your mates has made it, and Bonham as well. So they sort of set the way, and when we followed it, we sort of had a built-in audience, if you like. People wanted the new Zeppelin or wanted to hear more of that kind of thing. And I think we took it to a whole other level."

"Well, there was some crossover stuff that went down between Sabbath and Zeppelin," affirms Bill, adding a bit of intrigue in a different direction. "Only in the sense that collaborations started to sprout up between members of their band and members of our band. I think the strongest collaboration was between Geezer and Robert Plant. I mean, they were working on songs together and working things out! I do know that (laughs). I'm just thinking of John right now, God bless his heart. I do know that John came down to visit with me one day and we actually talked about it. John was actually a little bit concerned about the collaborations that were going on in the sense that, 'Hang on a minute; is this right? Where do you stand on this, Bill?' And I said, 'I don't know John, I haven't really taken a lot of notice. I know that Robert wants to do some stuff with Geezer.' But it all fell by the wayside; it wasn't heavy or anything. We were just sitting over a pint discussing it. But we never actually exchanged recordings, not that I'm aware of anyway. If there are tapes, then I'd love to hear them."

A good part of the discussed condescension towards the Sabs versus Zeppelin or Purple was fuelled by the band's fairly constant flow of bad press. It is very likely that there was some baggage on the part of the media, when it came to their dealings with Sabbath. It is well-documented, through articles letting us know this, that the band could blow off interviews, or treat them frivolously, or simply lack the organization around themselves to make sure they happen on time or at all. Then there's the band's insular nature, their particularly odd form of quietness, their brevity with words and their variously sardonic, ironic and grim senses of humour, especially on the part of Geezer and Ozzy. As well, you'd probably find some bald-faced envy on the part of the press, given Sabbath's quick, almost manic rise to the upper ranks.

To top it off somebody at "the office," had surely caused bad vibes by making the band unavailable. "We sort of, certainly in the early days, we had hardly done any press," remembers Tony. "We were kept away from doing press, really, purposely. They just didn't want to us to do press. Later on, of course, people would have input, saying, 'Do this, do that,' but we decided for ourselves what we did, really. That's why at one period we managed ourselves, took over the reins."

Of note, Geezer refutes Tony's assessment, saying, "No, not that I know. We did all the press we could. But then again, maybe Tony remembers it better than I do. I know the English press was against us at first, because a lot of it was based in London, and the press had never heard of us because we made our name outside of London, and we were the first band ever to do that in England. And I think just sort of, because we hadn't made it big in London at the time, they just sort of totally dismissed us. It's like, unless you've made it in London, you can't make it in England. And we totally proved them wrong."

Resoundingly so. *Paranoid* was to hit #1 in the UK charts and #12 in the States. Over time, *Paranoid* spent 27 weeks in the UK charts. Even its "reissue" in 1980 took it to #54, where it stayed for two weeks. The "Paranoid" single (backed with "The Wizard") would hit #4 in the UK and #61 in the US. By far the band's most successful album of all time, *Paranoid* has been certified quadruple platinum in the US, testimony to the power of hit singles, of which this album had a bonafide two, with "Fairies Wear Boots"… well, you can count that as at least a half. As the band gathered steam, "Iron Man" was issued as a single in the States,

October of 1971, backed with "Electric Funeral," no picture sleeve, with the centrepiece featuring the usual morose, war-olive Warner label of the day. The song, launched as a 3:33 edit, down from almost six minutes, peaked in the States at #52 the following year.

"Yes, *Paranoid* was even bigger than the first one," reflects Vertigo helmsman Olav Wyper. "We had our 12-month anniversary of the launch of Vertigo, and we had a big party at Ronnie Scott's club, and we presented gold discs to the band. That week, 'Paranoid,' the single, was on the charts, *Paranoid*, the album, was #1, on the 12-month anniversary of the launch of the label. And they were the fulcrum around which we built everything. Because they opened… oh, they're on Vertigo. Oh, here's something else on Vertigo. We'll listen to this because we like that and it's on that label. It was a more produced record, a more sophisticated record. Lyrically they had moved on again, and because they had more time to make it, it was more considered musically. Because on the first album, if they got two takes on anything they were lucky. Now because there was more money, there was more confidence. They had more confidence because of what they had achieved, so they could be more considered in the style, musically, that they were doing. And it was huge in America, too."

"They came out of an industrial urban area where life was fairly tough," reflects Wyper, "and to succeed at anything you really had to work at it. You also needed a bit of luck, but you needed talent, real talent. No matter what you were doing you needed real talent to make that work. Before then, there was the Liverpool sound, demonstrating the fact that fantastic music has come from different areas of Britain. It wasn't just a London-based thing. I mean I was at EMI when the Beatles came out and all of those records came out. I was head of advertising at EMI and promotions, so I knew all of them, and experienced all of that long before I moved to CBS and eventually to Philips. So it was quite common that things came from around the country. We're not a big island. We're a very small island."

But London always entered into the equation in terms of the next rung on the ladder to success. "That's right, because there were no labels outside London," explains Wyper. "I mean you've got to remember, in the time we're talking about, there was EMI, there was Decca, and EMI had Harvest, Decca had Deram. There was Pye which was a small-ish company, very much based on hit singles that delivered their records to the dealers in vans from a center point, whereas everybody else had a sophisticated distribution system. CBS was the first international company to open an office in England. RCA was still distributed by Decca in those days. So there wasn't a lot of choice, and there weren't a plethora of indie labels. There wasn't a label in Coventry or Birmingham that would say we'll sign you. Because if there had been a company like that, how would they have got national distribution? How would they have got the records pressed? How would they have got salesmen doing it? There weren't then independent record distributors. The business was totally controlled by the two majors."

"And so it became quite necessary for the Vertigos and Harvests and Neons of the world to step in and embrace this new music that was being made, because this heavier or more progressive music that was being made, they almost needed—we now call them boutique labels—to take a chance. But Vertigo was not just heavy metal because we had serious contemporary jazz bands on it, like Ian Carr's Nucleus, for example. We had folk acts. We had all kinds of acts. In the second release that we had, indeed when *Black Sabbath* came out, we had *An Old Overcoat Won't Ever Let You Down* by Rod Stewart. Now Rod was out of a deal. I knew his manager and he came to me and said look, we've got this album, we need to get it out, we need to get his career going again. He's solo, he's not with the Small Faces, and I listened to it and I thought it was fantastic. So we put it out. So we weren't just heavy; we were looking for people with, if you like, a broadness of sophisticated musical taste. At one end can be heavy metal, at the other end can be contemporary jazz. And folk, because we had contemporary folk in there as well."

"My opinion is that the best two albums Sabbath ever made were the first two albums," concludes Wyper. "And I think that not just because I was involved with them, but because one was their opening card in a game, which was the first album, and it was a brilliant card, and it captured absolutely the live element of the band, which was very important. And as their career continued, of course, they became not an album-selling band, but an audience-drawing band. A Black Sabbath concert even today will sell out because people want to go and see it. Ozzy will sell out in his way because people want to go and see him, because they generate an excitement."

Touring for *Paranoid* found the band visiting the US for the very first time, Sabbath touching down in New York on October 29, 1970, playing their first gig the next night—Traffic was on the plane with the boys and a right drunk was had. Preceding these dates, the band hit Europe, Chapter III and label mates Manfred Mann as support, before a handful of dates back home in the UK. The US stint saw the band play upwards of a couple dozen dates, highlight being an extended stay at both the Whiskey a Go Go in Hollywood and Bill Graham's Fillmore West in San Francisco.

A Circus article from the mid '70s had cited a Warner Bros. executive saying that when Sabbath "first came to Los Angeles, the Whiskey was packed two shows a night. I don't know where people heard of them. The word just seemed to be out." Indeed it had. Upon the release of *Paranoid*, it had been said that the debut had already shifted 40,000 units stateside. Tony also had said in the press that playing European festivals, especially in Germany, had been a boon for the band, although logistical hassles made touring America preferable.

With regard to the Fillmore shows, Bill Graham initially booked the band at the Fillmore East, for November 10, 1970, and reportedly saw them and hated them. But when he saw the size of the crowds they were bringing, he relented happily, proceeding to sell out the ensuing Fillmore West run three weeks in advance.

Notes Geezer, "Yeah, I remember the Fillmore West and Fillmore East. I remember we supported Rod Stewart at Fillmore East; Fillmore West, it was the James Gang and Love. I think we were in the middle; Love was headlining, we were second and James Gang was third. It was one of the few places we had heard of. Because coming from England, we hadn't really heard much about where you would play in America. There was the Fillmore West and the Fillmore East and the Whiskey in L.A., and I think that was about it; those were the most famous places, for a band coming from England."

And what surprised the guys most about going to America for the first time? "The women," laughs Geezer. "That was really a surprise to us. I mean, we get to our hotel, and we go to the bedroom and they'd already be in the bedrooms waiting for us."

"The first US gig ever was a place called Ungano's, in New York," recalls Tony. "And we came over, brought all our gear, sound system, the lot. It was all big stuff then. We weren't aware of what sort of sound systems you'd have over here, you see? Which is obviously far better than what we'd brought over. And so the first thing we do is plug all the amps in, and they blow up! Because of the power difference. We were so thick; we didn't know what we were supposed to do. So promptly, bang! The stuff blew up. And here we are stuck in this little spot called Ungano's, a tiny little place. Oh no. And these were the sorts of places we'd be playing at. We were really disillusioned at first. Because we were playing those small clubs; we'd played them in England and all around Europe. We thought when we got to the States, we'd see these big venues. And we get to this place, which is about twice as big as this room. Bloody hell! We were there for two nights."

"I mean, we heard all this stuff about America," interjects Geezer. "Like you know, you've got to make it in America. That's the place to do it, Carnegie Hall, Madison Square Garden. And at that point, we'd had a #1 album in England with *Paranoid* and a #2 single. So we were playing like the real decent gigs in England and Europe, nice places. And we got to New York; we're thinking it was going to be Madison Square Garden, and it's like the worst club we've ever played in! I think capacity was 300 or 400 or something. It was this horrible, dingy dump. I'll always remember, I don't know whether it was at the club, or at this place where we went to eat, there's this guy frying hamburgers. And a fly landed on the wall, and he smacked it with the thing that he was using to pick the hamburgers up with. I've never seen anything like that before! Killing flies with the hamburger spatula."

"And we just thought, 'What the hell is this?' But what we didn't know is, the whole club was filled with agents who were there to see what we were like, and to see if they were gonna book a tour on us. And that's all we really played to, is all these agents and record company people that we'd never even seen before, or heard of. That was our welcome to New York."

"So anyway, the third night we did the Fillmore East," continues Tony. "And of course, that was great. We were like, 'Oh God yeah, this is more like it!' And we'd never used a monitor system before. We didn't know what a monitor system was. So it was great for us, because we could hear what everybody was doing through his monitors. It was real good fun to see all that, to build up to these stages, learn about things like that."

Additional support on the *Paranoid* tour came from an impressive batch of acts including Savoy Brown, Curved Air, J. Geils Band and Humble Pie, as well as lesser known "baby bands" such as Freedom, Patto, Quatermass, Sir Lord Baltimore, Jonathan Swift, Cactus and Steel Mill, which included among their ranks a young Bruce Springsteen. Eight months of touring this venomous, garrulous record ended in late April of 1971, the band exhausted and exasperated at the distances a band needed to travel stateside to get across one's point. "I had to go to the hospital, my nerves were getting in such a state," complained Ozzy. "It was all that travel that shook me up. Flying 3000 miles from New York to Los Angeles and then back again…"

Headliners over Sabbath included Canned Heat, Fleetwood Mac, Jethro Tull, Emerson, Lake & Palmer, Rod Stewart & The Faces, Alice Cooper, James Gang, Mountain and at the L.A. Forum in late February of 1971, Grand Funk Railroad, who Geezer recalls, 35 years later, as the band who treated them most shabbily throughout Sabbath's long touring history.

Gearing up for the release of the next record, Ozzy spoke a bit about his early influences, as well as his impression of Grand Funk Railroad. "I used to like what everyone else did: the Beatles and Rolling Stones. Geezer was into heavier things like the Mothers. We just started playing 12-bar blues and 12-bar jazz about four years ago. I used to like anything that was heavy. The Kinks' 'You Really Got Me' did something to me, and I used to dig the early Who and Led Zeppelin. I dig anything that makes the hairs in the middle of my spine stand up. We just started writing our own stuff and our sound just evolved into what it is today; it wasn't planned. I suppose we are similar to Grand Funk Railroad, but I hadn't heard of them until our third tour here. Nobody knew who Grand Funk were in England. We didn't realize how big they were until we played The Forum with them and they just packed the place—two nights! They turned the crowd on, but musically they didn't do anything for me. I'm not saying they're a bum group, because they've got to be a good group for people to dig them. Personally, I like to hear music which is considerably different than what we play."

"When we played with Cactus," recalls Geezer, "that's when they got some of their Sicilian friends down to shoot us, because Tony had beat one of them up. Because while they were on stage, they came off stage, and their dope was rolled up in a towel, and they accused us of stealing it. Meanwhile, we hadn't even been there. And this guy came in, I think he was the singer or something, and started shouting at Tony, which is the wrong thing to do, and the next thing, the guy went straight through the wall. Tony smashed him around the head. And we just beat hell out of them, and because they thought they were tough and we found out that they weren't. And so when we went on, we had all these motorbikes turn up outside, and somebody passed us this message that we were going to be shot in the middle of the set. So we went on and we just kept our eyes open, and we saw all these guys making their way to the middle of the hall, and just at that moment, somebody tipped a can of Coke into Tony's amp (laughs), and blew it up, so we had to finish the show. So we'll never know if we were going to get shot or not (laughs)."

"There was a wee skirmish, aye, aye," recounts Cactus bass legend Tim Bogert, with a chuckle, going on to actually invert the key detail of the tale. "What happened was, we were on stage. And our roadie went back, who was a little, tiny guy—smaller than Vinny (Martell, Vanilla Fudge) is—a really thin man. He went back to the dressing room to get us… and I can't remember what anymore, came back out; we're continuing the show. Whether it was towels or water or whatever it was. And he goes off stage, doesn't come back in the appropriate amount of time. Rusty (Day) goes back and he's all beat up. They had accused him of taking their stash, which we did not, which, he wasn't a user; we couldn't care less. And Rusty went flying off the stage when he found out what went down. And Jimmy went flying off the stage and by the time Carmine and I got there, most of the melee was over. But yeah, it got heated. People got pushed around."

And was there a death threat from some bikers or something?

"That I don't remember, honestly. Who was threatened? Us or them?"

Them!

"Oh, cool (laughs). Well, I am a Harley rider, so I hang with those people. No, I mean, I don't remember. I was only involved in this particular section of it, so I don't remember. I've come to know those guys over the years; they're all nice people, and no problem. It's 35 years ago. There were so many moments, so many thousands of really cool moments, and there were millions of moments; I just can't remember all of them, unfortunately. Memory is selective. It's funny, legend grows in and of itself, once an event has occurred. And I don't know what legend has grown on our behalf. If there has been one, hey, cool! (laughs). It's like Woodstock is thought of as this wonderful occurrence. It was a mudhole! It was a mess! (laughs). It was like living in a dungeon for three days. But now it's just, oh, how wonderful it was. In retrospect, you forget all the punky things in that respect and you remember the good stuff. That's why when you asked me about the Sabbath story, that was kind of a punky thing. So I don't really remember a whole lot about it. Because I have so many good memories of the early years. It was such a good time."

Turns out there was actually a protracted piece in Circus about the Asbury Park incident in which the story is related as follows: Sabbath had two towels, Cactus one, in a joint dressing room, and Sabbath took an identical Cactus towel, identical, save for the fact that Cactus' drugs were wrapped up in it. Parties were summoned to the scene of the crime and Tony punches the Cactus roadie, having taken offense at being called thieves. Returned towel, apologies all 'round, but tensions simmered, with Cactus sticking up for their 110 lb. helper. Rumours now fly that Cactus is getting a gun and/or that a hundred guys were being gathered to attack Sabbath, possibly onstage. Then turpentine was said to have been added to the band's onstage water glasses. Guards were posted, songs were played, the power went out… twice. Five songs done and the show was knocked on its head.

It's no surprise Black Sabbath haven't forgotten Cactus.

As it turned out, another New York band, Mountain, would also make an impression on the Sabs, this one a mite more positive. "The first real band who I really loved, before we got to America was Mountain," says Geezer. "I just loved their album… 'Mississippi Queen' and all that stuff. And they were really good guys, showed us the ropes. It was great for us, because we loved that album, and when we came to America, we didn't know who we were going to be on tour with, and when that was put together, we loved it."

Indeed, one could add Mountain to our previously discussed trinity of heavy acts, in terms of bands who had considerably heavy records out, Leslie West and crew having made their deafening mark through two albums as of spring 1970, the Leslie West – *Mountain* album from September of '69, and the classic *Climbing!* record from March of 1970, which did indeed include the molten guitar tones of the man mountain's "Mississippi Queen."

"Nobody would touch Black Sabbath," recalls Mountain drummer Corky Laing. "They were too heavy in those days. We had a theory, that when you're a headline band, get the strongest opener you can, because it keeps you on your toes. And Black Sabbath, they weren't a great band but they were very cutting-edge, the gothic thing. Nobody went near them. Because don't forget in those days you had Nixon in the White House; it was a very Republican, very conservative era. As a result, the underground was very underground. And Black Sabbath were having a very hard time cutting it in America. In those days it was pretty heavy stuff. You go down to Texas in those days with Black Sabbath and you can get your car blown up. And that's where we were. We were one of the few bands to take them on the road because we were hooked up with an English agency that had Jethro Tull, a lot of English acts, Humble Pie, Ten Years After. It was great, but if you play with those kinds of musicians you tend to be competitive."

"But yes, nobody would touch them. In 1970, the summer of 1970, no one would go near them. And they had a hard time, because they were trying to break them over in America. And especially in Texas, nobody wanted to know about Black Sabbath—just too freaking weird. So Felix (Pappalardi), myself and Leslie got together and decided it would be a really cool idea to have a group like that open the show. And Ozzy was just so thankful after every show. He would run back and give us all kisses on the lips and stuff. He was just so boisterous, even though the crowd booed him; the fans really didn't understand Sabbath. The cops were looking at Ozzy like he was some kind of fucking alien. They were just a very different kind of band; the first gothic band to come out. This was a whole month, in the south and in Texas. We were still touring Mountain *Climbing!*. *Climbing!* was actually recorded in the fall of '69, and came out in the first quarter of '70, and we toured it about a year."

"It was just very awkward," continues Corky. "The police were there. Don't forget, they looked pretty strange. They weren't your pretty boys. And they were pretty strange. The only thing was, we had to keep an eye on Tony Iommi because he lost his fingers. He has his fake fingers. So one gig, we had to look for them; that was kind of weird. I just remember that because we found them like a minute before the show. They didn't really know what they were going to do without his fingers, because he only had one set at that time. We had crew, three bands on the floor in Texas, Texas Arena, looking for his finger. It was great. What I'm saying to you is that he was in tears. Tony was in tears; he said I can't believe it; he wouldn't be able to play. He just had to play every gig. They had nothing else in their life. Yeah it was wild. I gotta tell ya, he was very upset. You lose your finger... and he had the prototype over in Birmingham. You know it sounds funny now, but at the time it was very, very traumatic."

"Black Sabbath were so fucking focused it was unbelievable," recalls Corky, asked to put what they were doing in context. "They only had one beat, they had one guitar riff and Ozzy had one thing that he did. But they did it so well and they did it in different dynamics, that they had 45 minutes. It was unquestionable that... I think they would admit that they had their limitations, and as part of their success they were able to stretch out, but they were smart enough not to get clever or not to get smart. They kept their repertoire at a place that just built and built. They were pioneers, innovators of that brand of rock 'n' roll, because you don't change a good thing and they had it."

"It didn't start off as a good thing. It started off, probably to a lot of people, as a mistake that came over from England. But somehow people grabbed onto it because of the uniqueness of it, and again because of the conviction. Those guys went up there, they didn't have a penny in their pocket, they came over and they toured with nothing and they worked very hard. It was a statement. If you listen to some of the records, they are very simple. The changes are simple but it's the execution that's very, very well done."

"And they had thing thrown at them. It took about an hour to clean the stage after for us to go on. But I gotta tell ya, they didn't give a shit. That's where the conviction came. Ozzy knew what he was doing. He didn't care.

Matter of fact, he came from Birmingham where my dad's from. They don't really give a shit what people think, and that's partial of the name of the game. If you're going to do that kind of music, if you're going to step out that way and be that extraordinary and that loud, you have to think like that. It was very interesting, it was a branding, it was heavy metal."

"Bill Ward is a very solid drummer," furthers Laing, speaking with obvious authority. "He never considered himself a well-rounded drummer. He was just really great with the Sabbath. He had a way of playing, a plodding nature about the way he played. Everybody would bounce their heads really slow, you know, like sort of dolls or dogs at the back of the car, the way that doll goes up and down. He had a nature of playing like that. He wasn't a speed freak at all. He's a plodder. He started that whole plodding drum thing."

Mountain also hooked up with the Sabs on their own turf. "Yeah, when they were in England, they invited us over," notes Corky. "They played so loud. I'm serious, they played so loud, I was a block away driving to the studio. And in London, it's a very strange town. I just followed the sound. It was like three or four blocks away, and we're talking about these buildings. And it was so loud, you could open your window and all of London could hear it. This was when they recorded the second album. We were over there touring or something. I remember going to the studio over there, with their manager and their agent. We hung around quite a bit. For some reason there was an affinity there. Oddly enough, my father was born in Birmingham, and this is where they're from. They're all from Birmingham. It's a real blue collar worker upbringing. It's a tough place, like Manchester—these neighbourhoods were tough. These guys had to be hard-assed. And that's where they're from. I don't know, I got along with them very well and so did Leslie. It was just one of those things and it wasn't that we were big fans of their music or anything like that. Quite frankly, I always thought Ozzy could do better singing-wise. He didn't consider himself a singer as much as an entertainer, you see? So that's why he sort of did all that stuff at the front of the stage, but I thought he had a great voice."

"Oh yeah, Mountain were great," says Bill in closing. "I mean, we knew all the guys. Sabbath were a breaking band; we had a sound of our own and I think there was a mutual respect for each other. No, they were just a really good fucking rock band, coming from a lot of blues. I mean, to this day, I have my Mountain CDs."

Earth 1968: Geezer Butler, Ozzy Osbourne, Tony Iommi, Bill Ward. Courtesy Joe D'Agostino Collection.

Early Warner Bros. promo shot.

The record that invented doom.

Industry ad for the debut, Billboard magazine

Singapore issue of "Paranoid"/"The Wizard, vertigo 6059010.

Swiss issue of Sabbath's second album

Warner (WWA) tour poster; note Tony without moustache.

Portuguese issues of "Changes"/"Sabbath Bloody Sabbath;" Vertigo 6165 001.

German issue of "Tomorrow's Dream"/"Laguna Sunrise;" Vertigo 6059 061.

Ozzy, Tulsa, Oklahoma, October 22, 1976. © Rich Galbraith.

First date of the *Technical Ecstasy* tour; support came from Boston and Moxy. © Rich Galbraith.

Warner Bros. promo photo; note Blizzard of Oz t-shirt.

The master of the heavy metal riff, Tony Iommi.
© Rich Galbraith.

Alternate cover for *Vol 4*, featuring the gatefold shot of Geezer.

Geezer, Tony, Bill (not shown) and Ozzy take on America. © Rich Galbraith.

Album 3

Master of Reality

"War and paranoia, death and hate"

We begin the examination of Black Sabbath's warm and fuzzy third record, *Master of Reality*, with a bit of a summary of experience, as it were, from band manager Jim Simpson, as he would soon be shunted aside, as Black Sabbath become too big for Birmingham.

"Immediately we knew we had something special," recalls Jim. "Up until then we knew we had a good band, and we all got along well together, we all knew how to work together. But to get some gigs we had to do something different and we knew that. But from the moment "Black Sabbath" came up, the moment the style emerged fully formed, really, from that moment on we were on a crusade. We knew that we'd got something really, really special, and from that moment on it became really serious."

When it became "serious," that's when reservations about what Jim could offer the band became paramount and distracting. But, as Simpson explains, the fans were taking the band to the top. "It was a guy's music," chuckles Jim. "It wasn't a girl's music by any means. But immediately guys would... first we got Ozzy to suck them in. Ozzy had this great image onstage, great persona. I mean he's one of the world's great innocents. He's a very honest guy, and onstage that honesty always came through—you couldn't ignore Ozzy. If Ozzy were onstage in the room, you shut up and you listened to him. I mean people criticized the band—the band were incredibly criticized by the media in the early days—but we didn't care because we knew we were right. We knew we were onto something really special. I keep coming back to it—it was a crusade. We knew we had something great right from the beginning."

Further on Ozzy Osbourne, Jim explains that, "Ozzy had a crisis at times. I guess he felt like because other people could pick up an instrument and make noise with it, that they were in some way sort of qualified musicians. And he worried whether or not he could sing at times, and they had many late night conversations here about that with him needing reassurance that what he got was something special. And he, more than anybody else, wanted to listen to other singers to sort of learn his trade, I suppose. So he could say other singers influenced him. And the singer I played to him more than anything else was Jimmy Rushing, the Basie band's singer, who I played for everyone, of course. Who else should you play to people? So I could say, yeah, there's an influence from Rushing there, but you wouldn't identify it. I could point out similarities that you'd agree with but you can't say Rushing shows through."

"You have to understand that as far as I'm concerned all great music starts off with the Count Basie band. For me, all my jazz sort of stems there. I think it's the greatest aggregation ever. You think Basie is known as a riff band in jazz. It's the greatest riff band in jazz. They've got repetitive riffs that build up and create an effect. Well, metal does that. Jo Jones rides on his high hat in a very distinctive style. Well, Bill Ward did that in the early albums. And like I say, Basie band had Jimmy Rushing, this big open-throated bellow of a vocal. Apparently that man was standing singing in front of a 16-piece band with no electrical amplification whatsoever to assist him. So he had to have a big voice. Well, Ozzy's got a big voice. And Ozzy's one of the few singers who makes himself heard above a band. So there are lots of connections there. The sort of ponderousness and real metallic heaviness is inherent in what the Basie band are."

Back in the rock world, concerning the critics, Simpson figures, "First of all, the ones that weren't interested in music, they jumped onto the black magic thing, which wasn't helped by another band around at the time called Black Widow. And they got involved with England's number one white witch. How anyone gets to aspire to a title like that, I'm not sure. They got in with Alex Sanders, and they'd get the double-page spread in the Daily Mail, they'd get all the radio interviews, they got all the press coverage, yet didn't get any gigs. We were out there doing the gigs; we were always a hard-working band.

But Sabbath's own image, as well as the brand confusion caused by Black Widow caused witches to come out of the woodwork for the Sabs. "Yes, we had so many cranks come to us at every gig, and letters and phone calls," says Jim. "All sorts of cranks. Especially Americans. They seemed to get deeply into that Satanic thing more than we did. But we knew nothing about that; it wasn't a game we played. I think Boris Karloff was about as far as Geezer got into the occult, horror movies. I mean people on the outside who didn't listen to the music could be excused for going off on that. The publicity in the end was good, but it annoyed us at the time. We thought we were a music band. We thought the music was pretty good, and we really wanted people to listen to the music and appreciate the band for what we believed they were. And in retrospect, we were right. I keep coming back to this. We were on a crusade, and anything that took the attention away from the music was annoying, especially when people talked to you about Alex Sanders and white witches."

"But I don't think anything else was going on like that. But if you listen to the music, if you forget the lyrics for a second and you listen to the music, what other lyrics could it have had? I mean they came up with something absolutely original and it was them that did it. There was no outside influence. Obviously we were all influenced by the outside, but they came up with the lyrics and the style of the music, the riffs; everything was theirs and the entity was totally original. I mean, a musicologist may prove me wrong and play to me stuff that came before, but that was not a steal—it was pure, original music. And the fact that they were from Birmingham, people keep pointing out industrial city and things affecting the music, but I think that's pretty nonsensical. It's a reflection of the serious, heavy styles of music which emanated from Birmingham anyway. I mean a lot of industrial cities produce tough, urban music. Chicago and Detroit are two obvious examples. And I suppose you could say that San Francisco produces light, airy-fairy, sweet-smiling, sweet-smelling music. And you could say New Orleans produces funky music reflecting the city, and it probably does."

"But what we were listening to in those days was blues and that's what Sabbath came from. They could not have come from London and the home counties, that's for sure. Sheffield had a couple of good metal bands, but I couldn't imagine them coming from something like Manchester. I could imagine them coming from Yorkshire, Sheffield, Leeds, places like that. I suppose Birmingham was stronger in all those things than the northeast anyway. They could be a Geordie band, they could be a Newcastle band, but they're not—they're the archetypal Birmingham band."

Tongue firmly in cheek, Jim continues, explaining that, "All the talent in Britain, all the quality, all the innovativeness, all the ideas, all the aspirations came from London. If you didn't think so, just ask them and they'll tell you. London as a whole tended to shut the door. If you wanted to make it in London, you had to go off and live in London, which I always thought was a terrible thing to do. They just strip talent from all over the country and cram them in one area where only a small amount are going to survive anyway because there's too much in one area."

As for Geezer's estimation of London town, "I don't know because we didn't go there," deadpans Butler. "It was okay but there was a big clique kind of thing in London. They didn't take you seriously. It was a bit like L.A. If you're a movie actor, if you want to make it in movies you have to be in L.A. Or New York. And Birmingham is sort of like St. Louis or something. 'Where you based?' We'd say Birmingham and they'd say, 'Oh, see you.' It's like you were from Mars or something. So you had to get to know all these people in London on the London music scene, and the record companies, because they wouldn't go out to Birmingham to see you. You had to go see them. It wasn't like it is today. If there's a great band up in Scotland they'd take 12 A&R guys rushing them to Scotland. Then, if you weren't in London, they just didn't want to know. So you had to go to them. And like I said, everybody we went to see to audition for, they just treated us like scum. They'd say, 'What clubs do you play in?' We'd say, 'Henry's Blues House in Birmingham.' 'No, what real clubs are you playing in?' 'We're not.' 'See you.'"

"I always had a lot of envy," adds Bill, of London, "because I felt like they had a lot of firsts coming out of there. Well, talking about Jimmy Page, and that's just there with Zeppelin, but the Yardbirds, and any of the great blues bands like the Animals or Them, everybody would go to London. They wouldn't come to Birmingham. It was all there; everything was created in London. And they had a huge jazz scene there and their blues players as well, so there was a much richer culture. I think it was the stronger of the cultures at that time in the mid '60s. But I did, I envied it because I could hear the sounds, and we weren't necessarily spending a lot of time in London during the mid-'60s. We were playing in the Midlands and further north. So yeah, there was a lot buzzing there."

"So I felt a little bit intimidated," continues Ward. "I'm trying to think about my age at the time, maybe 17, 18 years old; so I'm this rough kid that would have strong opinions about certain things, including anybody that I thought was looking at me the wrong way. I felt intimidated by them and I wanted to retaliate immediately. So that was the mentality. But the bottom line is that I felt a little intimidated when I spent time in London, at first. I love London today, but at first, many years ago when I was still quite young, it felt different, a bit unreachable. Who made it reachable for us was Ian Anderson from Jethro Tull and Alvin Lee from Ten Years After, and suddenly I realized that the veil for me was lifted. It was a bit cliquey and I didn't feel a part of it, but suddenly I realized that we were in London talking to some very famous artists who were embedded very, very well into the London jazz and rock scene, and of course I felt like we'd reached a level of approval."

"So we, the bands I'm involved with mostly, have stuck in Birmingham," continues Simpson. "It's an hour-and-a-half away; it's not the other side of the world. You had to crack it in London, and the worst area to crack were the people who knew everything, like the people at record companies and newspaper editorials. The media found it hard to take anything seriously. Now and then things broke through. I mean the Beatles broke through, but they broke through because that was a certain region of the country which really had a great partisan-style following for things they produce there. You look at Wales. Anything happens in Wales, it'll get on Welsh TV and they'll support it and the Welsh newspaper will support it. Anything Irish, the Irish will stick together and they'll support it and give it a platform from which to launch further. Most of this country's very bad at that except Liverpool. Now maybe because it's got an Irish influence in it, but Liverpool people are very clannish, very proud to be from Liverpool, very supportive of things that come from Liverpool."

"But Birmingham bands seem to have to do it on their own. We have a great scene up here, and the amount of bands that came out of the city, a phenomenal amount of gigs I told you about earlier on, there had to be enough bands to play them. And we had some tremendous players out there. But most of them moved south. When we had a hit with Locomotive at EMI, the guy who was working for two years on it, one night he drove us to the station and said, 'How long is it going to take you to get back to Manchester?' I said 'Birmingham.' 'Oh, same thing.' They didn't care. London didn't care what happened north of the Watford Gap. We're all the same. Manchester, Birmingham."

But despite getting no love from London, Jim says, "We knew the kids liked the band. We knew the kids knew about the band because of the fan mail we were getting, but it was very hard to break in. Eventually I persuaded a guy called John G or Simon G, who ran The Marquee club;

that's the first date we played in London. And we were there on not a very good deal on a Friday night, and I'll tell you at four o'clock in the afternoon the queue went down Wardour Street into Old Compton Street. There must have been three times the capacity of The Marquee out there on the pavement standing waiting to get in. The kids knew it. Of course suddenly after that we got all the posh festivals, we got the TVs, all the clubs. But they were very reluctant. See, nothing had gone before Sabbath. I think they thought they were savages of some sort. If you're brought up on pretty girly music then I suppose Sabbath is a bit of a scare when you've never heard it before. I guess we're quite proud of that. I think we probably worked on that in some ways, but in some ways it worked against us in the early stage. But once people saw the band, there was never a problem going back. The problem was always getting the first gig. We put the band into Hamburg. It was a real struggle the first time but afterwards everybody wanted them, in Star club."

"I don't really feel qualified very much to talk about *Master of Reality* because I lost the band," continues Jim, bringing the story up to date. "The week I lost them the single 'Paranoid' was #2 on the singles chart. The album *Paranoid* was #1 on the album chart, and Black Sabbath's first album had come into the Top 20 at #16. I believe those are the two greatest albums they ever made, and I also think they were the two greatest metal albums that were ever made, and I'm very proud that they were made when I was managing the band and managing the band's affairs."

"The second album you gotta remember was made in about six months. All the formative years of the individuals, and the formative couple years of the band together in their various titles before they became Black Sabbath, all of that resulted in the album *Black Sabbath*. Six months later we had to do it all again, and I think it's a remarkable achievement that they did. Having said that, if I've got to play any Black Sabbath album to anybody, it will be the first one. Because that, for me, was organic. That is the seminal heavy metal album for me. I think *Paranoid* was a remarkable achievement, written whilst on the road, rehearsed in sound checks before gigs. Because the band had a day sheet. I mean anyone who's ever worked with Big Bear Records will tell you we work bands. We want bands to be on the road. I've never been involved with studio bands that go home to comfy lifestyles and come together for three months in the studio. A band has to get it together on the road and go into the studio and just record it. Trying as much as possible to capture what makes them a successful live band—that's what you've got to do in the studio, which I think we did for the first two albums. And the second album was a remarkable achievement."

Which set Black Sabbath up for imminent success, says Jim. "Yes, and not only the record company was ready for it but the audience was ready for it. I mean you think about it. If you discovered Black Sabbath, you buy the first Black Sabbath album, what do you want to do? You want to go straight out and buy another one, and that's what it was. The demand was there. It was like mad, because you couldn't go out and buy alternative bands because there weren't alternative bands. I mean Zeppelin weren't doing what Sabbath was doing. People would talk about Zeppelin and Sabbath together. I have nothing against Led Zeppelin, against the idea that they had the temerity to challenge Black Sabbath for their crown. I still see Robert Plant—I've known him for years and years and years. John Bonham, the drummer, was in my band. He was in Locomotive, and he left Locomotive to join Zeppelin. But they didn't have the same emotional impact that Sabbath had. They weren't as… what's the word? They weren't as brave as Sabbath. They were developed from the Yardbirds; they were developed from what had come before. And incredibly successful as they are, they didn't quite have the depth of emotion that Sabbath brought."

"Sabbath took a big, brave step. Lots of energy and time and life was put into Sabbath. And all of us, and those around us, had to suffer because of it because it was a very dedicated thing. They were never lazy. I never knew anyone who worked as hard as they did. If they weren't rehearsing they were around here worrying about the next step. We were very business-like. I put in my influence, I guess, but we had weekly band meetings with agendas and meeting notes. Often they were quite wild, but they were all very, very serious. They would never—as many other bands have been—they would never come drunk to a meeting or they'd never come with a can of beer to a meeting. They came for a serious meeting, and we'd drink tea and argue into the night. Not that they were puritanical but they were very, very serious about all aspects of the music."

"And their rehearsals, they'd rehearse hour upon hour. I don't think there's a living… they hardly got time off to do anything except drive to gigs, play gigs, rehearse and worry about gigs. And we were all the same. We were very driven people. But for us, I suppose looking back, you might say gosh, that was a huge investment, a huge risk of all of you to put all your resources into Black Sabbath. Well no it wasn't, because we knew we were right. We knew that we were right. We had no doubt whatever that Sabbath was going to crack it. None of us."

"And a lot of that was created by the media that ignored us. The London clubs and the record companies that ignored us. The more time people say no to you, the more stubborn you get, the more resolute you get, the more determined you get to prove them wrong. And I have to say, I mentioned earlier on that our mission was making Led Zeppelin sound like a kindergarten house band. I suppose a psychiatrist might say that's reflective of, I don't know, not an insecurity but the opposite. Of a determination to prove other people wrong. A lot of our drive came from the fact that we wanted to show those buggers. We were right, they were wrong, and we wanted to show them. We wanted to prove to the world that what we had was important."

"But what made it easy for us was the kids, the audiences. They loved the band. The audiences were never, ever reluctant. A good example. There's a gig we used to play in Carlisle and for the summer; we played for £25. The next day the guy got on the phone and booked the band for £40. The next day after the next gig he booked them back at £75. Now to anyone in the music business—and forget those figures, we're probably going to talk about £150 and £300 and £600 in today's currency—but people in the business don't naturally come back and rebook bands. The amount of times you phone up after a gig and say, 'How did the gig go?,' the guy says fine, and you say, 'Do you want to book them again?' And he says, 'Oh, okay, I will.' Those days, it wasn't like that. They'd phone up and say, 'Yeah, we'd like the band back.' And there's nothing that gives you more courage than that. The audiences loved you, promoters that had booked them loved you and that's all we needed. For us it was only a matter of time. And looking back it didn't take any time at all in the greater scheme of things, although it seemed to take forever for us. We knew it was great, why didn't you know it was great? We can see it's wonderful, why can't you see it's wonderful? It seemed to take forever. I mean no one ever despaired, but I suppose had we gone on another six months, despair might have crept in."

And then suddenly Jim was out, the band wrestled from him by Patrick Meehan under somewhat bullying tactics which Simpson could not counter. It would be a decision the boys in the band would live to regret fantastically as the '70s wore on. And yet, Jim admits that he was losing enthusiasm.

"You cannot keep making the same Black Sabbath album over and over again," reflects Simpson. "Had they kept the same formula the first couple of albums... I don't know, they had to change. In music, you feel reluctant to go and do the same… warm the same soup over and over again, so it had to change. I didn't find myself desperate to hear the next album any more, after about three albums. After the fourth album, I got hold of the album when I wanted to. I didn't feel a compulsion. Album three, album four, I didn't feel a compulsion to go out and buy, and that's not unusual."

"But you've got to remember, they weren't the only band I handled at the time. When I lost Sabbath it was a real blow, but it left me with a determination to make sure the other bands succeeded. So I was off the ball also. I'd invested a lot of my life into making Sabbath happen. I had a great relationship with the band, particularly with Ozzy. We never actually fought or squabbled or had a disagreement. They were lured away, there's no question. They'll tell you this. They were lured away by promised riches which never materialized. In fact they were badly treated by the subsequent people they were lured away by, and they will tell you this."

"But I suddenly realized a vulnerability," says Jim. "Here I am working from this very room and we had the band on top of the charts, but I was managing them from this very room. And I suddenly realized the next time I found a band and built them up similarly, the same thing would happen again. Someone would come with promises of champagne dinners at the speakeasy and first class rail travel and you would have your friend measured up for a chauffer's suit and you'd have this day with a limousine to travel around in. It would happen again."

"So I decided I was going to enjoy myself a bit more. So I immediately went to my jazz and blues roots, particularly blues, and I got involved with an American blues band and that sort of took my eye off the ball. And of course whatever you're involved in at the time is what you're enthusiastic for at the time. If I'd stayed with Sabbath for a length of time I'm sure I would have had some input in what they did later. I did tend to drift away. I was losing interest in it because it got away from the essence, the pureness and the honesty. I keep going back to this but the first album was a very pure, honest statement, wasn't it? It was a band playing exactly what they felt at the time."

Back in the Sabbath camp, there was a record to make. And so with the shuddering hack from Tony that opens "Sweet Leaf," Black Sabbath found themselves back in business, the bulldozing *Master of Reality* slamming into record store shelves, July 21, 1971. By this point, the band's first two albums had been certified gold in the US for a couple months, and sold-out shows had become commonplace. Advance orders for *Master of Reality* already had the album shipping gold, with official certification sorted out by late September. As testimony to the band's unorganized business dealings, long overdue platinum certifications wouldn't be obtained until 1986.

Featuring a now iconoclastic (but at the time, sort of stupid) pitch-black cover, band name eerily painted in purple, title of the record neatly but obscurely embossed, *Master of Reality* looked as ominous as it sounded. Printing the lyrics on the back of the album was a nice touch however, and original UK issues of the album had the sleeve constructed as a thin box, opening with a flap at the top. Housed inside was a large psychedelic poster featuring a sinister shot of the band standing under a tree. This photo was taken by Keef, who was responsible for the cover shot used on *Black Sabbath*. Some later non-box issues also included the poster. Black and purple were chosen as the theme to represent the colours of mourning. Many variants occurred around the world, with the majority intention being to make the name of the band more readable beyond the straight embossing.

"During *Master of Reality*, we were moving so fast," says Bill, when asked about the cover. "When we completed that album, we were, as far as I'm concerned, truly veterans, multiple world tours under our belt, nonstop, absolutely nonstop. There were signs of exhaustion showing. We'd not come off the road, and in some respects, I see *Master of Reality* as the ending of one era before we entered into another, but I didn't know it at the time. But I know that when we saw the album cover, we just loved it. We thought it was great, purple and black. Everybody loves fucking black in our band. We do; everybody loves the colour black. We saw it and we thought, yeah, that's great. I think we took a glimpse of it between an airport and a limousine. It really was like Spinal Tap (laughs)."

"We were still a very tight unit," continues Bill. "The things we'd learned in Hamburg in 1968 were still with us in 1971, '72, '73. We still had each other's backs. If one of us went to the bathroom, the three of us would go to the bathroom. Which brings me to one of the things I always talk about, is the Four Musketeers syndrome, where we did everything. We'd sit down and eat together; we did everything together, and it was still like that."

Nor did the guys pay much attention to the competition. "We just got on with the next thing, which would be what's the next song to write?

We didn't socialize a lot with other bands. Back in those days, we were in our own hurricane. And when you're in the hurricane, sometimes you don't even get a chance to stop and see who else is riding on the road with you. So we would bump into a number of people in down time, but a lot of the times I honestly didn't know where they were or what it was all about in that sense."

And with the music press, even at this juncture, "It still felt very un-positive," says Bill. "I mean even when we got a #1 record, which kind of caused all kinds of trouble in England. I don't think they were particularly pleasant towards us. When we did *Master*, I thought my God, surely this has got to get some credibility. Because I love *Master of Reality*. It's one of the best albums I've ever heard. And I hope I don't sound begetting when I say that. Just to me, it still is one of the best albums I've ever heard. And I think we started picking up a bit of, 'Hmm, they're not going away, are they? We need to talk about these guys.' And we'd been packing the houses, we'd been selling out in Europe everywhere."

Master of Reality found Sabbath recording in better facilities—Island Studios, London—than the locales of its two predecessors, and the band was rewarded with a fat, powerful and round guitar sound, yet still in possession of a gorgeous separation of brilliant tone with that of Butler's bass frequencies. Which is fortunate for us, because Geezer turns in a truly inspired performance, groovy, bobbing, slinky, yet still precise—picture the man's excellent stage presence and that's what these songs sound like.

"We had a lot more time—we had a week to do that album," laughs Geezer. "The first album was two days. *Paranoid* was five days, and I think *Master of Reality* was a whole week. Plus we'd been on nonstop touring, so we knew the direction we wanted to go in. We got used to the studio. It was the first like, real studio that we'd been in, because the other ones were sort of like four-track demo studios, and this was like a proper 24-track professional studio."

In truth, the band did much of the work on the record between February 5th and February 16th before being interrupted by a US tour, after which they returned to finish up the record in early April (roughly the 5th to the 13th), polishing up material written in December 1970 and January of '71. Indeed "Into the Void" was played live January 14, 1971 in Sheffield, albeit with different lyrics (a week later, Ozzy's first daughter, Jessica, was born). Of particular note, the January rehearsal sessions produced an unused composition called "Weevil Woman," which is unrelated to the earlier "Evil Woman." The song, issued on the expanded

2009 reissue of the album, nonetheless sounds dated, framed upon a rudimentary tribal swing and topped with a repetitive vocal that gets annoying fast. It's nice to get a fully-formed unreleased studio session track, although in this case, we're fortunate "Weevil Woman" didn't make the final track list.

April 26th would count as the last show of the *Paranoid* tour, and two weeks later, the band would be awarded with a gold disc in the US for that album, followed by gold certification for the debut on June 14th, all before the release of *Master of Reality*.

As the band prepared for the studio, Ozzy warned the press that the new record was gonna rock, telling Nick Logan that the third album was going to be, "the heaviest we've done. It's going to be heavier than before because that's what people want. I don't know whether Led Zeppelin made a big mistake or not with their third album, but personally I think a lot of people were disillusioned. If we ever decide to go acoustic with the band, we would do it gradually. But at the moment, people want heavy music, the heavier the better."

Rodger Bain was again at the production helm, third record running. Says Tony, "Up 'til then, we had such a restricted amount of time in the studio, he could really just sit there and record us live in the studio. It wasn't until then where we had much of a chance to put in extra instruments and stuff on. But Rodger was great, just like a member of the band, same kind of humour as us; he was really nice."

And that title? "I came up with that," says Geezer. "Because when you do an album, you've got the master tapes. So it was the master of the album, and all the lyrics were about reality."

Explains Tony, "From *Master of Reality* on, it got more and more bloody complicated. Every album was getting longer and more involved. *Master of Reality*... we used to experiment a lot in the studio, so consequently it took longer. Because in those days, you had to make all your own effects. You couldn't go buy a machine where you could press a button and get an anvil sound or water or whatever. So we had to create them ourselves. And some of those would take bloody hours just to get a little sound. That album in particular, we used an anvil. We tried to create a 'deeeoooo' sound, so we had to get a big tub of water, fill the tub with water, and then lift this anvil over it, hit it, and then drop it into the water slowly to get this effect. I mean, there were lots of things like that that we used to do to make a sound."

"Yeah, we always used to do mad things," affirms Geezer. "We used to lower a gong into water as well, this great big gong, and have the bottom of the water tank mic'ed up. Because back then, there were no synthesizers or samplers, so any obscure sounds, you had to make them all yourself. We used to do a lot of experimentation like that, playing about with sounds."

Bill puts into perspective the band's recording career thus far. "I think *Paranoid* represents the late '60s, and where we were in the late '60s. Because a good portion of the material on *Paranoid* was actually starting to be written, or was written, in '68 or '69. We started writing together in '68 and it might have even been earlier than that, '67. But *Master of Reality*, when you listen to that, you're hearing a band, a band that are already pretty much veterans. I think we probably already had at least one tour of the world under our belt, tours of America, multiple tours of Europe. So the band on *Master of Reality* was a band that had lived together and had been playing together nearly every single day. I mean, we hadn't left each other's sides. So with *Master*, I think you're listening to what is a definite upgrade in the musicianship. Ozzy's voice at times… I mean his voice is just incredible. So there are some, what I would call physical differences. We were probably at that point at our peak of working the hardest we had ever worked. When *Master of Reality* was completed, it was necessary for us to kick back a little bit, because we hadn't stopped. We had been on the road on and off for three years. We hadn't stopped work at all."

Addressing the huge, enveloping sound of the record, Bill says that "recording procedures, they change, as I'm sure you're aware; they change quite a bit very quickly. The equipment that we used with *Paranoid*, in comparison with the equipment we used for *Master of Reality*… *Master of Reality* was done on a 24-track board so that brought us up to a kind of Beatle-esque level, whereas *Paranoid* was done on an eight-track board."

The album, as alluded to, opens with a hacking cough from none other that Mr. Iommi. "You really want to know?" laughs Tony. "I was doing some guitar part in the studio, and Ozzy brought me a joint out, and I took a couple of tokes on it, and I choked me bloody self. And I started coughing, and of course, they let the tape run, and that tape became 'Sweet Leaf.'" The cough is looped, with distortion added, and it pans left to right accompanied by a high-pitched electronic tone. Tony further recalls that he had been working on one of the acoustic tracks when Ozzy handed him the joint. Fittingly, the band admits they were quite stoned during the recording of "Sweet Leaf."

After that legendary but jarring intro, Tony rips into another massive, highly tuneful riff, Iommi doubling himself, one track in the left, the other in the right. "I will probably cut my own throat by saying this but I have never had any problem coming up with riffs," said Tony looking back years later. "It seems to be easier than ever now. I don't know what it is. I must have written some horrible ones; I'm sure I have. I have thousands and thousands of riffs here at home that will never see the light of day. I may just play something and tape it into the box and it never sees the light of day for years."

Tony's "Sweet Leaf" riff is said to be inspired by the central guitar premise of "Hungry Freaks, Daddy," from The Mothers of Invention's *Freak Out!* album issued the summer of 1966 (both Zappa's song and Iommi's were album openers). Whether this similarity is slight or coincidental is up for debate, but it's quite likely that the Sabbath guys knew and appreciated that groundbreaking album. They were known Zappa fans, and Zappa admired Sabbath as well.

"Sweet Leaf" was indeed a keeper, turning the lumbering paean to pot into son of "Iron Man," but without that track's cold and rusty clank. Oddly, another Vertigo act recording in 1971, Clear Blue Sky, had as the opening track of their self-titled debut, a song (actually a song part), called "Sweet Leaf." Although Ozzy sings economically to the song's plod, his vocal melody is acceptably complex against Tony's riff, one that Geezer follows but also doesn't, Butler throwing in a few arcane notes and even playing with the rhythm at times. The tribal jam section that begins at roughly the 2:30 mark finds Bill busy on the toms and Geezer soloing, soon to be joined by Tony. A tam-tam (not a gong) is struck during this section and then is used again repeatedly at the close of the track.

"We were in Wales, I remember, when we wrote that," says Bill, of Sabbath's eminently more famous "Sweet Leaf." "And I think it was either Geezer or Ozzy, when they first came up with that lyric: 'When I first met you, I didn't realize.' And I realized it was about having a relationship with marijuana. And I thought, you know, this is fucking incredible. At the time it was like, man, this is real hardcore, because back then it was hardcore to be talking about a relationship with oneself getting high. It was basically us saying, 'Hey, we stand up for marijuana,' which was what we were doing back then. And then we did 'Snowblind,' which again was like putting a seal of approval on yet another drug. Which, in hindsight now I can look back and go, I mean, I'm certainly not ashamed of that because we went through that, we did that, but as you know, I'm an addict as well, so in my life now that is something that is absolutely discouraged. But back then when I was going through it, it was like 'Yeah.'"

"'Sweet Leaf' was obviously about smoking dope," affirms Geezer. "I'd just come back from Ireland, from Dublin, and they used to sell these cigarettes over there called Sweet Afton (laughs), and I used to smoke these Sweet Aftons at the time, and we were trying to think of a title for that song, 'Sweet Leaf,' and on the packet of cigarettes, it had, 'It's because of the sweet leaf that they taste so good.' And I went, 'Oh yeah, "Sweet Leaf," that's good' (laughs)."

An alternate version of "Sweet Leaf" can be heard on the 2009 reissue on the album, Ozzy turning in more of a conventional love song lyric, casual and with phrasing that would seem to indicate that it was mostly a placeholder until something better came along. There are versions of "Children of the Grave" and "Into the Void" that do this as well.

One of this writer's top five Sabbath tracks of all time takes the #2 position, "After Forever" winding up one of the heaviest songs Sabbath ever wrote, insanely groovy, pounding and with an excellent hippie-fried solo break. Raising eyebrows is the fact that this one is credited solely to Tony Iommi, who nonetheless has never claimed credit for the lyrics, and in facts talks about Geezer's messages in it as he does all the other Sabbath songs. The nicely layered, eminently hummable intro section is pure genius as well, as is Geezer's bulbous bass work through out. Here we get the tam-tam recorded in reverse along with a synthesizer drone. Tambourine and shakers are added as Geezer deftly jumps octaves on bass. Later in the track, Tony peels off a solo that is manically panned back and forth between left and right channels.

"We tuned down on that album," answers Tony, when asked why the guitars are so hard-charging on *Master of Reality*. "I think as time went on, I spent more time working on the guitar. The first couple of albums were very, very quick; we didn't have time to work on the guitar sound (laughs). We were in, done it and out. But as time went on, from *Master of Reality* onward, we had more time to work on sounds, on everything, really."

Asked to clarify if this was indeed the album where the practice of down-tuning started, Tony answers in the affirmative. "Yes, and I got it more from myself, because when I chopped the end of my fingers off, I found it difficult to bend strings. And on the first couple of albums, of course, in those days you couldn't get gauge strings. They were all sort of heavy strings. So I had to make my own set-up. When I had chopped the ends of my fingers off, I had to come up with ideas that would work for me. So I made my own set of light gauge strings. And how I did that was I got two first banjo strings, and then I got a regular set, and I dropped it down, until I found the right gauge for me. You know, instead of using the sixth string that was in the set, I would throw that away and then use the fifth as the sixth, and do it like that, until I found one that was comfortable for me."

"And of course, it was a problem tuning it. My old Gibson in those days, you could bend the neck, you could move it easily, as soon as you touched it. So tuning was very awkward at that time. But I had to do it. I realized that I had to change my whole style of playing, play in a way that suits me and not anybody else. So that's what we did. And of course, later on, I tried using every string tuned down, to get the same effect. But it worked also in the sound as well. So I'd done it… again, it's an experiment, just to get a different mood for songs. And of course, when you do it live, you have to do the same live. The last tours we've done with Ozzy, when we play 'Into the Void,' I had to have a guitar ready that is tuned down a step."

Specifically "Into the Void," "Lord of This World" and "Children of the Grave" are tuned down one-and-a-half steps. An intended by-product of down-tuning was that it made the range for Ozzy's vocals lower and more forgiving, but Tony amusingly says that Ozzy basically ignored the accommodation and would sing high anyway.

Also on the subject of down-tuning, Tony has stated the following, having been asked specifically about the number of guitars he was using live on the reunion trail of the late '90s. "Probably about six or eight, that I use throughout the show. We use different tunings because some of the albums were played in different tunings in the early days. We never went by the rules and just tuned the way that sounded right for that track or that album. We've always tuned a semi-tone down, but on the *Paranoid* and *Black Sabbath* albums, we tuned to pitch. On *Master of Reality*, we tuned down three steps. We didn't have any rules, because everybody else made the rules up. We just broke them. Onstage we tune down a semi-tone. We had always experimented with Black Sabbath. That's the greatest thing we've done. We always tried things that weren't the norm. We were the first to tune down, and nobody could understand that. I also went to many guitar companies years ago when I wanted light gauge strings and was told they couldn't make them because they wouldn't work the same. I had to explain that I'd already been using them and that I'd made up the sets myself."

Offers Bill, with respect to "After Forever," "I really liked that one, especially Geezer's, 'Would you like to see the pope on the end of a rope?' line. At first I thought that song was a little too poppy. But I really like the backwards gong at the beginning and the phase-shifting. I still have that gong. Man, I've had that the entire time, since Sabbath began. But the gong, we just washed it up a little bit with the sound effects and we put it on backwards."

With respect to other sound effects the band got up to, Bill recalls the following. "I think one of the nuttier things from over the years, there was a studio right behind The Marquee club in London, and we were recording there, and I forget which album it was now, but somebody came up with the brilliant idea of let's all walk upstairs at the back of the club. There was a lot of echo and reverberation on the stairs, and so we were walking up and down the stairs (laughs), trying to record what it might be like, give the feeling of like an army marching or something. There were so many stupid things we came up with (laughs). But I don't think they ever got used."

"I've tried all kinds of different things," continues Bill, asked about the recording of his actual drum set. "I've used what we called a cannon effect on the bass drums, in the sense that... when the sound comes out of the bass drum, the sound starts to reach its strongest point about six to ten feet away from the bass drum; that's where you get the real gut reaction. So that's where we put all our mics. I have a couple of mics inside the bass drum, but that's not my favourite pickup point. I like to feel, when you hit the bass drum, you move the air, and the sound comes out, and the sound is peaking about six to ten feet away from the drum. So we used to build columns that were six to ten feet long, so the sound would travel down these columns and we'd have microphones placed six feet away from the bass drum heads, picking up the sound at that point. But the sound of my drums, I've never really enjoyed the sound of my drums, on any of the Sabbath albums. They've either been compressed or... you know, at the time they sounded okay. But I'm like that; I'll never be happy with the drum sound (laughs), probably until the day I die."

"That was the Christian song wasn't it?" queries Geezer, on "After Forever"'s curious but provocative… proselytizing. "We had a lot of Satanists and Jesus freaks and everybody showing up at the gigs and it was just a reaction to all this wild religious stuff at the time, all this peace and love. I have a very open mind. I was raised a strict Roman Catholic but I am very tolerant of other people's religions. Believe what you believe; I don't like preaching to anybody and that song just says that once you get to the end, are you going to be prepared for what you find? Have you lived a good life?"

Geezer also once put it this way. "We were getting accused of all sorts of things, the whole Satan thing and everything. And 'After Forever' is just about all these people that were following us around that were into the occult, and all the so-called Jesus freaks. I used to talk to these people that supposedly had like, dedicated themselves to Jesus. And I knew more about Jesus and the Bible and God than they did. Most of them had, like, done too much acid. So as a response to them, I wrote 'After Forever.' It raises the question: 'When you're on your deathbed, who ya gonna call, God or the Devil?"

So yes, Geezer's lyric is point-blank pro-Christianity, further demonstrating the enigma that was Black Sabbath, the brave lack of boundaries. Still there's an edge, an incongruence, even a bit of misguided motivations. That other great doom band, Trouble, would tread this slightly aggressive, confrontational path a decade later, to similar creepy, almost thug-ish effect.

Like Geezer, Tony rolls his eyes when recalling the strange situations Sabbath got into with both the far right and those doomed to the left hand path. "We had all sorts of people. We have witches, Bible-pushers, the church, of course… lots of different types of people. The churches, for a long time in different places, tried to ban us, because they thought we were extremely evil. And then we had witches started coming to the shows and camping out in the hallway of the hotel and all sorts of different things."

But the complaints form the far right tended to have the opposite effect. "I don't think it did work, actually," says Tony. "If anything, it created more interest. It made people more interested to see what was going on, especially the young kids. The parents of course, would stay away (laughs)."

One mustn't forget that the late '60s and early '70s were a boom period for Satanic hysteria, with very real good reason. The hippie era resulted in all sorts of spiritual experimentation, and both white and black magic were at the top of the list. The horror movies were particularly chilling, with Roman Polanski's *Rosemary's Baby* leading the way and *The Exorcist* to come shortly—in the press Ozzy would claim to have seen that devilish classic 25 times, also professing that he would have appreciated if

Sabbath had been asked to score Kenneth Anger's *Lucifer Rising*, a job that went to Jimmy Page. *Race with the Devil*, starring Peter Fonda, was also a trip, documenting a fairly plausible chain of events that might reign down had one purely by happenstance witnessed a Satanic ritual. British writer Dennis Wheatley, with his book *The Devil Rides Out* among others, was an influence on Geezer's very earliest lyrics, Wheatley enjoying renewed fame (as well as movie adaptations of his titles) due to all things devilish being in vogue.

Back in the non-fiction world, Charlie Manson and his bald, cross-headed posse were all the rage as well, with Sabbath having to answer tiring questions about whether there was some sort of affinity or like-mindedness there (in defense, Bill had said that the band had tried to put a peace message into the *Master of Reality* album). In any event, this was the post-hippie landscape in America, and Sabbath's music thrived in it, more so even than back home, where depravities were much more conservative and mundane.

So yes, the righteous harassed Sabbath but so did the damned. Once at a theater show in the US, the band had to contend with the threat that they would be shot when they got to their third song, three being a significant number in occult studies. Indeed all the lights suddenly went out as the evening's third selection arrived, but the band survived the occasion, spooked for a time thereafter.

"Yeah, in the early days, there was the Druids," recalls Geezer, citing another episode regarding witch folk. "The black magic people were doing like a Walpurgis, which is a Satanic black mass, at Stonehenge. And they'd heard about us and wanted us to go down and play some songs while they were doing it (laughs). And we just didn't want to. You know, we weren't involved in all that crap anyway. And then the head of the white magic church in England phoned us up and says, he's heard that they're gonna curse us, and that the only way for us to ward off the curse is for all of us to wear crosses. And that's where all the crosses came from. We still wear them now."

Noted Bill on the band's lyrical motivations, "Our music was true to our hearts and it was about being on the level. We feel this way about certain things—how do you feel about it? There were a lot of bands that were singing and making music that was what I call on the level. But there were also a lot of bands that were singing about things that were going to happen in the future, or things that we ought to be doing, or should be doing, which is a great expectation word; that can actually be very dangerous if used incorrectly. But we weren't doing that. We were singing about something that's in the very day today—do you feel this? Do you ever feel crazy? Do you ever feel like you want to die? It was a lot of questions about do you feel the same way we do? But in a very poetic and realistic way. It was very valid."

"And I have to give absolute credit to Terry—that's Geezer—and to Ozzy. Because Ozzy as a vocalist can consume lyrics. He's so theatrical the way he'll take one word and make something huge out of it. And without those skills I don't think those songs would ever have been the same. So Ozzy is incredibly important. And Geezer is incredibly important because Geezer was honest enough with himself to go inside himself and start to ask some of the questions that he needed to ask. And he was almost like a spokesman for all the rest of us as well. Because we all liked the questions he was asking; he provoked a lot of thoughts for all of us."

Some issues of *Master of Reality* include the same sort of extra titling we saw with *Paranoid*. "After Forever" has "The Elegy" attached to it, considered to refer to the floating instrumental intro, which, granted, recurs throughout the song. "Children of the Grave" is followed by "The Haunting" to demarcate the closing portion where Ozzy is whispering the title with echo over ominous whammy bar-generated guitar squalls and feedback. "Into the Void" included "Deathmask" and "Lord of This World" is preceded by "Step Up."

Next on side one of the original vinyl is "Children of the Grave," preceded by 26 seconds of medieval instrumental music called "Embryo" (embryo, children… get it?). "Embryo," drenched in the medieval, takes only two guitar strings to play, and the effect is violin-like. Tied perhaps with opener "Sweet Leaf," "Children of the Grave" is *Master of Reality*'s big hit and perennial concert staple. Like "Paranoid," it re-establishes or underscores a heavy metal trope, Sabbath perfecting the archetypical heavy metal gallop previously explored on Deep Purple's "Hard Lovin' Man" of 13 months earlier. The song is introduced with Tony playing only in the left channel and quite palm-muted. There are tympanis as well, and once the song kicks in, Tony loosens up on the left channel playing, while adding an accompanying rhythm track in the right channel. Ozzy turns in a complex vocal melody, an improvement over the conservative and mostly unison approach used on the previous track. Later in the sequence, a jam before the last verse, there is an unspecified keyboard used that is likely a Mellotron, just as texture, while the guys build a wall of tribal instrumental doom.

"Children of the Grave" is notable for its extra layer of percussion, which lends the track an inexorable apocalyptic critical mass. These are timbales, with the lower one sent to the left channel, the higher-tuned drum to the right. "Yes, on the album I used two tracks of drums," affirms Bill, "but now I just play all that live. We use timbales on stage, and we'll be bringing them out again this time (this chat took place during a later reunion). I just play them with my left hand and keep the groove going with my right hand."

"I liked some of the things I was doing on *Master of Reality*. There were chops that I was using that are fairly popular these days; you hear them all the time. But there were things like… I'm not sure what you call it technically, but I was doing stuff with my bass drums and toms which were things I hadn't heard anybody else doing. At different stages I was learning different things. There's a lot of counterpoint drumming on *Vol 4*. The 16th note bass drums that are being played against a four cowbell, which was again an interesting combination and not that common at that time. I'm not saying I invented it or whatever, but it wasn't that prominent."

"There were some great drummers that I knew at that time, John Bonham, Carmine Appice, quite a lot of others. I've known Carmine since 1968. So those influences would rub off. But I found myself always staying with the jazz and blues roots. I'd use big band swing drumming a lot in our music. I think I went into drumming that was pretty technical at the time. Ginger Baker I felt had gotten into some really good stuff as well. But again, my stuff just came out. It was orchestrational, reactive drumming, just reacting to Tony and Geezer. You have to work when you're playing with such great players; one has to react. So keeping focus and energy was incredibly important."

"They're all the same theme aren't they?" laughs Geezer, examining the "Children of the Grave" lyric. "That was about how if we don't watch how we're polluting the earth we're all going to end up dead. I think there was hope in most of the lyrics, so it always had a positive ending. In 'Children of the Grave' you have to do something, or otherwise you wouldn't have it, sort of thing. So it was all like, there is still hope for the human race. I mean, there is some bleak stuff, like 'Hand of Doom,' but you try to vary it. There is a lot of talk about pollution and climate change going around. There was a lot of talk about the end of the earth and there was a lot of fear-mongering about nuclear war at the time. The Cold War was still going on with Russia back then. It just seemed like that if we don't do something then, we've all had it. It is going to be the end for all of us."

"I think a bit of both," answers Butler, when asked if his focus on pollution issues came from his immediate surroundings or from what he read in the newspapers about happenings in the wider world. "Because where we were, Birmingham, was the industrial centre, the first place to have a factory. In fact, where we lived, in Hansworth, that was the actual original place to build a factory; Matthew Bolton built his first factory there. And that's where the Industrial Revolution started. So, where we grew up, it was all factories and a lot of smoke and grime. Basically, everybody I knew used to have asthma and suffered with colds, emphysema, that kind of thing. So it directly affected us. I mean, politicians weren't too bothered about it, because they were safely ensconced in the Houses of Parliament away from all that stuff, but we had to go through it. Me uncle died; the thing is, where he used to work, he inhaled a lot of vapours from rubber, Dunlop Tires, so he died of this thing on his lungs when he was only 50. And there was a lot of stuff like that going about, so it did directly affect us. Plus it was on the news as well. I was training to be a custom works accountant, in a factory. This was just after I left school. I left school when I was 15, and then I went to college and had this job in the factory at the same time, in the offices of the factory."

"Terry, he's just brilliant," adds Bill. "I don't know what else to say. He's a great writer with so much vision and we were in a stubborn band. We wanted to stay away from certain subjects and we didn't want to talk about hope in the sense of everything's just going to be great once we get over the hill, guys, and so on and so forth. We wanted to be in the place where we felt most suited, which was that place of being able to say what we wanted, say what we were thinking and have complete freedom in doing that. We didn't want to be sending messages of hope. In fact we did, but we wrote it and played it in a way that was Black Sabbath's way. 'Children of the Grave' is about all kinds of things, but to me there was a message of hope."

Side two of *Master of Reality* opened with a two-minute acoustic instrumental called "Orchid." Says Tony, "That was something I had done at home and played to the others, saying, 'I've got this little acoustic bit.' Because with Sabbath, you never know exactly what you'd like to put on; you never want to get too far the one way. And I played these things to the rest of the guys, to see what they would say about it, and they liked it and said, 'Why don't you put it on the album?' So that's what we did. Those are little trinkets I do for my own self. And then they suggested that I try it on the album."

"Orchid" is played with diminished chords more characteristic of classical music, and finger-style picking more characteristic of classical guitar. Despite its brevity, the song includes a seven-second intro completely unrelated to the rest of the track. Along side Tony, Geezer adds warm delayed bass swells. Ozzy would joke in interviews that the song, debuted live in America before finishing the album, is actually called "Awkward" and that it was about Bill.

"Lord of This World" (working title: "Spanish Sid") is introduced with a watery bit of guitar, but very quickly the majestic full band explosion occurs, Bill highly groovy, until the band settles down for yet another oppressive doom verse pattern. Ozzy is recorded thin, frantic and urgent, perfect for the storyline, which finds the Devil himself gloating over yet another damned soul. "'Lord of This World' was about Satan," explains Geezer. "Because, the way the world was going at the time, it wasn't God's world, it was Satan's world, which is the way it is now. Just putting that into lyrics, I suppose."

Indeed, Geezer returned to fatalistic, apocalyptic themes repeatedly and gyre-like—to Butler, the Final War was laconically inevitable. No surprise need register, that would smack too much of hope destined to be smacked down. Ozzy could flash peace signs all he wanted, and the stoned witnessing throngs could flash him right back, but all of that wilted amidst the sonic carnage billowing from Sabbath's war-like stage.

An alternate version of "Lord of This World," recorded May 25th, includes faint unison piano, a prominently doubled Ozzy vocal and amusing slide guitar licks from Tony. These distractions stripped from use, Bill's cowbell however made it to the final version.

After "Lord of This World," things get eerily quiet. "Solitude" is essentially the sequel to "Planet Caravan," containing the same gloomy wandering vibe, a nomadic depressive lyric, similar musical structure, even flute. Surprisingly, the vocal is Ozzy—it has been suggested that "Centre of Eternity" from Ozzy's *Bark at the Moon* solo album is a second example of Ozzy sounding this considerably non-Ozzy-like. Bill can be heard brightening the proceedings with finger-cymbals put through a delay. There is also uncredited piano, which is likely performed by engineer Tom Allom, who also added piano to "Planet Caravan."

Closing out *Master of Reality* is a song all about finality… and new beginnings. Tony Iommi's favourite song on the record ("a real cracking track"), and an undisputed heavyweight champion among the five mountains of muscle that make the album so classic, "Into the Void" has also been collared by Bill as his favourite Sabbath track of all time and in fact, Tony picks "Sabbath Bloody Sabbath" and this one as his favourites across the Sabbath catalogue, appreciating its structure, its colours and its tempo changes.

"That was Black Sabbath at its absolute height, when it was absolutely coming alive," enthuses Bill. "At that point Geezer was writing really strongly. And the band at that point was unbelievably tight. We were really becoming confident, due to all the touring we'd done."

Says Geezer, with typical succinctness, "That was a science fiction one about how we were all fed up at the time and wished we could just get into a rocket ship and blast off."

On "Into the Void," Tony's guitars heave to a stressful breaking point, Bill and Geezer struggle to hold the inevitable implosion in check, and Ozzy turns in a terse and monotone vocal, in other words, one of his less imaginative vocal melodies. Tony recalls that Ozzy was quite frustrated with how many words he had to cram into the verses. Tension mounting, Geezer's message of our doomed planet reverberates long after the bad vibrations have waned. Tellingly, as the album was taking shape, Tony had indicated that "Into the Void" and "After Forever" were the first songs the band had come up with, and that they were a bit funkier—but still heavier—than the songs on *Paranoid*.

In press at the time, Geezer came off like a bit of a hippie, but with a disposition blacker than black—"Into the Void" seemed like a solution to the man's commonly, sincerely held views. "It's a Satanic world," reflected Butler, speaking with Rolling Stone shortly after the release of *Master of Reality*. "The devil's more in control now, and happier than ever before. People can't come together; there's no equality. The higher you climb, the more people you have to cut down. You feel you're better than other people, that they're inferior to you, and it's a sin to put yourself above other people, and yet that's what people do. Even in freak communities, people are trying to be freakier than the other person, to be one up on them, to be better. That's the devil's work; that's why there's war. We all live with a shadow over us—the shadow of the next world war. You're not going to get out of life alive, so it's not worthwhile. And people don't live a spiritual life. They only live for now; the devil rules them. That's what my poems are about, things that are happening now. War and paranoia, death and hate. It gets people thinking about what's going on."

Sabbath wasn't yet dreading the prospects of their next American tour. The *Master of Reality* tour in fact kicked off in the States, in the summer of '71, Tony, summing up the experience thusly, shortly after the fact. "America was amazing. Although we'd been there before, the impact is more impressive this time. Our first trip was to tell them what Black Sabbath was all about. A high-pressure promotional tour, if you like. Same as everybody else does. This time though, we were really able to take stock of the States and get to know how the scene works. Avenues were a lot bigger for instance and because of the album's success we were more widely known. American fans will travel miles to see a group. They think nothing of traveling 50 or 100 miles, even by air to catch a concert. Then they're patient and orderly and make the gig really great for us."

"Even really bad reviews haven't stopped the albums from selling," began Tony, in another *Master of Reality*-era interview, this time with Julie Webb. "I don't know why they sell so well. Maybe people like the songs words-wise or maybe they buy them because they're simply heavy. I'm also pleased with our tours. Apart from one time in New York where we were really tired and just couldn't get into it, the reaction we got was great. We have one or two gigs where they were screaming, but the rest, they are just quiet and appreciative. Maybe the critics go to the 6:00 shows. If you're doing two shows a night, it's a known fact that the second one is better. Another thing you've got to consider about the critics, is that if someone is looking for an audience reaction, they may not think we're going down so well, when the kids don't rave all the time. In certain places in America, the kids are afraid to get up and rave because the police might hit them over the head with a truncheon! The police can be very cruel like that."

"We've still got a hard core of British fans and our records do well," defends Tony against accusations that—as was leveled at Deep Purple and Led Zeppelin—Sabbath had somehow abandoned the host country fans to concentrate on America.

"I don't think we are being unfaithful to them by going to America. You can only play certain venues in Britain; the Albert Hall in London is great, for instance. But we reckon it's worthwhile going to America and it's not just because of the money. The first tour we ever did, we made very little money. Now we do make some, and our records sell well. The albums get advance orders of around 200,000, which isn't bad at all. But then America is such a vast place. With each succeeding tour, we like to cover parts that we haven't already visited and even this way, we still haven't been everywhere. We've done well in America, the gold discs and all that, and the American kids seem to know more about the band. When we play England, we get slugged by the journalists, but not by the people. *Paranoid*, that LP got bad reviews and sold well. But we can't complain about English audiences. They've always been good to us."

Actually both the UK and the US were good to Sabbath, with *Master of Reality* rising to #5 in the UK charts (a residence of 13 weeks in total) and #8 in the US. No singles were issued from the album, which didn't stop it from being the second most successful record of the band's career in America, where it currently sits at double platinum, along with platinum in Canada and gold in the UK.

"We're working out a new show," said Tony, about an intriguing idea that never came to pass, "although it's not finished yet, and we're hoping to do visual changes. We did have thoughts about doing a special Black Sabbath show, like a play before the group goes on to perform. But that's just an idea going around in our heads at the moment. There are no plans to change our musical policy. If people like you, why change? We wouldn't be Black Sabbath if we suddenly changed to another kind of music. If there are any changes, they'll be gradual, so gradual we won't even notice. We're hoping to get more into recording now, but we'll always do live gigs. If the day ever comes when we stop doing live gigs and just want to record, then Black Sabbath will be no more."

Tony says touring for Sabbath didn't include the extracurriculars, like say, Deep Purple with their soccer. "For us, we took music very, very seriously. And it overtook our lives, really. Geezer had an interest in football. I don't know if he actually went out and played, but he certainly watched football a lot, Aston Villa. Bill and Ozzy and myself weren't so much into soccer. I was into more gruesome sports I suppose, boxing, wrestling, anything where there's beating somebody up (laughs). But as I say, most of our efforts were channeled into music. Everything we were interested in before got pushed aside when we went into music."

With the relentless added experience of playing so many shows being notched, were there still confidence issues within the band? "I think we all had problems to a degree, in the early days. Because you know, we worked as a band. We weren't the sort of musicians, certainly in those days, to get up and jam with people. That didn't exist that much anyway in those days. So we tended to be like a unit and work as a unit. I think inside, everybody was, 'Oh, I'm not very good at this or that,' but you work as a band and you work as a team and it works."

"I saw one the other day (laughs), and I can't believe I wore it," says Geezer, addressing the subject of stage wardrobe in the early days. "It was black and silver trousers that were like about 40 inches wide at the bottom, and I'd totally forgotten about them. And at an autograph signing, this kid came up and showed me this picture. I had totally forgotten about them until I saw this picture, and it was like, God, it's unbelievable I went onstage with them things on. It was like curtain material or something. You used to have to have things made back then; you couldn't really buy them. Nobody would want to buy them anyway, nobody else. So you would have somebody make them for you."

Usually band wardrobe was the domain of one of the band's wives or girlfriends. "It started off that way when we couldn't afford it," agrees Geezer, "like the first album. Bill's wife, she made us all the leather stuff, but it was out of old car seats, so like, the leather was about three inches thick, and you could hardly move in it. And then the more money we got, the better tailors we found. But this leather, it was mainly like the trousers. You can't really see them in the photographs because it's usually the top half of us. Yeah, old car seat leather. Because there again, she worked in the factory in Birmingham that made car parts. The whole car industry in England is based in Birmingham, and she worked on the car seat section, so the stuff from the car seats, she would turn into leather trousers for us."

Dragging themselves across America, both Bill and Ozzy tried valiantly to keep their long distance marriages alive. Letters from home would be delivered, issues would have to be dealt with slowly, and at geographical odds.

"It's all so horrible," said Ozzy, speaking in the midst of the US tour, "flying around and around, landing again. The hotel room's the same, everything's the same, the walls… it drives me mad. I really freaked out on the last tour. I got pissed-off, those hassling bastard groupies screwed me up for one. We have a lot of nervous trouble in our family; I'm very high-strung. On the last tour I had blackouts. But I don't care what happens as long as everything goes well in January." January was when his wife was about to have the couple's first baby.

"I'm quite sane now, but I won't be sane for long, after I take this pill," continued Oz. "Metrospan, they're called. They really give you a hit on the head. A doctor gave them to me for depression a few days ago. They must have some ups in them; they make me crazy. I'll be okay as long as there is me and my wife, and my kids and my group. But sometimes I start to wonder if my family's going to wait for me. I wonder if she'll get pissed off while I'm running around, recording and all. I don't know what I'd do without her."

"Our music is aggressive; people can get off on it," added Ozzy. "It gives them a release. I can see it happen at concerts. We get people's aggressions out. Then they won't go out and beat some old lady over the head. It works for me too. Like when I'm at home for awhile, not working, with no outlet for me energy, my wife and I are hammer and tongs at each other 'cause I'm all pent-up. But our music gets it out, for me as well as the audience."

"They're crazy mad in love," volunteered Bill, on the drama in Ozzy's marriage. "He really can't stand being away from her. The problem they're having is something too complicated and personal to talk about now. It has to do with something that happened some time ago."

Temptations on the road were most definitely causing resentment—the band, each raised conservatively but flung into this wicked world, seemed to be in a fight for their very souls. "Fucking groupies," spat Ozzy. "I'm telling you, the next one who pushes herself at me, I'm going to piss all over her. Me and Bill decided to do that. Ain't that right, Bill? Just piss all over them. They're disgusting. Remember Bill, that time in Atlanta, Georgia? This bitch calls me on the telephone and said, 'I'm the best plater in the world'—you know, blow job—'Can I come up to your room?' So I gave her Geezer's room number, and told her to come up, just for a laugh. Well, she went up to Geezer's room, and without a word took all her clothes off and lay down on the bed with her legs apart, Billy, me and Geezer looking on. 'Well, isn't somebody going to fuck me?' she says to us. We all just stood there looking at her, kind of horrified. She looked pitiful and disgusting. Finally, she got pissed-off when no one went near her, got up and dressed. 'You English boys are disappointing.' A bunch of fags, she called us, and left the room. But the next time I'm not going to stand there. I'll fucking piss all over them. Wait 'til me mother reads that; she'll never speak to me again."

"We used to have fun in the old days," sighed Bill, Ozzy adding, "before we got all exploited and things. It used to be anything goes and we'd have fun. But now it's more of a business. We've got to watch what we say and do—more people watching. You've got to be clean English boys. Well, not exactly, but we've got to be more cautious now that people are aware of us. Before we really didn't give a damn. We played small clubs in England and Germany. Like the Star-Club in Hamburg.

Remember that night that chick gave Geezer some pills, told him they were ups? But it turned out they were laxatives, and Geezer had to run off the stage to shit every five minutes. His ass was fucking raw! We finished playing, we did five sets a night then, and we'd go out on the town and tear the place apart. We could have parties then, but we can't do that anymore. We have to get up early and fly somewhere to do a concert the next day. It's more a money thing now. I'm going to make as much money as I can, then shoot myself. I'll die before I'm 40."

"Oz gets up too fucking early," groused Bill, "8:00, and turns the TV on. One time the hotel was on a lake, and Oz was fishing out the window. I'm sitting there, having me tea, and a huge fish flies through the window. He caught a mudshark. We put it in the tub, but it died by the time we got back that night. We cut it up and threw it out the window, back into the lake."

On the *Master of Reality* tour, Black Sabbath shared stages with a myriad of acts in a myriad of styles, as was the tradition in the '70s. Along for the ride were the likes of Alice Cooper, Humble Pie, Yes, Three Dog Night, Black Oak Arkansas, Bloodrock, Gentle Giant, Ten Years After and Nazareth, along with acts now forgotten to various degree, such as Brewer & Shipley, Grease Band, Sweathog, Eleven, Ultra Violet, Stoneground and White Witch.

Prominent from the basket of obscure acts was Wild Turkey, who greatly exceeded any other band in number of Sabbath dates logged on the tour, the bluesy, fairly hard-hitting and Free-like act being the band of choice for the UK leg in January and February of 1972, and then a second US leg in March, Yes also part of the bill for that tour-closing stint. Press reports at the time found Wild Turkey and Yes getting the good reviews while Sabbath got most of the "bread," the reporter also making note of the divide between the Sabs' young fans and the older folk who preferred Yes, with Sabbath getting the final just desserts, crying all the way to the top of the charts.

One intriguing final point, Black Sabbath has been reported to have also opened for the mighty Led Zeppelin, twice, in Western New York, mid-September of '71—according to Geezer Butler himself, this never happened.

Album 4

Vol 4

"Vials of pharmaceutical cocaine"

Already gravely burnt-out from the long, continent criss-crossing tours behind them, the boys in Black Sabbath decided to court a fully crisped form of burn-out by writing and recording their fourth record in three years lounging in the den of iniquity known as Los Angeles.

But below the madness that would ensue, there were sincere creative intentions. Three records in, the band was starting to take to heart criticisms that they were musical brutes. It was time to prove that there was substance and depth to what the guys were writing and recording, even if on the face of it, *Vol 4* would still sit squarely within the parameters of bruising, bulldozing heavy metal.

"We didn't want to just stick to the same old thing," reflects Geezer Butler. "We thought after *Master of Reality* we wanted to branch out and get a bit of a different sound. We were experimenting. We were buying keyboards and stuff like that. Tony was getting good at playing piano. And we just wanted to experiment a bit more. And we took a lot longer to write and record albums by this time. So it gave us a chance to experiment in the studio and try to get different sounds out of things, and to make it much more of an enjoyable experience in the studio. Because up until then we had like two days on the first album, five days on *Paranoid*, a week on *Master of Reality*, so it was just another gig to us. We'd go in, play, and then go back on the road. So by the time of *Vol 4* and *Sabbath Bloody Sabbath*, we thought let's spend a bit more time in the studio and experiment a bit more. And we had enough money by then to be able to not be on the road, to be able to go into a studio and spend more time."

"So we wanted to branch out a bit more," continues Butler. "We'd always put in things on the albums, slower stuff and ballads, but we just wanted to get more involved in different sounds. You want to move on. You don't want to get stuck in the same old rut, which is the trouble these days, I find. A lot of bands get known for something and then you get the same old thing album after album and it's hard to get away from. Once you're known for a kind of music, the record companies, that's all they want to hear you do. It's really hard. But back then the record companies didn't have any input whatsoever to the music side. They just let us get on with it. You didn't have any A&R guys coming in saying, 'Oh, you can't do that.' If we liked it, we'd do it. If you don't move on, then you feel like you're stagnating, and that's what we wanted to do to keep going. Otherwise we would have had nothing else to give, nothing new to prove or no more challenges left."

"We were totally mental," recalls Geezer, shaking his head at the memory of the May 1972 sessions at the Record Plant, and more egregiously, off-time at the band house in Bel Air, northwest of Beverly Hills. "It was when we were really into cocaine. We used to have like queues of women every night outside the house (laughs). And the studio was the downer part. We just like, enjoyed the rest of it (laughs). Completely mental. That was probably Sabbath at our most debauched. I remember when Ozzy sat on the alarm bell, and the police came up to the house. And we had a great big bowl of grass on the table and loads of vials of pharmaceutical cocaine all over the place. And we didn't know that Ozzy had set the alarm off, because it was a silent alarm. And all these coppers turned up outside, and we flushed everything; it was like a mad dash. We must have flushed about $10,000 worth of cocaine and two grams worth of grass, and it was just like a false alarm (laughs). The police came. They were outside, knocked on the door; we thought they were busting us, but they said, 'Your alarm's going off. What's wrong?' And we said, 'Nothing.' And they just left. Didn't even come in the house."

"I can't even remember the lyrics on that record. We were all cooked out of our brains every day. I mean, it was just mad. That was the peak of our lunacy then. It was like the first three albums had been incredible successes and we were all like young kids with loads of money and loads of drugs, living in a great big house in Beverly Hills and just going wild (laughs). And I think the album kind of wrote itself. We were very productive, because we were all living together at the time. As I say, we had this great big house in Beverly Hills, parties every night, more drugs than the average drugstore, and we were experimenting. We had a grand piano in the house; that's where 'Changes' came about. We had a Mellotron, all different kinds of instruments at our disposal. So we were experimenting a lot with different sounds; it was good."

"Oh, that album for me… we had such a great time," adds Tony. "It was fantastic, like Disney World really. Because we had moved to a house in Bel Air, and we all lived there. It was a lovely house, had a ballroom and everything, fantastic. And we just set up our gear downstairs. There was like a bar downstairs and we set up the equipment in there and just wrote the album. We'd be up all bloody night tooting coke... oh, we just went berserk. It was just like a joyride, really. We had a fantastic time. And then when it came down to seriously recording the album, we got down to it and done it. We recorded it in Los Angeles as well, at The Record Plant."

Bill is quite fond of the resulting album, but adds, "I think what overpowers me when I'm listening to it is the circumstances that surround it. My second wife and I were going through some rough times. We weren't fighting or anything. There were just problems going on with her being American and thus living in England. And the use of cocaine had escalated, especially with me. I had really, really become completely and totally involved in cocaine at that time. Looking back, when I listen to the album, I can feel all the eeriness of the cocaine."

Tony denies that this was one of those apocryphal rock star situations where dealers are so plentiful, no one can get any work done. "Well, at the time, to be honest, we used to have stuff flown in privately. So that wasn't such a problem for us, I don't think. But actually, yes, all around the studios in those days you'd have somebody trying to sell you one thing or another."

Bill figures that *Vol 4* marked yet another notch up in sophistication for the band, but in truth the big leap wouldn't occur until the next record. "That was the first album we made where we were in this new change of attitude where we had decided to slow down a little bit and take our time and feel less hurried about getting an album out and going out on tour. So this is basically the beginning of a new era. As we've said, a lot of the writing took place in Los Angeles and we recorded a majority of the album at the Record Plant on La Cienega Boulevard in North Hollywood. At that time, in my life at least, my cocaine addiction was pretty heavy, to say the least… it was pretty darn heavy."

"I try to be careful—and I know I'm not successful at this—but I do try to be careful about talking about the other guys, the way they might have been partying. But I don't mind speaking for myself. I was pretty much loaded. My cocaine addiction was pretty much in full force. And I think a lot of the songs are influenced by the narcotics we were using. 'Snowblind' for instance; I mean, give me a break. That was a direct song that came from the use of the narcotic, cocaine. For the most part, the making of the album felt good. I think we were thinking more about what we were actually going to put down, whereas before, on the first three albums it was more responding to each other. There was some thought going into the album. It was the first time we ever used strings; at the end of 'Snowblind,' there's a little string quartet. From a drummer's point of view, I got into some new things and I thought I had progressed into some new bass drum work. I was pleased that I was coming along a little bit as a drummer."

"That was the first album also where I nearly got kicked out of the band," continues Ward. "We took the remainder of the album and we went to London and I was pretty solid gone. I was good at getting so far out of it that I was forgetting what we were doing in the sense of the album. I guess I was pretty critical of the songs and I said, 'Look, let's get into some old-fashioned blues. Let's do some blues jams.' And that didn't go down too well at the time and there was kind of a cold eeriness in the studios and I definitely realized that I was under the gun. It was like, oh oh, I think I'm causing some trouble here. And at the time I had nowhere to live. I was with my girlfriend at the time and we were leading like a Sid and Nancy lifestyle. We were living in hotels and wherever we could, just running around London and doing stupid things. We were loaded like all the time."

Continues Bill, "The Record Plant was such a weird time for me because my cocaine abuse had probably reached its peak. I was definitely, definitely peaking. It was just ruining me, a day at a time, pretty much (laughs). I thought it was making me productive, but it would take ages to get anything done, and I can remember laying a track down for 'Tomorrow's Dream.' I think we did that at The Record Plant. I know we laid a lot of track at The Record Plant, but I know at the same time, it was almost the ending of my cocaine abuse, because I was just burning out. I was like 23, 24, 25 (laughs), and I was just burned-out. Bel Air was nuts. By that time we were a pretty major band, and we were pretty big in Europe but we were still real young and having a party. It was just a nonstop 365 days a year party. So Bel Air was just a target, as far as I was concerned. A lot of the time I was pretty out of it. I know that everybody got their fair share of cocaine, I guess, over the years."

Vol 4, issued September 25, 1972, opened with a lumbering, yet markedly less malevolent epic track for the band called "Wheels of Confusion." The song was originally titled "Illusion" and it deals with moving from the imaginary and fantasy-filled world of childhood into the hard realities of adulthood. Ozzy's vocal is starkly melodic, and there is a slight increase in nuance and subtlety to the band, especially come the jammy closing section, which is actually separately named as "The Straightener," but only on some copies of the album. Revolving Leslie speaker cabinets are used for this textured portion, prompting sentiments that this was quite a psychedelic record for the band.

Also with respect to "some copies of the album," *Vol 4*'s gatefold existed in variants. The full version features a stitched in booklet, a Geezer page and a Tony page as the actual inner gate, an Ozzy page and a Bill page as part of the booklet, and then a live shot from behind as the centre spread. Later issues deleted the individual player pages, leaving a standard gatefold using the live shot. But some issues went out with the booklet simply removed, leaving, curiously, the Geezer and Tony pages as the sum total of the inner gate. This is the version the author bought as a new release as a nine-year-old headbanger-in-waiting; it was a Canadian copy, purchased in Trail, BC, shipped into town from Vancouver.

Geezer's "Wheels of Confusion" lyric, despite the paean to lost youth, seems to sum up the loss of innocence and the fatigue the band had experienced over the whirlwind few years since their debut album was recorded in a day. It might be about growing up, but it also seemed to be about the band.

It is of note that Rodger Bain, producer of all three Sabbath records thus far, had been ousted. *Vol 4* was produced by "Patrick Meehan and Black Sabbath," which essentially means it was self-produced, as Patrick was the band's manager. At the time, speaking with Howard Bronson, Ozzy dismissed Rodger as "someone the record company gave us when we signed with the company. It was really a clash of egos. He got it into his head that he was more responsible for our hit status than we were. He wanted, to a moderate extent, to control our music."

"Tomorrow's Dream," which can best be described as a deep album classic—not a hit but a well-known and well-regarded song—comes next, the band once more underscoring their penchant for rumbling, massive, elephantine structures that seem to shake the earth when they move. Bill calls the song, "a great one to play, a drummer's dream."

"Wheels of Confusion" on this record was already like that, and most of *Master of Reality* did much the same thing, meaning slow, hypnotic, doomy and bulldozing heavy metal before such a thing was codified. Geezer's "Tomorrow's Dream" lyric can be seen as a break-up story, but one with hope, one that includes the promise of fulfilling dreams to go along with the hopefully fleeting sense of grief. "Tomorrow's Dream" was launched as a single, backed with acoustic instrumental "Laguna Sunrise." It failed to chart, although the album proper rose to #8 in the UK (with a total residence of ten weeks), #13 in the US, with the record eventually reaching platinum designation in America. Again, indicative of the band's assertion that there is a little more detailing on this record than past albums, there's additional percussive tracking, including use of cowbell and tambourine, amidst a frantic barrage of kit from Bill, achieved by busy snare and a sense of double bass drum.

Next up was "Changes," a track so saccharine that it became bitter, especially in context of who this band was. Piano, Mellotron… are they being used ironically or with sincerity? Certainly the melody and the lyrics possess a mournful quality, but, unlike "Planet Caravan" or "Solitude," this was emphatically not a dirge, although one can still envision "Changes" being played at a funeral or somber church service. Despite the song's simplicity, it's apparent some thought was put into it. Geezer accompanies Tony on bass, Ozzy multi-tracks for the chorus, and as the song progresses, the Mellotron lines exhibit a level of melodic complexity, even though they remain washes.

"Yeah, I'm afraid so," laughs Tony, copping to the fact that that's him playing piano on the track. "Actually, that was the first thing I'd ever played (laughs). Because I'd never really played piano. We were in Los Angeles and we all lived in a house together, to write an album. And they've got a piano there in the ballroom, so I used to go and play that at one and two o'clock in the morning and I'd come up with this idea for 'Changes.' And I played it for the other guys, and they liked it, and we ended up recording it that week. First thing I'd ever done."

"I tried other things, other instruments," says Tony on the subject of branching out away from the guitar. "I think everybody in the course of playing tends to get to the stage of trying to play a lot of different instruments and trying to play everything at once. And I did—I am included in that. I played the piano and flute, I bought a sax, and I made a right row with that! Then I bought a sitar that I couldn't play at all. Violins… I remember Geezer and myself when we had done… I think it was *Vol 4* or *Sabbath Bloody Sabbath*, we were going to use strings on a track. So we never thought of hiring anybody—we were going to play them ourselves. So we got a violin and brought it over. Geezer was going to play the cello and I was going to play the violin, and we started trying to play these things and the sound was fucking horrible, sounded like dead cats, like someone had trodden on a cat! We just assumed we would be able to play them, you know. We got these things and there we were in the studio trying to play them, and I thought, 'Oh fuck it, let's get a string section in.' So we did; we got a string section in. But it was funny. You know, you get to that stage; you want to be like Roy Wood and play everything."

Upon the impending release of *Vol 4*, Ozzy addressed with Howard Bronson the subject of changes in the band, as well as the incendiary new track "Changes." "I think everybody peaks. Not only does the crowd get fed up of hearing the band, but the band gets tired of gigging. It's not like we're jukeboxes or records that can play forever. When you're a new band, it's like you get a tinge of stardust on you. It's born, then accepted, and after levelling it off, it dies. Anything's like that. Our new album still has the Black Sabbath sound, but it's more melodic. Instead of me singing the guitar riff like on 'Iron Man,' I'm singing different melodic things and it's all building up. Tony just composed a guitar piece with strings. It's a nice piece of music, and we wanted to write a happy song. People call us 'downer rock'—you take the reds, man, and drink the wine, and blow out, get high on the decibels. All that's a lot of rubbish. Whatever people do at our concerts is none of our business as long as they enjoy it. I'm just up to entertain people, a good old show business trip."

"So there'll be a lot of gentle things on the new album," continued Oz. "One song, 'Changes,' about a guy—whether he's with the band or not, I'm not gonna say—who quits with this woman, is the ultimate in the way I feel about things. It's more of a song rather than a frustration-reliever screamer. It's just a pretty, slow ballad."

Ozzy goes on to address the novel, contrary nature of the band's lyrics. "When we started writing things we didn't want to present rubbish like, 'I'm gonna see my chick and we're gonna get it on.' It's all hypocritical. Let's face it, you only remember the good times because you don't wanna remember the bad. You can have a whole month of downer and only one good night, and you remember the good night. If you feel positive, that's fine, though we wanted to write things the way they really were. Geezer furnishes most of the lyrics. This love trip is so grossly distorted. One week you fall in love, the next week you fall out and start doing dope and blow your mind out. I don't believe there's anyone in this world who is 100% in love. I don't think anyone is totally happy; you can't really wake up in the morning free of hassles and do what you want as long as you don't harm anybody else. If you wanna stick needles into your arm, it's your own life. Like I'm not into taking heavy dope, although I have taken dope. People who take it just have hang-ups that they can't deal with."

"If you haven't got your own mind and you can't do what you want, you're not an individual, just part of a mass. The society trip in England is that you go to school, then get a job, and at the age of 21, you get married. You work the rest of your life in a factory and when you retire at the age of 65 you get a gold watch; 45 years in a factory with stinking oil, polluting the land. I used to work in a factory and I used to see these blokes dying on their machines. That just blew my mind. They're saying you should cut your hair and get a good job—for what? So people can suck off you? They're picking your bones, getting all that energy out of you, when it could be put to much better use. But I'll tell you one thing, I've got children, and if such a day ever came, I'd dig holes to feed them. I believe in giving your children a good start and a lot of love."

Ozzy next tackled with Bronson the incongruence of delivering the band's "downer rock" with such giddy abandon, when it comes to the concert stage. "When someone identifies with the downer song that I'm singing, they're able to put their energies into the music and relieve their frustrations. It's good therapy. If I make people feel good, I feel good. The band and the crowd gets off on each other and it's a tremendous trip: peace power. I don't wanna see people get busted on the head. I've been through that whole trip, been knifed a couple times and it's not much fun. Music is my life; I am music. It gets into your body. The stage becomes like a cancerous growth in your mind; if I'm not working for a time, I get so aggressive because the frustration builds up to a tremendous level."

Back to "Changes," Ozzy told Circus, "I sing on it and I'm so pleased with it because I'm able to sing in a different way than like, screaming. It's a gentle, sad song, very un-Black Sabbath."

"It drove me nuts in the end," says Ozzy, on constructing *Vol 4*. "I used to freak out. I was dreaming there was like a tape machine coming into my room and eating me. The album's not a change from heavy to soft. It's heavy, it's still very heavy, but it's just going in a different direction. It's more worked-out, if you like."

“English bands tend to play dirty, earthy, vicious type music,” continued Oz. “Like our type of music, it’s like trying to get back or get at or blow it out at someone. When I’m on the stage, my feelings come out when I’m singing. Like for instance, if we’re playing the song ‘Black Sabbath’ and somebody annoys us or something goes wrong, I just sound against the guitarist. Bill, once, we were playing a jam, and Bill, he thought we were going to kill everybody. You see, we’re just four ordinary guys and we come from a really rough area of Birmingham, you know, all the Irish people fighting, everybody always fighting everywhere. It shows in our music. Our environment shows in our music. And when you’re playing, you can build a little wall around yourself. You just play and your emotions come out. You know, you really go mad.”

“Changes” was actually brought into the live set during the Tony Martin era in the 1990s, for performance on the *Forbidden* tour. As well, in 2003, Ozzy’s duet on the song with his daughter Kelly hit #1 on the UK singles charts, the track showing up on Kelly’s album *Changes*, a reissue of *Shut Up* from the previous year, re-named, with that track added.

A short spell of sound effects called “FX” arose next, as preamble to “Supernaut.” “That’s Tony standing and playing his guitar in the nude,” laughs Geezer, remembering “FX.” “He took all his clothes off in the studio and he was hitting on his guitar strings with the crosses that he wore around his neck. That’s what it was on the whole track (laughs). If you wanted anything different or any weird sounds, you had to do it yourself from scratch. You had to sit down and work them out and make something that sounded different. One time be brought some sitars in and tried them on some tracks.”

“We tried different things,” adds Tony, in the same 1999 Vintage Guitar feature. “We’d spend all day farting about and end up with nothing useable. We’d end up making all these cabinets and coming up with all these brilliant ideas, like trying things going off the piano, into the piano and then miking up the piano strings to hear different sounds. In those days we’d make up ideas and try things. Now you just go buy a box and press a button and you’ve got that sound. We tried violins and cellos, bagpipes. But it was just ideas—sometimes it worked, sometimes it didn’t, but it was fun. It used to take a long time but at least it was original. You wouldn’t hear it anywhere else.”

Other versions of the “FX” story have the whole band naked or mostly naked, with Tony saying that they all danced past the guitar, hitting it. The nakedness likely came from the fact that the guys were either on their way into the Jacuzzi or on their way out of it. In any event, the piece begins with guitar tones, but then converts to the straight rhythmic, extensive echo effect used to establish the flow.

"Supernaut" is another classic great escape lyric from Geezer. Filled with (drug-fueled?) motion, the song sounds like a rocket taking off, Supernaut laughing maniacally as the G-forces paste him to his seat. The lyric feels like a sequel to that of "Planet Caravan" but at higher speeds, paralleling a shift from smoking dope to snorting coke. It is said that Mr. Frank Zappa himself loved this song—Zappa was known to have appreciated what Sabbath was doing, and the guys in the band were all fans of Frank. Both artists were on Warner Bros. in the US.

I asked Bill what he remembered about this mid-level Sabbath riffster. "That John Bonham really liked that song," laughs Ward. "It was one of his favourite songs. And he came to Morgan Studios in London one time when we were recording, and they wanted to jam. There was Planty and Bonham; they came down and they were jamming, and we got together and Bonham wanted to play 'Supernaut,' and he had it down. It sounded great (laughs). We know there's never been a recording of it, but it just sounded really cool. I love it because I think we originally did 'Supernaut' in California. We recorded it right here where I am now, in L.A. It was a great time in our lives and I love the beginning. Tony's riff on that one totally rips. And I love the lyrics. Again, Ozzy and Geezer were totally on. 'The dish ran away with the spoon'—I love that."

Further features of "Supernaut" include an opening riff where there are two channels of Tony, with a slight wah-wah applied to his part in the right channel. A third guitar is added so that Tony is briefly harmonizing with himself. Later in the action, Tony performs a killer yet often overlooked solo over this harmonized rhythm track. "Supernaut" also features a wholly unexpected Latin jam that is almost Santana-esque.

Side two of *Vol 4* opens with the aforementioned "Snowblind," this album's most famous song, a track that lumbers and then lilts through strings of chords individually played, the band turning in melodic acoustic-structured passages rendered full electric, the band's oft-purported but elusive bluesiness making a rare if obtuse appearance. In the latter half, a simple string arrangement is added, the band refusing to get out of the way, in other words, playing full volume heavy metal along with the classical. Lyrically, the track is about the demon cocaine, without the cozy words of love we saw back at "Sweet Leaf."

"We were originally going to call the album *Snowblind*, by the way," offers Bill. "At the time I thought it was a good album. It was a little bit tighter than our other albums. They tended to be… go into the studio, slap them out. We spent a bit more time on sounds. You know, we would take a few takes rather than like three takes and that's it. So there was a little bit more time to use overdubs, a bit more time to get a steadier, tighter sound. And I think it's quite noticeable as well, on songs like 'Snowblind.' I'm still glad that we made 'Snowblind,' which was about cocaine the same way that we did 'Sweet Leaf' about marijuana. I think *Vol 4* stands up."

"That was our cocaine song," affirms Geezer. "We were going to call the album that but the record company wouldn't let us (laughs). We'd been through grass and hash and acid, and cocaine was the big new drug at the time and we were recording in L.A. and coke was very big there so we wrote about it."

Big indeed, as Ozzy can attest, speaking with High Times back in 1999: "We rented this house in Bel Air and we just had the fucking packages up to here. It would come in like big gallon bottles with a spoon on it, covered with a seal of wax. This coke was the best coke that I've ever had. I'm lying by the pool one day and I met this guy and I asked him, 'You wanna do some coke?' He goes, 'No, no, no.' I'm whacking this stuff up my nose, it's a brilliant sunny day, and this guy is sitting there with one of those reflectors under his chin getting a suntan. I say, 'What do you do?' He says, 'I work for the government.' 'Uh… what do you do with the government?' 'I work for the drug squad.' I sez, 'You're fucking joking.' He shows me his badge. I fuckin' flipped. I was fuckin'… flames were coming out of my fingers, man."

"He says, 'Oh, you're all right. I'm the guy that got you the coke.' We got all fucked-up, but me and Bill went fuckin' a little bit further. Bill ended up in a psychiatric fuckin' place. Bill's anti-drug, anti-drink, anti-everything now. He don't mince his fucking words either, you know. With the coke and all these chemicals, I got a chemical imbalance in my brain. I'd become really shaky. I have to take Prozac and various medications just to stabilize me. One thing about cocaine though, it used to isolate you and you used to stay in your room paranoid. You buy a bag of white powder and the paranoia soon follows. And when you hear those birds going in the morning, tweet tweet, you want to get a fucking machine gun and shoot every bird in sight. When the day breaks, it's horrible. And what do you do when you wake up? Snnnniiiiffff! Like a fiend, you know."

Back on *Vol 4*, "Cornucopia" follows, and the doom gets blacker. Beginning as a denigration of consumer society, the track ends with an anti-war message, apparently incited by Geezer hearing about the latest casualties in Vietnam, a report that "only" 25 Americans had been killed that week. Cornucopia means horn of plenty, and the term is used ironically here, Geezer saying that a life of little toys, plastic ways, mortgages and frozen food eaten in concrete mazes isn't any life at all.

Another one of the band's solemn, possibly grave mellow moments comes next, with acoustic instrumental "Laguna Sunrise" sounding so peaceful, one fears that death is near. Tony puts a sort of root, rhythmic acoustic track panned hard left and on the right, he plays what is essentially a vocal part, also acoustically. Flooding the sound picture is the album's most complex string arrangement. At the close, the song seems to settle on an infinite loop but then ceases.

"I don't play acoustic guitar that much so I'm not a very good acoustic player, quite honestly," says Tony, but the song achieves its goal, calming the band's crazies, before the practical joke of volume kicks in with a cackle, in the form of "St. Vitus' Dance," named for a childhood affliction related to involuntary muscle spasms.

The song's lyric, however, is surprisingly this-worldly, revolving around love gone wrong, the music, almost funky, the song all but forgotten in the catalogue.

"Yes, I think it does. Things come out in the music," mused Tony, doing press at the time, on whether the band's increasingly complicated lives affected the music at all. "Your scope widens. Like from the early days of Sabbath up until now, we've seen a lot of the world; we've seen a lot of everything that goes on. Like in this last album, there's a thing called 'Laguna Sunrise,' which is over there, Laguna Beach. It's about the beach and the sea. You just write about things which are in your environment at the time. Obviously we all live a lot better. In the early days it was a lot rawer because of the environment we were in. We were all down in the dumps and that had a lot to do with it. It certainly changed the music. At the time of the first album we were pretty much upset as I said and it was all very aggressive. The new album is different, really. It's basically heavy but it doesn't have the rawness like the first one."

"St. Vitus Dance" demonstrates ably Bill's idea of "orchestrational" drumming, where he is accenting often and in odd places. Also of interest is the way that during the verses, he lays off the cymbals, backs off on the aggression, in particular, his snare being played (or recorded) quieter than is evident in the "country hoe-down" section or the pre-verse doom chording. There's also a charming "floundering" element to Ward's performance, with a few whacks close to being blown shifts, quite likely so given Bill's own admission that he was barely holding it together at the time.

Closing *Vol 4* is an epic called "Under the Sun," appended with a frantic closing section called (on some of the printed copies and in some of the printed locations on those copies) "Every Day Comes and Goes." Lyrically, this one is akin to "After Forever," Geezer proposing this philosophy of tabla rasa through nihilism, or on the positive, freedom from all creed through belief in oneself, maybe just through drugs, maybe from care-obliterating cynicism. The over-riding message is one of atheism, Ozzy bleating out exasperation at both the Jesus freaks and the black magicians that want a piece of the band. Most amusing is the assertion that not only does he not believe in violence, he doesn't believe in peace either.

"Bill had a terrible time trying to get that song," laughs Tony. "It was probably a time when we were pretty stressed-out then. Certainly I know Bill was. And he had gotten this thing in his head about playing that particular song. He brought it on himself, I think. He just couldn't get it right. Every time we would start to record it, start playing it, he would mess it up. And of course, after a bit, he would just lose his temper—'Ah fuck it!' you know? So we thought we would try another studio, because somehow the studio got blamed. So we moved to a different studio and we tried it again. But Bill definitely had his hang-up with that one. Eventually, of course, he got it, but it did really drive us nuts. I think we tried three different studios recording that one."

"Bill's fantastic. He's such a nice guy, Bill," muses Tony, during the same conversation. "You couldn't wish for a nicer guy. Especially these days. Years ago, he was a real... when he used to drink, God, he was a different story. But he's such a lovely guy, such a funny guy. Drummer, I think he's great; he's fantastic. He's such an unusual drummer, so unorthodox. He plays all these little bits that you don't hear drummers do nowadays. Most drummers say, 'Oh, I'm a good drummer and I'll just play the beat,' you know? And they think that's great. But Bill will really get involved in it, really look to it, the percussion side of it. I think he's great."

"I hated the bloody thing," affirms Bill. "Tony had this lick (sings it), and at that time I thought it was just horrible. I couldn't stand the song. Oddly enough today, I think the song sounds great. But at the time I just couldn't find a drum part for it and I thought, 'Oh God, anything but that song!' But you know what, Tony, even as far up until today, he'll turn around and play that lick, because he remembers what trouble it gave me years ago. But man, it was such a struggle with that particular riff that what I wanted to hear was a blues jam more than anything (laughs). But I think we made some new ground. Geezer was writing really strong on that album, good lyrics, it was very much a band effort."

Musically the song is another vaguely blues-doomed freight train, yes, almost entirely metal, but definitely tinctured by the blues, perhaps mostly in the vocal melody. Mournful passages emerge later, and then there's the strangely sing-songy "Every Day Comes and Goes" section, not entirely successful, but indicative of the band's wild creativity for this involved record. This part bears similarities to Deep Purple's "Flight of the Rat" from 1970's seminal *In Rock* album, but the variation this section brings to the song just might be inspired by the spate of recent dates the band had played with Yes, not to mention other shows logged with the likes of Curved Air, Gentle Giant and earlier, King Crimson and ELP.

Other upticks in sophistication for the band are more subtle. As Ozzy telegraphed in interviews, his vocal melodies across the record are more independent of Tony's riffing than in the past. The song closes with the band bashing away behind Tony's epic descending but non-doom chords, slowing the tempo in unison before one massive last punctuating chord.

Rhythmically, it's apparent why Bill had trouble with "Under the Sun." Although not difficult, it's a strange cross between a shuffle and a gallop. And then Bill brings upon himself another challenge by introducing tom toms into his beat come the second verse. There's also a solo section, at 2:16 and again at 2:41, where he fires off some rapid-fire triplet combinations. This portion also includes some of Bill's most assertive and exacting snare work, on an album where quite often the usually metronomic whack of the snare on two and four is subsumed in a gauze of guitars and crash cymbals.

The problem with the drum track on "Under the Sun" lingered to the point that it eventually had to be tracked when the band was back in England, in June, at Island Studios in London. Ozzy says that every time they played it, Bill played a different beat, and by the time they were done, they were calling the song "Everything Under the Fucking Sun."

All told, *Vol 4* was not well received by the critics, which is somewhat understandable. The album has a strange uniformity to it, despite all that supposed studio work done to it. The brunt of the album is slow, almost fatigue-inducing, and it has a coldness and dampness to it, unlike *Master of Reality*, which had a certain charm and assured songfulness. Vocally and lyrically the band sound a little haggard and desperate. The doom doesn't leap out of the lyrics as much even if it is certainly there. More so, it seeps from the sounds, almost at walking pace. Several tracks would slouch off the record into the band's set list for years, even decades, but certainly few fans would characterize these as live favourites. "Snowblind," "Tomorrow's Dream" and "Supernaut" would act more as the glue that held the show together, as one prepared for the blast-off of the band's more beloved anthems.

Wrote Max Bell of Let It Rock in his December '72 review of *Vol 4*, "Despite Black Sabbath's protestations that they have spent both a great deal of time and money on their latest album, the end product still manages to be a monumental bore. In the past, say the Sabbath, their discs have suffered from a lack of the above essentials and, as a result, they have failed to do themselves justice on record. I am inclined to think that even with unlimited resources they would be hard put to make a really good album. They just don't have sufficient talent or musical direction. The monotonous riff, the clichéd drumming, the heavy bass work and the flat vocal are trademarks of their style, but where's the attraction? With this album one can leave the room for ten minutes and not miss anything interesting."

"And now for the good news!" continues Bell. "Two tracks, 'Supernaut' and 'Under the Sun' are effective. 'Supernaut' has some nice bass and lead work, with the two guitarists working well in unison, while 'Under the Sun' has the whole group cooking together. Maybe this is what their live act is about because, these tracks apart, *Vol 4* is a real bummer and leaves one wondering why the Sabbath are so popular. Their great American following is doubly difficult to comprehend because they are, basically, very English in their approach, and there are many other bands who are equally exciting visually and far superior musically. Their success in the States is, of course, partly attributable to the number of hours on the road and the live gigs they have under their belts. Too many, as recent events have proved, but this enforced curtailment may well be a good thing—at least the band will have a chance to spend more time in the studio and think more about the future of their music. They desperately need to widen their scope and, as a start, the addition of a regular keyboard player wouldn't be a bad thing. Black Sabbath have long assured their critics that they have the talent to make an album of real worth; I'm still looking forward to hearing it."

Jim Esposito from Zoo World, also reviewing the album at the time, underscores this idea that *Vol 4* is not really that different from what came before: "It's not that I really care that the few people I've talked to about *Vol 4* like it better than the other three, it's just that I don't see how anyone can tell if one Black Sabbath album is better than another. Furthermore, I think anyone who says they can is lying. After all, there's no medium of comparison with which you can rate the four Black Sabbath albums. What are you gonna do, institute some sort of weight measurement to see how heavy each one is? Then again, you might see how many hours of constant exposure to Tony Iommi's fuzz tone chords it takes to disintegrate a Ford LTD or possibly, if all else fails, you can try to register them on a seismograph using the Richter Scale (but you'll have to have a pretty good stereo)."

"That's the main problem with Black Sabbath. Almost everything they do sounds just about the same. I'm not putting them down either because every band tries to create its own distinctive sound and it would be foolish for Black Sabbath to change just to satisfy a bunch of dilettantes that are still pissed-off 'cause the Beatles broke up. I never heard the Beatles try to drown out New York City—from London—and no one expected them to. You don't buy a Black Sabbath album to be carried away into the heavens on the wings of an angel, after all. In a way, that's what the group is trying to say when they call it *Vol 4*. Volume four. The same old stuff, just volume four. And if you can dig it, outta sight. There's a real market in driving people's heads right into the ground and those people now have another album to do it with."

There's an interesting wisdom in what Esposito says there. If you read between the lines, there's the idea that *Vol 4* serves a purpose that few other records at the time could, save for, of course, volumes one, two and three. By this point, America had coughed up little more than Mountain and Cactus and the Stooges; maybe Bang and Sir Lord Baltimore if you were willing to dig. Sure, Deep Purple had issued the well-received *Machine Head* album earlier in the year, there was Zeppelin's fourth, and Uriah Heep had issued the fine *Demons and Wizards* back in May, but nothing drove "people's heads right into the ground" like Black Sabbath did.

"We just thought we were a hard rock band at the time," indicated Geezer. "That's what we liked. The term heavy metal wasn't used at all until probably the mid-'70s. And the first I heard it being called heavy metal was somebody being derogatory to us. I read this interview when we were on tour over here in the States, criticizing us as usual, and they said it sounded like a load of heavy metal being dropped, not musical whatsoever. And then after that I kept hearing it more and more. And then particularly when Judas Priest came out, they were instantly a heavy metal band. That was the first time it was really applied to anyone. They embraced the term heavy metal, yeah. But we used to think of it as an insult because of that one review that we had."

Still, regarding the value of *Vol 4*, a hard truth cannot be avoided: it wouldn't be out of line, if one were to rank all the heavy songs across *Master of Reality* and *Vol 4*, to say that the top five are "Sweet Leaf," "After Forever," "Children of the Grave," "Lord of This World" and "Into the Void." It's arguable, sure, but not unreasonable, and in the telling, quite the indictment.

In America, summer of '72, the band included in their set list "Tomorrow's Dream," "Under the Sun," "Cornucopia," "Supernaut," "Wheels of Confusion" and of course, "Snowblind." The album wouldn't actually be issued until September of '72, at which time the US leg was over, with Gentle Giant being the main support constant. The last two dates of the American tour had to be cancelled due to Tony collapsing at the Hollywood Bowl gig on September 15th of '72.

Somewhat recovered, the band was off to a memorable one-off festival date in New Zealand (with a ton of unknown locals, only Fairport Convention joining the Sabs from away), followed by five Australian dates. German dates kicked off the European tour in mid-February of '73, followed by UK dates in March, Sabbath backed by Badger and Necromandus, with which the band shared friendship and business ties.

But the guys were burnt to a crisp, the exhaustion of touring the US causing plans for a major rethink of the whole process. It was reported in the press that the band had decided to quit touring the States, Ozzy not winning any friends telling Circus that "America was the most Satanic country in the world. They'll do anything for a dollar. People are living nightmares over there. Everybody in America is crazy." Ozzy was also known to remark that he was surprised fans in America didn't bring their own coffins to the gig.

"We thought we'd go over anyway," said Tony, of the band's reluctance to tour the US. "So we did a couple of gigs and Ozzy's voice went. We had the doctors in, everything, injections, throat sprays, the lot.

Anyway the doctor said he should have time off, and he did take time off for two days. So we thought it's getting better, we'll try again. So we did another gig and then he had to have a week off. It just makes me fed up hanging about. It had been just all rush from the beginning, and we just weren't ready for it and then when his voice did come back, we were going out onstage wondering if it was going to go again, all worried like in case it goes. Eventually it all came to a head, and the last night, I collapsed at the Hollywood Bowl. We'd just finished the last number and I come off and I'm just gone. The doctor was in, and he said we'd have to go home, so we had to cancel the dates. I didn't know anything about it. Completely out, I was."

An interesting bit of trivia comes with press reports in January of '73 that Sabbath had plans to issue a live album called *Fire on the Mountain*, in time for US dates in June. The label however, was said to have not liked the tapes, sending the band off to L.A. to write the next studio album instead.

A man by the name of Markus Payne had enjoyed a unique perspective on life with Sabbath on the road during the early '70s. From a broken family, Markus found himself tagging along to many Sabbath shows as a nine, ten, 11-year-old hanger-on to his bigger brother, Bernard Colgan, nicknamed James, who would roadie for the band, mostly on the eastern seaboard but also in Europe.

"My brother told me he met Sabbath when he got home from Nam, and that's where he got a chance to help Sabbath out because they felt bad for him, because he came back really into the pot and heroin, and the war had basically fucked him up. But he was a good, decent, honest person. And word is that is why Sabbath asked my brother to come out on the road and help them out on different occasions. But his drug habit eventually became too much, and he died at the age of 46 of massive heart failure."

Payne saw the rise of Sabbath essentially from the front row, offering the following survey of the growth of the band's concert business, as well as how the guys were coping with the rigors of the road.

"It all started with their first show in New Jersey. My brother, at first, would just buy a ticket for me, and sit me down somewhere and tell me not to move, and he would come and check on me, and ask me if I needed to go to the bathroom, wait until he had a free moment, and he would come check on me. Basically all he did with Sabbath was stage production. He wasn't a tech or anything. Back in those days, Sabbath wasn't travelling with 18-wheelers or nothing. They were travelling with vans. So it was like a garage band situation. Because Tony Iommi only had the tube amps and the head, and the PA was usually just put up by one of the local bands, or if it was held at a bar, the bar had a PA."

"But when it came to the second and third albums, Sabbath started picking up an audience here in the States. And by the time we got to like California Jam, I helicoptered in with Ozzy and Bill Ward, to California Jam, and I mean, it was, what, 500,000 people? Then I was a little bit older and I kind of stayed in the background and knew not to get in anybody's way. But Ozzy was very friendly with me. Ozzy was cool to me, and he would pat me on the head and disturb my hair. I had like a shag haircut, past my shoulders, and he would tussle my hair."

"Tony Iommi was friendly," continues Payne, "but I don't think 100% approved of a kid being around. And Geezer Butler was friendly. He would talk to me and stuff. But I do know, 100% for a fact, Bill Ward was not cool having a kid around, because at one point, I forget where we were, they were having a meeting, and they were all going into this one room. This was at a larger place that had backstage rooms and stuff, and they were having a meeting, and Sharon Arden was on the road at this point. And I went to get up to go into the meeting, and Bill Ward put his hand on my forehead and said, 'No kids allowed.' Really, Ozzy is the only one I can ever recall making an attempt to associate himself with me and to make an effort to keep me entertained."

"But it's funny, that first show, or one of the early ones, was in a church—and an Episcopalian church sponsored it. But it was held in like a VFW hall. They were nothing in the States at that point. They would open up for bigger bands, or it was just Sabbath themselves and they would play high school auditoriums or VFW halls and people would sponsor it. But at the time, being a kid, I just thought they were some of my brother's Vietnam buddies. I did. They had long hair, they were listening to hard music, so I just figured it was like people that my brother was hanging out with that he had done time with in Vietnam. No, the whole spectacle did not dawn on me. I guess that's why, in my whole career, I've never been star-struck, because I was brought up being around Sabbath, and they were just normal, regular individuals to me."

"And the drug use was normal to me too," remembers Payne. "Because my brother and sister, growing up in the house I grew up in, were all on heroin and pot and were pill users. So it didn't seem strange or odd to me. It seemed like a bunch of average guys. And my brother played in garage bands, so when I first started hanging out with Sabbath, I just figured they were some sort of garage band that was going on shows around the country. That's how it seemed to me, as a young kid."

Indeed frighteningly early, Markus soon found himself immersed in the band's drug scene.

"Ozzy did coke with me," remembers Payne. "We were sitting on a bus, and we were at the fold-down table, and there was a mirror on the table, and it was Ozzy, my brother and me. And Ozzy was doing lines, my brother did a couple lines, and I got up and I went over, and I snorted like a little section of a line, and fucking started choking. Wasn't aware of what I was doing. But that was my first endeavour into doing drugs."

It gets worse.

"To the best of my knowledge, I think Bill Ward was doing heroin. I think Ozzy experimented in heroin. And everybody smoked pot, everybody popped pills, everybody did coke. Those were the three big things. To be honest with you, I can't remember what pills were being done, but I remember a lot of pills were being exchanged. There were always pill bottles laying around and I don't think they were necessarily for sleep. I think they were recreational pills. But it wasn't until I got like 13, 14, with like California Jam, that I realized that they were like God to me. These people that I would see getting dressed or would see backstage, and they would be walking towards the stage with the manager and the security from the facility, they were turning into demi-gods to me and I was looking up to them. And I was kind of afraid of them at the same time, because they were so big and powerful."

"But around the time of the California Jam, I switched from being a kid tagging along into like a man. I always went in front of the stage and joined the audience and partied with the audience. And the audience was always pretty cool. 'Oh my God, check this guy out, he's smoking pot.' And I was smoking joints with all the 17, 18-year-olds, getting high, throwing around beach balls and everything. It was just something completely different."

Eventually Payne would go on to work for Sabbath in the *Heaven and Hell* era, Ozzy as a solo artist and then Ronnie as a solo act, but for now, he was watching all this happen as a kid with wide-eyed wonder, there at his ringside seat watching the band become superstars.

"First it was like folding chairs set up in front of a stage that was a foot off the ground, like I say, a VFW hall or a high school auditorium.

And everybody sat down and just watched the show and smoked pot and popped pills and did whatever in the bathroom or whatever. It wasn't until like when *Master* came out that they started going to places like the Capitol Theatre and the Academy of Music, turning themselves into a concert act. But before that, I mean, a lot of times, Ozzy would fuck up and not sing his parts correctly. They would be drunk or high, and it just didn't seem like it was taken all that seriously."

Fortunately, the band soon began to get more professional, but it was still always working against the drugs and booze and sheer fatigue of hauling all this across America.

"Yeah, Ozzy was just silly, because he was high all the time. But there was also a very dark side to Ozzy's getting high. He knew exactly what to take to feel good on stage, but after the show was over, when the girls and the groupies and everybody came around and the crew was breaking down, when they were backstage, that's when all the really dark drug use came out and all the dark really heavy shit was going on."

"Bill was a user," says Markus. "Geezer, I don't recall Geezer being very dark. Geezer was a pot smoker. To be honest with you, I don't even have any memories of Geezer doing lines. But I do know he did lines. So maybe he didn't do lines because I was there. But one thing with those guys, when shows came out bad, Ozzy, Tony, Geezer and Bill would personally feel very, very shitty. If the show went bad, or people didn't seem to be getting into the show, they took it very personally. They made a really bad scene and would cuss a lot. They would slam doors and shit if the show was a flop."

Then there was dealing with rednecks.

"Yes, I can remember being on the road in Kansas and over at this diner, like this whole shitty truck stop. And everybody had long hair at the time, and we went into this truck stop and believe it or not, the waitress' name was Flo. One of the guys turned around and he's like, 'Flo, do you have any scissors? Looks like I've got some haircuts to give.' And then I remember a fistfight out in the parking lot."

"And I also remember religious protests at Sabbath shows," continues Markus. "Which is why it's so funny that I was just seeing those posters and the ticket stubs that had the band sponsored by this like St. Paul's Episcopal Church. It's just such a bizarre dichotomy. I remember it wasn't taken seriously by the band—it was taken jokey. Nobody considered it serious, because nobody considered themselves Satanists or like anything that was evil. They always had dark imagery, but it was all about war and government and stuff. But when we would pull up to a place, they'd be waiting for the cops or whatever to show up so they could get into the venue and play. There would be churches, kind of like the Westboro Baptist Church, but in very small numbers, picketing wherever they were playing, and I remember them having this jokey attitude about it."

Asked for a bit of a psychological profile of the guys, Markus ventures that, "Iommi and Geezer were both very smart. And I know Tony and Geezer are both animal lovers. I know Geezer is very into mysticism and Aleister Crowley and all that kind of thing. He was always reading, and always checking stuff out for his lyrics. Things just seem to come natural to Tony. I mean, Tony just personifies this god-like image that was just super cool and suave. I've never, ever heard Tony raise his voice and scream and yell. I never heard an argument come out of him. I've heard Ozzy argue with a lot of people but I've never heard Tony argue and scream. Even with the coke and the pot and everything, I've never seen him be mean or have a mean bone in his body."

In general though, on the subject of tension between the guys, Payne explains that, "there was a lot of dissension over money in the early years, a lot of discourse about money, and the direction they were being led in, and playing shitty gigs for very little money. When Don Arden came into the picture, that was when they started taking off and sort of playing huge shows and festivals and stuff."

Ah yes, Mr. Big, who is still a few years off at this point.

"Don was much, much, much older than me," recalls Payne. "He was much, much older than Sabbath too. I would say he was probably in his 40s when Sabbath were in their 20s. So he was kind of like an authority figure. But he wasn't an authority figure that was a dick. He was pretty cool about things. But he had the business end. When it was business time, he meant business. He knew that a lot of stuff was going on that probably shouldn't be going on. I'm not saying he condoned it, but he knew what was going on, and like, I don't ever recall him confiscating drugs or anything. But he also wasn't the manager that would open up his top desk drawer and have a fucking kilo sitting in his top drawer. You know, he wasn't that kind of manager. He knew what was going on, he was aware of the times, the 'sign of the times,' and he would tell them all the time, you know, you shouldn't do it, don't do it, you're gonna ruin your career, you're gonna waste your brain away, and you're so talented and stuff. He would especially say that to Ozzy. But he never, like, forced anybody to go into rehab or anything."

"I would like to think so," muses Markus in closing, asked if in some way, he had been raised by the Sabbath camp—no father, mentally ill mother back in Germany, heroin-addicted brother, and finishing with school by about grade four (he would later get his GED). "I would like to think so. But you know, not a lot of people gave me attention because they were basically kids themselves. Like I said, the only one that was really fun to be around was Ozzy, because he was such a juvenile and he was so wasted all the time."

If it wasn't for Ozzy, who knows what would have become of this kid thrown to the wolves? "Do you remember the Circus magazine cover, shaved head and he wore Mickey Mouse ears?" laughs Payne. "That sums it up. Ozzy's a total sweetheart. I've been at his house in England. I've been to the house in California, where the TV show was staged. I've been to the newer house, the newer little cottage that they live in. I have no problems with Ozzy. I've never had a problem with Ozzy. Ozzy is one of those people, if you're kind him and you treat him good and you show him a little bit a dedication, he'll repay you back for that. He will. He will. But Ozzy's just one of those characters—he's like a three-legged dog. You know, you can hear the dog running around the house, but you don't really pay attention to what he's getting into."

Back to our tale, with respect to the grueling nature of Black Sabbath's early tours, now despite being a much more substantial draw, nothing much had changed in terms of the band finding solace with any of the creature comforts available to them.

The griping and the drama of the *Master of Reality* tour reached a fever pitch on the *Vol 4* tour. Sure, the number of US dates was reduced, but Sabbath also covered off two other continents. The band's gaskets were blown. They clearly couldn't handle it, and quite possibly they weren't quite mature enough mentally and psychologically to deal with the organization's rising fortunes.

Then again, the drinking and drugging, as Markus describes, didn't help, shortening fuses. Ozzy was, as previously characterized, literally haunted by America, scared of its audiences, horrified at its string of identical hotel rooms and meals, at its groupies, at its stoned throngs wanting nothing more than to drive him crazy and away from his wife and kids (Ozzy's first wife Thelma and family are essentially now estranged). Ozzy would voice as much publicly, which would cause a bit of a press skirmish through early '73, with Oz in a more sober state, finding himself backtracking and clarifying that he maybe did not loathe

America to the extent that was portrayed (most notably in a Barbara Graustark piece in Circus called, aptly, *Why Black Sabbath Hates America*).

Relations weren't much better back home, Ozzy telling the NME's Keith Altham, "I just cannot understand the critics in the UK or why they have been so unfair about our recent tour. We hadn't played in England for over a year, and we had no idea what the reaction would be. Believe me, I'm not handing you any bullshit when I say the audience were incredible—we've never had scenes like it. I was staggered. Some of those reviewers go to the concert knowing they won't like what we're going to do—they've got their reviews written before they see us. They know we hit hard and play loud and what our material is like from our albums. Now why bother to go at all if you know you are not going to like it? Why waste space on a band you think is crap? Surely there are other bands who need encouragement."

"It might be an age gap," figures Ozzy, asked by Keith why this is the case. "Most of our audiences are in their late teens, and certainly not many of the critics are in that bracket. It may just be that they cannot identify with us. But if that's the case, why can't they admit it and at least put the case for the 99% who gave us standing ovations and sell out concerts on this tour? We've never had a good press in England—never. We work our bollocks off in America and bring back thousands of dollars into this country, but no one even gives us credit for that."

"I really don't feel that anywhere has there been a fair reflection of the sort of reaction which freaked me out on this last tour. The reporters who really piss me off are those who come backstage afterwards and say how much they like it, and then go away and crap on us in their papers—two-faced bastards. We work really hard at our music. I spend hours at home with a cassette getting songs together, and we put a lot of extra time in because we care and like what we do. We give 100% energy, high power rock for an hour to those who like our kind of music. Where's the harm in that? If I believed what I read in the press about us, I'd pack it in."

In any event, despite the band's battles with respectability, a wholesale refurbishing would be in order, resulting in a pronounced maturation and variation in styles across the Sabs' next album, a mind-blowing masterpiece called *Sabbath Bloody Sabbath*, a record that would have the band back on track and more importantly, on a trajectory toward 1975's *Sabotage*, a record considered by many to be the Sabs' finest hour.

Album 5

Sabbath Bloody Sabbath

"I've always referred to him as The Irish Poet"

There's a whiff of finality to the title *Vol 4*, or at least the nuance that the music enclosed will be more of the same, or at minimum, part and parcel of a set. As it would turn out, in retrospect and set against what came after, that sentiment would ring loud and clear. Ultimately there's an immense gulf between those that came before, capped by *Vol 4*, and what Black Sabbath had up their collective sleeve to close out the decade. Indeed *Sabbath Bloody Sabbath* would mark a second wind for the band, an explosion and an expulsion, in the process the band being rewarded with a record that is often cited decades later as the finest album Sabbath has ever crafted.

But its origins were a scramble. "I remember one particular time, when we came over to California here, we'd recorded *Vol 4*, and that's all ready to go; that was out," reflects Tony, with a shudder. "For the next album, we thought, 'Well, let's go back to create the same thing.' We came back, we got the same house, same environment, same studio—and I couldn't think of anything. I just had a block. I couldn't come up with anything. And everybody's looking at me, 'Oh, you know, he can't come up with anything' and it was just too much pressure for me, to have to be the only one that was coming up with ideas. And it's very difficult, too, when you can't get someone to exchange an idea. Nobody else wants to do it; then you're stumped. You get to a certain level, and you might come up with a riff and it leads nowhere. Because I'd done it for so many years, of just coming up with this stuff and everybody playing it. Just that one particular time I had a mental block and I just couldn't get around."

"So we all went back to England, and it was all dismal, you know. And I think they might have tried to get rid of me at that time (laughs). I remember something going on there, as they thought I couldn't come up with any more ideas. We had nothing at the time, not the album title, not even a riff. And it just didn't happen. So we went to Wales and rented this castle, the whole castle. And we rehearsed in the dungeons. And I got ideas then! I started getting ideas! I was going again. You see, that was the problem back then. I didn't have anybody else who was creating, to bounce things off of. And it was very hard. I mean, they'd have ideas vaguely, but not ideas as far as riffs or anything else. Or if they did, they wouldn't say anything. It would all be left to me. And it was just too much of a strain."

As was often the case with Sabbath doppelgangers Rainbow, a castle came to the rescue, in this case Clearwell Castle in Gloucestershire, the band's new and temporary home, complete with practical jokes, hauntings and fires. Clearwell became a regular writing, rehearsal and recording location with bands in the '70s, playing host to the likes of Led Zeppelin, Bad Company, Mott the Hoople, Badfinger, Peter Frampton and Deep Purple, who wrote both *Burn* and *Stormbringer* there.

"I really like *Sabbath Bloody Sabbath*; I thought that was a great album," muses Tony, reiterating the above and adding to it 30 years later. "I really do like that album, because it sort of lifted us up a bit different from what we'd done on the first four albums. We experimented a bit more. It was interesting, and the whole thing about that album was, we went back to Los Angeles, back to the same house, tried to create the same vibe we had with *Vol 4*, but of course we didn't. We couldn't create the same vibe. And even the studio changed, that we were going to go into. So we were basically right in the shit. You know, we went back there to write it, and I got a writer's block. I couldn't think of anything (laughs). It was like, 'Oh my God, no!' I mean, we had a couple of songs, but not an album. And then with the studio change as well, being smaller, we weren't happy at all. We couldn't get in the studio we wanted to get in."

"So we just basically packed up and came back to England. So I just got home and I felt really depressed, and I thought, 'Oh God, now, that's it.' And we left it for a while, and we had booked Clearwell Castle, in Wales, and that was an experience and a half again, different again. We all moved down to this castle and set up in the dungeons. Because we want to be miles from anywhere and we want just to concentrate on what we were doing. So we set all the equipment up in the dungeons there, and bloody 'ell, things started happening just like that. I wrote 'Sabbath Bloody Sabbath' first, and that was the benchmark for that album. From then on, it was not a problem. But just the vibe of being somewhere like that, created an album. Each one of those means something special, but I like *Sabbath Bloody Sabbath* because it was different. It was a phase in our lives where we tried something different and I enjoyed it."

"As far as fires were concerned, pretty much Ozzy and I were always lighting fires," recalls Bill. "This is difficult for me to recall. Because we played in different rehearsal spaces and there were times where we actually did rehearse in a castle or castles. *Sabbath Bloody Sabbath* was made in a castle. And I can remember when we first did that track, man, it was phenomenal. I loved it. But the fires, that could have well come about through myself or Oz. It wasn't unusual for me to get drunk and just light a fire whenever I wanted to light a fire. I don't know if you've seen the movie *Sid and Nancy* and sometimes him and Nancy would go on the nod, and that one part of the movie, they didn't even know there was a fire. And when I watched that particular part of that movie I thought, oh my God, I totally identify with this. Sometimes the room could have been on fire, and I would have just looked and watched the flames, totally oblivious to the fact that I could be in danger."

As concerns the reported hauntings at the fortress… "Well, we're always seeing ghosts anyway," notes Bill. "Seeing a ghost was not unusual. I mean, Geezer was always in tune to the phenomena of ghosts. And I've seen ghosts many times; I see them all the time. Even today, it's not unusual. My father had seen many ghosts. To me it's not an unusual thing. It's something that is normal, clairvoyance and stuff like that. I know that my mother had the ability to teach me and pass on things to me that even as a child, I had clairvoyant instincts and was able to answer questions before the person asked them. I did not understand why I was able to deduct. And I still have that with me, right up until this interview today. So of course, and the castle, yeah, there were some ghosts. That story sounds about right with Ozzy building a fire that might have been too big. It was either him or me. Him and I were the firebugs. I might have got sick of my clothes and just took them all off anywhere and just set them on fire; that wasn't unusual. In fact it was almost like ritualistic. At one point we had the famous burning of the coat. That was at a party and half of Led Zeppelin were there and all the Sabs were there and a few other people were there and I think either one of the guys set me on fire or I just might have set myself on fire, I can't remember."

Usually it was one of the guys igniting Bill with the aid of lighter fluid.

"Yes, that was the party trick that was an inside trick that we used to perform sometimes at parties. So actually being set on fire was not unusual. So that was one type of being on fire. And then there was the phenomenon where I might have been too loaded or Oz was like way loaded and we'd have these ritual burnings of clothing or anything else. And we'd build gypsy fires for campfires. And also now in reflection, things fell out of the fireplace and set Ozzy on fire and nobody knew about it. That was pretty much normal back then. It happened a lot. Unbelievably irresponsible. When I look back on it, we're lucky to be alive."

Bill had other problems as well, which saw him move onto Geezer's… lawn. "Yes, that was when we were doing *Sabbath Bloody Sabbath*," affirms Butler. "I just moved; that was the same house where I wrote 'Spiral Architect.' And the first day I'd moved in, I looked outside, and Bill had turned up outside, and he was just leaving his first wife and he was with his second wife at the time, soon to be second wife, and he'd been thrown out of his house by his wife, so he didn't have anywhere to live (laughs). So he came up, followed me home, just as I'd moved into my house. I've got no furniture or anything in the house, and Bill says, 'Do you mind if I sleep on your lawn? I've got nowhere to live' (laughs)."

Asked how long that went on, Butler says, "I think just the night. Until he sorted out his hotel or whatever he got. I said, 'Do you want to come sleep inside?' He says, 'Oh no, I couldn't do that. I'll just sleep on your lawn.' So he just slept on the lawn."

Adds Tony, "Yeah, well, again, that's another part of life we saw a lot with Bill, going through the different stages of his marriage. You know, when he broke up with one and went with another and had nowhere to live. I don't quite know the ins and outs of that, because I kept out of that, but I know that Bill was shifting around one or two places (laughs). Oh dear. I'll let him tell you that one. I don't like to talk about him."

Bill recalls the event this way, although pertinently, he thinks it was during the making of *Vol 4*. "I didn't know where to go, so one night I actually did leave the studio and the guys were just wanting me out of the studio period. I can't say I blame them at all. I'm not sure what kind of a state I was in. And I ended up going to Geezer's house and sleeping on his lawn, outside of his house. So I went there and slept on the back lawn and I don't think he was too happy to see me and my missus sleeping on the lawn when he got up in the morning. We were there and we just didn't know where to go. I was definitely in crisis. I think I was about 23 and I was big time in trouble, big time. I was a young guy, already a veteran of the road."

It is of note that even as Bill talks about thinking he was about to be fired for not being able to get his drum parts down on *Vol 4*, come *Sabbath Bloody Sabbath*, Tony mentioned at the time that because of his writer's block, he thought the guys would lose patience with him and send him packing. With Ozzy always down on his singing abilities, perhaps it's only Geezer who felt secure in his job.

"That room was just a good room anyway," adds Bill, on the recording values at Clearwell Castle. "Oh yeah! That was just like solid rock about ten feet thick. So it was good for drums; the drum sounded powerful throughout. I know we had good rehearsals, but I don't recall any special techniques."

But there was spookiness to the place too. "Oh yeah, thanks to Mr. Iommi and Butler and Osbourne," says Ward. "They used to tie little bits of fishing wire. You can't see fishing wire. So they used to tie... I mean, they spent more time, so elaborate, you know, but if there was a picture in the room, or a glass on the table; this is my room, of course. And they would wrap fishing wire around it. They would go to really elaborate lengths to pull off these tricks, even to the point of actually going up two or three stories on the outside of the building, so they could put the fishing wire from the outside in. And the fishing wire was under the door. So at night time, things started to move. And you couldn't see it, because it's like invisible stuff. I managed to get fucking scared to death at Clearwell Castle, as everywhere else, to be honest with you."

In fact after being told about the spirit of a maid who got pregnant by a past owner of the castle and killed herself and her baby there, Bill took to sleeping with a big knife by his bed. The predictable ribbing ensued, Bill being informed that you couldn't kill a ghost with a dagger.

Finally, Geezer pipes in on the case of the haunted castle. "When we were doing *Sabbath Bloody Sabbath* we rehearsed in this really old castle because the regular rehearsal place was booked at the time. We had been in America trying to write *Sabbath Bloody Sabbath* but nothing was working at the time. We felt like we were on the verge of breaking up so we came back to England. After a couple of months we went back to our regular rehearsal place and I think Free were recording there. We had to find an alternative place. They recommended this castle. We had to rehearse in the dungeon of all places."

Continues Butler, arriving at Sabbath's favourite ghost story, "We were in the dungeon playing away and all of a sudden we saw this person walk past the door that had a big black cloak on. We thought, 'What the hell is going on around here?' Tony and one of the roadies ran after the person. They saw him go into this other door at the end of the corridor. They ran after him and they were shouting at him because they thought he was some lunatic that got into the castle. They went into the room where he had gone into and there was nobody in there; he totally disappeared. We asked the owner of the castle about it and he told us, 'Oh that's just a ghost.' Apparently, he was the regular castle ghost. We all saw it. Tony went after him. You couldn't miss him wearing that big black cloak. I went home every night after that."

Tony also tells the tale, saying (slightly counter to Geezer's telling) that the guys were walking down the hall, and that the apparition appeared and turned left into the armoury, the weapons room. When they told the castle keepers about the experience, they not only confirmed that it was the castle's ghost, but they gave it a name. But of course some of the hysteria was conjured by the band themselves. Tony, for example, had specifically strung fishing line in Geoff "Luke" Lucas' room, attaching it to a model ship above the fireplace as well as the curtains, running it under the carpet so he could make it move from outside his door.

Sabbath Bloody Sabbath's stunning, incendiary cover art had Black Sabbath firmly sat back and stroked in Satan's downy, matted lap. "The front of the cover represents a man dying on his deathbed," said Ozzy, to Circus Raves in 1974. "There are all these distorted figures bending over him and gloating as he lies there. These figures are actually him at different stages of his life. He's a man of greed, a man who's wanted everything all his life and done all this evil stuff. But flip the album over, and the back represents the good side of life. The person dying on the bed has been really good to people. He's got all these beautiful people crying over him as he's dying. At the bottom of the bed, he has two tame lions guarding him. All in all, this represents the good and bad of everything."

Geezer has supported the basic premise of this interpretation, calling the artwork yet another in a long line of misunderstood anti-black magic messages from the band.

"Oh no, I thought *Sabbath Bloody Sabbath* was incredible," remarks Bill, on the cover art. "That's one of my favourite all-time album covers. No, I thought that was incredible. On just a personal note, I love the back of that album cover, really nice. I guess if I ever wanted to die, in a certain way, that's how it would be, with all the animals and everything, everybody just around me or whatever."

The cover painting, called *The Rape of Christ*, was done for Pacific Eye and Ear by Drew Struzan who was also responsible for the iconic movie poster art for the first *Star Wars* film, as well as the illustrations for Alice Cooper's *Greatest Hits* and *Welcome to My Nightmare* albums. A reading that approximates the above would make sense, given this vague idea of evil on the front, good on the back. As well, one might look at it as a battle for a man's soul at the point of death, with the demons falling away for a peaceful passing. Also, one might look at it as a case of possession, with good winning out on the back, no death involved whatsoever, but instead, recovery. An interesting and somewhat sinister interpretation has been floated, this idea of the man on the bed being tormented, either by his surrounding loved ones or by a demonic presence, and that what is going on in his head on the back cover, is depicted by the fury of the front. As well, meanings can be ascribed to the sex and age composite of the "watchers," and to the rats and snake on the front as opposed to the translucent God image and the "tame" lions on the back.

The typography for the album was executed by Geoff Halpin, who essentially had touched off a heavy metal firestorm with his slashing Nazi-esque lettering, this and the gothic typeface used on the back cover (and for the tiny band name on the front) becoming prevalent on heavy metal covers for much of the '80s.

On a perhaps amusing but real and personal note, I remember instantly as a young metalhead in the mid-'70s, spotting an optical illusion to the back cover that I've never been able to shake, that of a "headless" man turned away from the viewer, arms extended Christ-like. It works like this: the bottom dark blue rectangle is the "upper butt" of his jeans (the lion's paws could even be pockets), the light blue band above that is a belt, and then all of the orange is the back of a shirt, arms extended to the left and right, hanging down, the collar of the shirt being the area adjacent to the chest of the man on the bed. Get it? In order to see it, you have to essentially ignore all the blue, except for the mystery man's belt and jeans.

I asked Bill if the *Sabbath Bloody Sabbath* cover art fanned the flames of the occult controversy surrounding the band. Indeed, one wonders how Warner Bros. even let it hit the racks.

"Yeah, that was something we lived with all the time and I think it scared a lot of people. It was interesting actually to see what it did do to people. But we really did try in the press, when we did interviews, to really say where we were at and I don't think we did any interviews where we said we were demonic and really go into a black area. As far as I'm concerned, Black Sabbath went into enough black areas anyway that weren't anything to do with being demonic, and it was still Hell as far as I was concerned. We'd certainly been through all of that."

"To be honest with you, the people that I feared the most personally back then—and I don't think this is a very admiring name—you know, back then they were called Jesus freaks, and it's something that's not a particularly nice way of calling people. They're still human beings, you know? But unfortunately they were just caught up in this obsession and I feared them a lot because they could be very violent at the same time. Or individuals could be very violent. And if anybody was going to try to pull a gun and shoot one of us, I'm sure it would have come from there. But there were attempts on our lives over the years, through different sources and things like that. It's not something that happened all the time, but there were some incidents and we were well protected at the time, well policed, and the FBI were involved. But it was the people who believed in Jesus Christ who really bothered me; they really got to me. Only because I feared that they were mental enough to really go over the top."

"We had good and bad, funnily enough, for that album cover," adds Tony. "We won some awards for that cover. And then yes, there was obviously criticism from both sides, really." Again, it's surprising there wasn't more outrage at *Sabbath Bloody Sabbath*'s cover art, but then again, the early '70s was a decadent time in the history of popular culture, and the Satanism craze was all the rage. In fact, Sabbath's new record hit the streets one month prior to the launch of *The Exorcist*, that film fully scaring the hell out of everybody throughout 1974. "I was a big fan of it," muses Geezer. "We all were, but it didn't really filter into the music. It was pretty scary, at the time (laughs). I mean, people running out of the cinema in fear and puking and everything (laughs)."

Also of note, early copies of *Sabbath Bloody Sabbath* (and even later copies in certain territories) were gatefold, with an inner photo depicting the band transparent and naked, arms crossed in front of their faces (Ozzy doesn't quite get it right), in an old, nondescript, typically English house. Somewhat of a link is made to the cover art with there being a bed behind the band, and, I suppose, with the guys being naked. This photo can also be seen in the Castle mini-sleeve CD reissue of the album. Also of note, a lyric insert was included.

Sabbath Bloody Sabbath opened with the album's superlative title track. All sorts of uneasy abstracts revealed themselves with this song. Bill Ward torments the riff in what is actually one of the best illustrations of his "lead drum" playing, his Keith Moon-ness, Tony's summation of the man as more of a percussionist. An urgency verging on desperation is felt, double-underscored by Ozzy's frenetic vocal, the range in which it was housed destined to cause Osbourne grief for years as the oft-requested song would be attempted and dropped in the set, due to it becoming increasingly onerous to sing.

"That was about all the management hassles we were having at the time," explains Geezer on the song's lyric. "And the Sunday Bloody Sunday thing had just happened in Ireland, when the British troops opened fire on the Irish demonstrators. That was known as Sunday Bloody Sunday, but I didn't really want to write about that. So I came up with the title 'Sabbath Bloody Sabbath,' and sort of put it in how the band was feeling at the time, and getting away from management, mixed with the state Ireland was in."

So already you had broken with Patrick Meehan?

"Yeah, that was when we started to get away from him; it was a long process."

Looking back now at Meehan, what are your thoughts on him?

"He's horrible."

Tony contrasts life with Jim Simpson pulling the strings, versus Patrick Meehan. "Oh dear! Well, Jim Simpson, for us, in the early days, he did help us. We had nobody. He used to have a club and he got us rolling, playing at his club, really, a blues club, Henry's Blues House. It was one of those where he started looking after us and helping us, and he became our manager. Which was like having the guy next door to you; 'Oh, he'll be a roadie,' you know? And that's what it was based on. 'Well, Jim, you might as well manage us.' We didn't have anybody else. But Meehan came along with a lot more ideas and a lot more determination to take over the world, as opposed to take over England. And that was the difference. That Meehan had come in with that power at that time to get us out there. But I don't think at that time we realized how big we were becoming. In America the album was in the charts and whatnot, and when we first came to America, like I say, we knew nothing. So it was probably us as well that got us booked around the world, as opposed to us thinking that Patrick Meehan did it, because of the popularity we were building up."

Geezer has also explained that some of the venom of "Sabbath Bloody Sabbath" was directed toward the press, as well as acrimony over the emptiness of fame. It has also been said that the title came from a headline for a story on the band in the UK's influential Melody Maker magazine. Whatever its wellspring, Geezer also was hugely relieved when the dam broke and Tony started writing again, saying that hearing Tony come up with this was like seeing your first child being born.

The band's adversarial relationship with the press was underscored in a conversation Tony had with the NME's Keith Altham at the time. "I really think volume is the key to most of the bad press we've been having," reflects Iommi. "It's just that our generation of fans are used to that much more volume and like it like that. The critics, who are usually older, do not. What they say doesn't hurt us as long as they report the reaction of the audience fairly—after all we are playing to them. They're the ones who've paid to see us, not the journalists with the complimentary tickets."

"We keep our customers satisfied, and I personally believe in Sabbath," continued Tony. "Our fans are a very loyal bunch. I think some of the newer bands like the Sweet, Glitter and Chicory Tip have a much more fickle following. In the States for example we're in the top five groups along with Zeppelin and The Who, but in Britain the critics have kept us out of that ranking. On drawing power and album sales we can compare with groups like Zeppelin and The Who, although we seldom get recognition for the fact."

"I don't know if I was shut down towards the journalists," reflects Bill, years later on those times. "We'd had quite a beating so I think I put up a defense system. I honestly can't remember a lot of the comments that were made by journalists. I'd kind of gone past the point of needing their validation for something that I thought we were doing a really good job."

Musically, "Sabbath Bloody Sabbath" saw Sabbath adding some brave new textures. A daringly dovetailed mellow portion, replete with acoustic guitars, signaled that the rulebook had been ritually burned. Tony's guitar tone is newly driving and dangerous, Iommi adding to the effect with a mercilessly doomy section late in the song, after a freight train of a guitar solo that is musical and composed. During this nightmare, Bill gets truly percussive, a tambourine shakes like a rattlesnake, and Ozzy sings more harrowing than he ever had to doomy date. The song would be the subject of the band's first ever promotional video, in which the guys can be seen wandering through a forest-like scene which in fact turned out to be Geezer's garden.

"We did 'Sabbath Bloody Sabbath' in a castle in Wales, near Tintern Abbey," adds Bill. "I can remember when we did it. As soon as Tony came up with that lick, Terry and I just went full tilt. I mean, Geezer is such a great bass player; he just puts it where it's supposed to go, you know? I immediately went to the toms and I just love the power of the song. I think we did a good recording of it, but live, man, it was just so powerful. The lyric 'Bog blast all of you'... it's just such a neat way of saying screw you, because it's used in such a polite terminology. It absolutely got the point across. It's very difficult to pinpoint. Privately—and it's not very private anymore—but I've always referred to him as The Irish Poet. And I kind of romanticize like that when I think of him, because his descendancy is Irish. Sometimes I see him as this kind of almost impish, Irish, vagabond writer, lyricist, which is a nice way of looking at him."

Next up was "A National Acrobat," a malevolent arch-Sabbath track with a vague psychedelic feel to its lope, especially come its murky wah-wah moment. The song breaks into a caterwaul of a jam with all manner of layering, demonstrating again that this was a newly sophisticated Sabbath at work. There's a twin lead riff, doubled vocals from Ozzy with echo added, an extra percussion track, and then the aforementioned Latin break which recalls the jam from "Supernaut."

"'A National Acrobat,' Geezer came up with a riff in that," recalls Tony, "which I thought was really good. And we were starting to... we hadn't swapped ideas much before; it was always me who came up with the ideas. Certainly for *Sabbath Bloody Sabbath*... Geezer, you see, always felt a bit embarrassed to play me any of his material. That's the way he was. Really, it was silly, but he had this thing in his head, 'Oh, I can't play it to you.' And one day, I made him—'Come on, you've got to play; come up with something. It shouldn't be me all the time.' And he did, and he'd gotten some good stuff, Geezer. You know, he's had music that he's had way back 'til then, that he's still never, ever done anything with. He's had some stuff, and I've got loads of stuff, stuff that has never seen the light of day, really. I would hope one day it will."

Geezer confirms Tony's assessment of the situation. "Here and there I used to come up with stuff, but it's hard to do when you're in the studio and you've just got your bass. And every time I played a guitar, everybody would bust themselves laughing. And I used to feel intimidated, so I wouldn't play it. That's why I love it now. I can just do whatever the hell I like. But yes, I wrote 'A National Acrobat;' I did that whole thing at home. And Tony came over to the house one day and I just played it to him, rather than in a group situation."

As alluded to, the other guys had their own confidence problems to deal with. "I think Ozzy was never sure about his lyrics, which is why he always delegated them to me. The thing is, with Sabbath, we were like, whatever instrument you started out on, that's what you are expected to play, and never move from that. I mean, it took Ozzy a long time to play 'Who Are You,' for instance, on his Moog, for us. And the same as Bill; when he used to play 'It's Alright' on the piano, he came to us and he would say, 'I'm thinking about...' You have to say, 'I'm doing this as a solo album' (laughs), and hope that somebody would go, 'Oh yeah, that would be a good Sabbath track.'"

I mentioned this solo album talk to Bill, and asked him if he had ever seriously gotten that itch. "Yeah, in fact, what I had hoped, what my dream was, because there are a lot of different songs that were showing up, which might not necessarily be what one would call Black Sabbath, so right in the middle of it all, I know one of the ideas that I was pretty firm on, was for us all to do solo albums, but never touch the mother ship. In other words, guide the mother ship with our lives, still carry on with Black Sabbath, and put Black Sabbath songs in Black Sabbath, but at the same time, allow ourselves to do solo albums. I thought that would be a great way of using any pressure of trying to pack a lot of stuff into a Sabbath album."

"Geezer had a lot of stuff," continues Ward. "I would just sit there for hours listening to what he had, and I was just blown away. I just thought, oh my God, the stuff was so great, and it's just his own private... and in one sense it's like, well, this is where we are. There's always that internal argument, if you like; this is where he is in his private life—this is where Geezer is now. And if this is where we are, then surely we ought to show this truth in a Sabbath album. But the truth is that when we do get together, we pretty much like to rock. I love showing up and kicking the crap out of me drum kit. It's the only chance I get to play drums, because I don't play drums with any other band. But yeah, Geezer's stuff was great.

I used to listen to Tony's stuff, jazz, piano playing, all kinds of stuff! And I thought, oh my God, this is just really good stuff."

Told that Geezer said that he had a problem presenting stuff, because when he would, he would sort of get laughed out of the room, Bill says, "I know we would joke around a lot, and sometimes the jokes would hurt. Because, yeah, I know I would bring things forward and kind of like wait for the rebuttal. It's not like it was boo-hooed or anything, but yeah, bringing something that is vulnerable to three other guys who are just... you never know what kind of mood they're in that day. So I can totally appreciate Geezer saying that."

And he also said he was a little hesitant about playing guitar in front of the guys. "Oh yeah, I'm sure that's true as well, if he said that, yeah. I mean, I'm not that aware of it now. I mean, he originally started out as a guitarist anyway. Geezer changed to being a bass player after the first gig we did as Polka Tulk Blues Band. But yeah, my hope, or my dream, if you like would have been for Black Sabbath to remain with some hardcore rock and hardcore music, and allow all the things that we couldn't do in a Black Sabbath record to come out on solo albums. That was my thinking way back in 1975. But it was an idea that was a pipe dream, if you like. It never came to fruition. And sometimes I think it was kind of like a scary proposition to us. 'Yeah, but if we have a solo album, maybe that might tear the band apart.'"

"'National Acrobat' was about sperm," continues Geezer, addressing the album's reptilian second track. "It's just about what happens to all those spermatozoa—

is that what they're called?—the ones that don't make it to the egg. It's like it's their big moment inside this ejaculation or whatever, and nothing happens to them. It's like, what could've been? All those sperms will never meet the egg and turn into people (laughs). But I loved *Sabbath Bloody Sabbath*. I mean, I loved the first three, but they were almost done unconsciously (laughs) in every sense of the word. Lyrically I really like 'National Acrobat' and 'Spiral Architect,' my two favourite lyrics; and 'After Forever' as well."

And Bill's assessment? "I couldn't even imagine 'National Acrobat' on the album *Black Sabbath*. But that's where we were going to; these were the progressions. We were changing and very much taking risks. And if that's a bad thing or a good thing, one can only debate for the next hundred years, but it was what we had to do at the time."

"Fluff" followed, with Tony turning in an uneasy acoustic track, again, beautiful in a morbid manner, the song being so incredibly mellow that none could see it as anything but ironic. This was not the band being pretty, this was Sabbath playing a practical joke. Tony is credited with acoustic and steel guitars, as well as piano and harpsichord. The song begins with Tony building to three tracks of acoustic guitar. Then piano and bass are added, along with simple George Harrison-like electric licks. The harpsichord makes an appearance at the end, although it's hard to hear, given the similarity in texture to the most defined and crisp of the acoustic guitar parts. The title is a reference to British Radio 1 DJ Alan "Fluff" Freeman, Tony essentially thanking Freeman, who was a fan and used to use "Laguna Sunrise" as theme music on The Saturday Rock Show.

Closing out side one was "Sabbra Cadabra," a curious track that rocked hard but sounded oddly earthly, a bit conventional, with touchstones in blues and boogie. "That was our one love song we ever wrote," laughs Geezer. "We were probably all stoned out of our heads at the time." Geezer has also said that it was about a girlfriend he had at the time, and that the original lyric had to do with Ozzy cracking up over and repeating the English voiceovers from some German porn that had been worked on in the studio Sabbath now found themselves.

"Sabbra Cadabra" closes with another interesting, high relief jam, Ozzy 's voice captured hauntingly, Tony reprising his "Changes" and "Fluff" roles by tinkling the ivories, Rick Wakeman from Yes joining in as well. "I just did mini-Moog on two tracks," notes Wakeman. "'Sabbra Cadabra' was one of them. I did the mini-Moog on that at 1:00 in the morning one day. That was done at Morgan Studios, in London. It was exactly the same week we were doing *Topographic Oceans*."

"He was great," recalls Butler. "I mean, the whole thing was just totally accidental anyway. It just happened that Yes were in one studio and we were in the other, in the same complex. And I think he wasn't very happy as far as the rest of the members of Yes, and he would come over and spend time with us, hanging out in the bar and stuff. We were a lot more sociable than them. It just came about; he just ended up playing on the album."

"We liked Morgan Studios a lot, and we went there a number of times," adds Bill, leading to the meeting with Rick. "We used to meet people all the time there. Yes were in and out of there all the time. Ronnie Wood and Charlie Watts would come down and I used to play darts with Charlie (laughs). There's a nice little bar there. And of course, that's where we bumped into Rick Wakeman and we ended up with 'Sabbra Cadabra.' We became good friends with Rick. It was almost like Rick was part of our band but he was still with Yes. I don't know how that worked out (laughs)."

"It was fantastic," says Geezer, concerning having Rick involved. "He was a great bloke. He was a really nice person. The way it came about was Yes were in one studio, in Morgan Studios; they were in studio two or whatever it was, and we were in studio three. And we were trying to work this keyboard part out for ages. All of us were trying to play it, Tony was trying to play it, and it just didn't sound right. And there was a bar in Morgan Studios and we were in the bar and Rick Wakeman came in. Before that, because Ozzy didn't really get on with the people in Yes, we went over and threw about a hundred stink bombs into their air conditioner while they were recording and nearly gassed them all. So they were all out in the road getting all the fumes out of their studio and Rick Wakeman was in the bar. So we were in the bar trying to figure out how to do this keyboard bit. So we were talking to Rick, asking his advice, and he said, 'Well, what are you trying to do?' And he came into the studio and was like, 'You mean like this?' (mimes playing keyboards). And we went, 'Yeah! That's it!' So we got him in and he did the keyboard parts."

"First of all Rick's a good friend of ours, and so is his son, Adam," explains Bill. "So the Wakemans are like family. We initially met him with Yes and we got on very, very well to the point where on tour Rick spent more time with us than I think he did Yes at certain points. And we all loved his playing, so obviously the day came when we wanted him to come play something there. It was like okay, well we've got this song and it all sounds okay, more like a huge jam but really well done. So Rick I think enhanced the music. And I'm glad that we went through that. I'm glad that we played with other artists on our records, especially keyboard players. It allowed us to say okay, we've got this song, let's do it this way. So instead of being inside some very scared place about oh, we can't do that, we're changing it too much, we had to smash through a lot of what we might have originally been."

Officially, Rick is credited only on "Sabbra Cadabra," with Tony and Ozzy being credited with the synthesizer work on "Killing Yourself to Live," Geezer and Ozzy on "Who Are You." Tony says that Rick refused to accept pay for his work, so he was remunerated with beer. Also on the subject of credits, Spock Wall is thanked prominently on the back cover.

"Spock Wall, a big help he was," confirms Tony. "All around, he was great. Spock was with us from the very early days. We brought him in as a tech, really, to do guitars. And eventually he was doing the mixing, and he had become really good at it. But he was like an extra member; he was so, so helpful, and a great help in the studio."

Back at "Sabbra Cadabra," Rick can be heard in the quite progressive break section marked by Ozzy screeching "lovely lady," which, given this vintage quote from Bill in Circus magazine, might have ended up as the title to the song (the band ultimately decided it was a little light for a Sabbath title). "We're getting into things which we relate to now. We're not fed-up or angry young men anymore. We're getting into much happier things now. On our new album, we're into songs like 'Lovely Lady.' We're actually talking about women, which is something we haven't gotten into before. With a lot of other groups, everything they do is related to women. It's hard to describe the album in detail. The title track's about big brother. It's a revolution song. We're having a knock at society. There's a lot of things that could be straightened out in it."

In the same interview to promote the release of the album, Ozzy mused that Sabbath "don't ever try to say we're a bloody downer rock band or anything. We just play music. For the past three years, all I've read about is the same old thing. We come from Birmingham, hard town, and we're a hard band and all that bull. It makes you sick. It's all too exaggerated. The *Master of Reality* album I didn't like at all. It was too rushed and the sleeve was a load of nonsense. It was done so quickly, in three weeks, and even the bloody sleeve had been printed. We didn't have the chance to do what we wanted to do. The first album was even worse. We did that in just two days! You know the Led Zeppelin second album, the one with all those incredible tracks? Well that was what we wanted for our album, but all we got was flat sounds. After the *Master* album, we said screw all of them, we'll do it ourselves. We didn't want to feel like we were putting out a load of bull. And we were pissed-off with people telling us what to do. We didn't start out saying we were going to conquer the world; that's a load of bull. We're trying to achieve quality. It's nice to do something different every now and then, and this LP we've just done has some nice melodic things on it."

Tony was in agreement. "It's probably less aggressive and raw than in the old days. The theme is wider too, and I think that with the passage of time, we've improved as musicians. Yeah, it's widening out."

"Sabbra Cadabra" closes with one of Sabbath's most freeform jams, carried on because the guys were having so much fun with Rick Wakeman. Tony says that Ozzy was ranting in the background, spewing various profanities including "Stick it up yer arse." After hearing it, it was decided to push Oz way back in the mix and put heavy phasing on his voice as to make his wisdoms unintelligible.

Opening side two is another Sabbath classic, "Killing Yourself to Live" possessing some of the inky blackness of "A National Acrobat," its synth pattern under the verse being almost as prominent as Tony's secret agent man riff. The chorus is all Sabbatherian power and might, the band collapsing in a pool of doom, Ozzy again forced to hit notes that would later cause him trouble. Bill's drumming is recorded exquisitely and powerfully, and Ward rises to the occasion with a groovy performance and spirited snaps at the snare. Come the solo section, Tony fires off two competing guitar solos, one to the left channel and one to the right, no rhythm bed. Then it's one solo over a rhythm track, then, briefly, two solos and a rhythm track. Supporting, one supposes, all this talk of the album being proggy, at the "Smoke it" signal, there's a new section (with synth), featuring Ozzy singing full unison with Tony's guitar licks. Then there's a completely new, fast third section that features Tony playing two independent guitar solos at once, with a fast left/right panning action uniting them.

As Tony told Keith Altham back in the day, "One of the best tracks is 'Killing Yourself to Live,' which is pretty much how we were beginning to feel after flogging around the States for the umpteenth time. We all started to fall over and get ill, and that's why we've been out of action since December. It was just the travelling and the food—nervous exhaustion really. We'd been working solidly for about three years. We've been established now for nearly four, you know, and we hadn't had a real break."

"These last few months have given us time to take stock and I think the band is changing slightly," continued Iommi. "The more evil and malevolent aspects of the first two albums have been replaced by a more aggressive but less sinister approach. We were never really into black magic or anything like that, but I think we were the first of the really committed loud and heavy bands. We just decided to go all out and let go. It worked and we've stuck to that policy. In America they seem to think we have the same kind of appeal as a horror movie. It's basically an act. Apart from the fact that I look after a management agency with a friend of mine up North—we handle bands like Budgie, Judas Priest and Necromandus—I don't listen to a lot of heavy music. I've got a few tapes of Deep Purple in the car but I prefer to listen to things like Peter, Paul and Mary, Sinatra, the Moody Blues and the Carpenters. We played a much more jazz-influenced music before we hit our present formula, but I get more satisfaction out of what we do now. If it all finished tomorrow I could never join another group after Sabbath. I'd just carry on as a producer or with my agency and give up playing."

"For some reason I just keep thinking of Ozzy when you said that," notes Bill, asked about the song. "I remember when he was first doing the vocals, it seemed like a really angry song." Adds Geezer, "'Killing Yourself to Live' was just about the rigors of the road and going through all the management problems we were having at the time. It just seemed like everything we were doing was going to line the manager's pocket, doing all this and seeing nothing for it." Geezer has also said that the song is about the boredom of hotel rooms, and in those waiting areas, doing too many drugs, or coming down hard off those same drugs, again adding that the situation was made all the more irritating and stressful by the siphoning off of the band's money at the hands of corrupt management.

Ozzy, when the album was but a month old, saw it quite differently. "Everybody is so governed by what they hear on television. Look at Watergate and all. It's hard not to be sensitive to what you hear and read about all around you. One night I was at home watching TV, when I heard some really bad news about people getting their heads blown off, and it was getting very frightening and sickening. So I started writing the lyrics to a song called 'Killing Yourself to Live,' which just about sums up the bloody state of affairs around us. The song is about people who are born to do just one thing in life, and then they die. They don't even care about trying something else. I personally believe that people are here for a reason, not to do what someone's telling them all of their life. I think that's why so many mindless acts are committed. It's like that painting of the man on the bad side of the album. You can give to people all of your life, but they'll never give to you. I guess it's just selfishness."

Subtitles for "Killing Yourself to Live" have been added on some issues of *Sabbath Bloody Sabbath*, namely "You Think that I'm Crazy" and "I Don't Know if I'm Up or I'm Down."

Sabbath really step outside the box for the record's next track, "Who Are You," which lives, loves and dies on the strength of a synth riff, although rhythm accompaniment is added to this rare Ozzy Osbourne contribution. The lyric charts typical Sabbatherian exasperation at religious issues, the narrator stung, like any misunderstood and outcast metalhead, by the workings of the world, asking an omnipotent being—God or the Devil—what in the hell do you want from me?

"Yeah, that's a total Ozzy song," says Geezer. "He'd just bought a Moog synthesizer, one of the first ones, and it was just like monophonic, so you could play with one finger, so he put that together and wrote the lyrics. And it was fine, so we just left it like that."

"When we did 'Who Are You,' I think that was Ozzy who was playing it," notes Bill. "Because when Oz originally came down to Fields Farm, he drove down overnight from his house, and fuckin' 6:00 in the morning, me and the wife are fast asleep, and he's a pretty loud guy, you know, and the door bursts open and it's like, 'Hey!' And I'm like, 'Oh God, it's him this time in the morning.' And he just set it all up, man. And the next thing you know, he's singing 'Who Are You' and he did the vocals and he double-tracked himself in our hallway, because it was a big farmhouse, so the hallway had a good reverberation of its own. And I was just in bed listening to him put it together and I thought, 'My God. What an incredible fucking song.'"

Geezer is also credited with Mellotron on "Who Are You," with Tony indicating that he himself played piano on the track. "It's about the song," continues Bill. "So it's like what instrument will make this song and enhance this song? So the Mellotron came out and that's where we would do that a lot. I still do that a lot today with my own music: what will suit the song? Sabbath took a lot of risks like that where we would look and go, well what might suit this is a string quartet or this or that, so we would go and get that and hopefully that would work. So that's how those sounds would come about, finding out what's going to go with Ozzy, the way things change. I don't think we could have picked better instrumentation. It's played very low on the piano, very sad notes, and Ozzy's voice and low notes on piano are absolutely a sound unto themselves. It's such a good match, so it makes a perfect musical picture. So I think Sabbath had that ability to be able to pick the right instruments."

"And we had the luxury of being in the studio," continues Ward. "We could afford to be in the studios and I think that played a huge part. We had idle hands, if you like. Being in the studio we had access to so much more. 'Well let's use this.' I can't see how we could have gone back down the tunnel and just played… well, there were songs that would come out where it was very much like those three or four first albums, but then we would go into something else where it just seemed like the right place to go. I mean, I've listened to Tony's melodic playing on piano, and Geezer wrote such incredible songs by himself. Ozzy had all kinds of really nice melodies and things, so there was almost like a departure from the departure. And at home we were going into different places, however when we came together it was as you understand it. It was as the world understands us."

Ozzy, speaking in 1974, called "Who Are You" the story of a person who is "confused about everything and didn't know who to trust. You can say that person was sort of like me. I wrote that number at home between bouts of insomnia. I couldn't sleep. I bought this synthesizer and all day and night I would fiddle around with it to keep me busy."

"Looking for Today" serves as a metaphor for this album as a whole, Sabbath, through this track's verse riff, finding a way to synthesize (no pun intended) their harder rock with overt melody, as well as integrating their challenging new palette of instruments into their central guitar/bass/drums format. On "Looking for Today," out of nowhere, the band plays acoustically, popping along at the same speed as the harder verse section, flutes even added to the mix. Then there's the chorus, which stood out as Ozzy's most sing-songy vocal melody to date. Bill turns in an interesting military march pattern for the verse and then grooves deliciously when we get to the melodic, descending riff chorus. A second track of drums is added for fill purposes come the lush close-out of this brave and under-rated Sabbath classic. Also of interest, the actual chorus doesn't arrive until after two verses and after the two shots at the elaborate acoustic pre-chorus. After the chorus comes a third verse, which collapses straight into another round of the chorus. Here's where we get a bit of soloing, along with the percussion augmentation, placed hard left and hard right specific to the drum.

Lyrically, Geezer offers that "I think that was about all these up-and-coming bands who thought they were brilliant and lasted for like about a week," although Ozzy, on the press trail at the time, contradicts Geezer's modern-day account. "The album was written in a very rural area, like a piece of nothingness, a void. I remember one night, I just picked up the newspaper, and that inspired me to write. One paper told how somebody had gotten blown up in Ireland and another paper I picked up told how somebody was blowing up a jumbo jet. There was trouble at the London airport, and all kinds of crap. I thought to myself, 'Well, what's it all about?' These people don't even know why they're doing these things. I guess that's the way I feel. Tomorrow comes and comes, but we're all still looking for today, searching for something that's passed us by."

Settling heavy metal accounts, "Looking for Today" was slightly pop, "Fluff" a full-on baroque acoustic, and indeed, as discussed, mellow bits sprung up like spring flowers in various other incongruous spots on *Sabbath Bloody Sabbath*. But the band was to end this boldly presumptuous album with what would be their most serious soft rock track ever, "Spiral Architect" sounding like the Moody Blues, albeit of a forceful, darkly pensive mood, orchestrated to the brim by Will Malone and "The Phantom Fiddlers."

"I had just moved into a new house in England," offers Geezer on the writing of this track, a process which happened quickly after fully three months of gestation. "And when we were recording *Sabbath Bloody Sabbath* in England, we used to commute back home on the weekend, and I'd just couldn't come up with the lyrics for 'Spiral Architect.' I was trying and trying but nothing was happening. So I got back to me new house about 6:00 in the morning, and it used to have these two great big pine trees in the front garden. And I went there and sat between these two pine trees and I was just watching the sun come up and I just started writing those lyrics. And it sort of wrote itself. It was like looking at the earth and knowing it was good and all that kind of thing. It was really good."

Bill takes credit for the chorus of the song, having piped up as having written some of the lyrics and the melodies at that juncture. "I came up with the title," notes Bill. "What was neat about that is that Geezer got that straight away. He liked the title and was able to work with it. I wrote the verses in that: 'Of all the things…' I wrote those parts and Geezer wrote the other parts."

Also of note, contrary to the credits, neither Tony nor anybody else plays bagpipes on the track, as Tony couldn't squeeze anything out of the instrument. Says Iommi, "During recording, you sometimes get these brain waves. 'Oh yes, let's do that.' We wanted this drone on a track, and I bought some bagpipes. I had this Scottish guy send them out. I started puffing on them and couldn't get a thing out of them. Nothing. So I sent them back and said they were broke. He sent them back and said that they were okay. I tried again. Nothing. I even got to the stage where I was going to hook them up to a vacuum cleaner, to see if it had got the wind. It was disastrous. They sit in the cupboard now."

At first the guys also tried to play the classical bits themselves. Geezer and Tony got a violin and a cello and thought they'd saw out some simple parts and multi-track them. But the sounds they got were deemed horrendous and it was quickly decided they'd get a proper orchestra in, one that is elaborately featured on the track, especially at the conclusion. Which in fact is not a conclusion—the band pull another castle trick, and begin what sounds like another song, accompanied, oddly by applause, an idea put forth by engineer Mike Butcher. But then again the vibe created by the clapping, and the fact that the ensuing piece is a sort of laid-back instrumental… the end effect is one of outro music at a concert.

So there you have it, Black Sabbath had turned in a record that fans might—and did—compare to Led Zeppelin *III*, despite Ozzy's earlier aversions to having that sort of record come out of his band. In essence, Sabbath were admirably above caring about things as base as weighing their records for heaviness. Or at least at this juncture they were. They were looking to prove themselves as artists, but one suspects, they were just as much looking to father some music that wasn't so hard on the bloody ears. And this shouldn't have been surprising. Despite, almost by accident, playing bookshelves of volumes of pages of heavy metal, as we've heard from Tony, the guys didn't listen to it. When you *are* it—and indeed when there was none before you to grow up on, drink your first beer to, shag your first bird to—where would you have gone to get it? Surely not your contemporaries. Who had time for that? When they're working, we're working and all that. No, bottom line, because Black Sabbath were making it themselves, there was no point listening to other bands making it.

So Sabbath did what they did best, randomly firing off on tangents, experimenting, jamming, picking up weird instruments, using everything, and almost as pertinently, balancing the topical and conceptual with touchdowns upon the drama of their own lives. And that's what we got with *Sabbath Bloody Sabbath*, an exotic amalgamation of the experiences of four lives lived fast and furious with a sense of the surreal inevitably popping out at the seams.

But *Sabbath Bloody Sabbath* included so many fake-outs, there really weren't any seams. Somehow the album came off as heavy, the biggest fake-out being its torrid emotional force, so at least it seemed heavy enough that there wasn't a massive revolt from the fans. As a further fake-out, the big and lasting songs from the record were the impossibly leaden rockers, the title track being launched as a single (and sinking like a stone), before it would become a (short-lived) live favourite, along with "Killing Yourself to Live." Chart-wise, *Sabbath Bloody Sabbath* outpaced its predecessor in both the UK and America, hitting #4 at home, where it stayed for 11 weeks (as mentioned, *Vol 4* peaked at #8) and #11 in the States, where *Vol 4* managed a #13 placement. *Sabbath Bloody Sabbath*, like *Vol 4*, currently sits at platinum status in the States.

Wrote Wayne Robbins, reviewing the album for Creem back in April of '74, "The question, Sabs, is where have you been so long? So highly irresponsible was their disappearing act over a year ago that heavy metal almost vanished from the face of the earth. Unlike every other gang of electric warriors, Black Sabbath alone retains ultimate dignity. Would they ever let Todd Rundgren produce them to get a hit record? You know that answer. Would they ever do a reggae to get some cheap airplay, like Jimmy Page and the Blimp that Pissed in the Continental Hyatt House? No way, man. The Sabs got integrity."

"Finally, salvation," continues Robbins. "*Sabbath Bloody Sabbath* is here, and you know, they didn't let us down. Even if when you put it on, and get engrossed in conversation for what seems like a half hour, you find out the first song is still going. Even if we had extended discussions with authorities when they found this kid in my English class on the sidewalk, having splattered in the parking lot from the third floor of our school. He did say that 'Spiral Architect' was 'Kahlil Gibran for Satanists,' didn't he? The dude's lucky he can still drink through a straw."

"No questions asked of the Sabs, though. They've been too busy making their most ambitious album to date. There is actually a chord change on 'Who Are You' and a certain amount of melodic inventiveness that some of the more Cro-Magnon-esque elements of Sab culture might have a hard time dealing with. The most difficult aspect of all this to relate to is the appearance of Yes' Rick Wakeman on some kinda screwy keyboard. You know what that smells like to me: attempted artistic achievement, and if the Sabs ever fall for that, they're sunk."

With respect to its launch, *Sabbath Bloody Sabbath* was issued in the UK in November of '73 and North America two months later. But at the time, there were reports that a vinyl shortage, due to the OPEC oil crisis, had delayed its issue, the more immediate source of this shortage having to do with Alice Cooper's hotly anticipated *Billion Dollar Babies* taking priority over at Warners.

Alice Cooper bassist Dennis Dunaway laughs when told that story. "You know what? If you ever talk to Warner Bros., anytime we were ready to go back into the studio, they would say, 'Oh, your career is over; you guys are washed up.' And we would have to fight tooth and nail to keep things going with the record company. I liked Warner Bros.; that was just the way they did business. They always made you feel like you were on your way out. I don't think they could believe that we sustained. Maybe that was a realistic point of view on their part. But yes, the price of oil went up, and yes, we were on the road, and there was the trucker's strike, because of the high cost of fuel. We had two semis on that tour, and whenever they would pull into the gas station, there would be all of these picketers, truckers picketing, and then they'd have to tell them, 'Oh man, this is for a band, rock 'n' roll' and everything, and then they supposedly—this is what I heard—they would be allowed to fuel up. But we had a few gigs where we had makeshift staging. And vinyl was threatening to be outdated, even though it did come back briefly before CDs took over."

Dennis adds a memory of Alice Cooper playing with Sabbath, rarer than one would expect, given shared label and stylistic similarities. "I do remember a gig where the bill was Black Sabbath and Alice Cooper headlined, and there was this opening band that nobody had ever heard of. And I remember walking into the arena and seeing the audience, basically people socializing and finding their seats, and this band was on stage that I thought, 'Oh man, we've got to follow these guys?' And it was Yes. And I was thinking, geez, these guys are playing so good and nobody is paying any attention to them (laughs). But yeah, I know that we played a lot of festivals where we were on the same bill, but that was the only gig that I can remember that was an actual concert-type lineup. We were pretty much running independently in those days."

Black Sabbath indeed had played many dates with Yes in 1971 and in 1972, and it's been said that Tony had been inspired by the band to expand their sound, hence the instrumental layering and progressive flourishes on *Sabbath Bloody Sabbath*, even if Ozzy said that the two bands didn't like each other and were worlds apart. The fact that Rick Wakeman lent his services was just a bit of serendipity.

Sabbath's tour for the album began in December of '73 in England with a brief trip to the continent in January before mounting a major American assault in February. Playing through April, Sabbath had on board a diverse selection of bands, including James Gang, Blue Öyster Cult, Lynyrd Skynyrd and Bedlam, whose drummer was future Rainbow and Sabbath member Cozy Powell. With respect to the band's touring set list, Sabbath tapped their latest album for "Killing Yourself to Live," "A National Acrobat" and "Sabbra Cadabra," with the title track to the record noticeably absent. A recording of 'Fluff' was played as a chill-out outro at the end of the show. In contrast, four songs from *Vol 4* were still part of the band's set list at that time. It is said that "Who Are You" was attempted then knocked on its head because temperature fluctuations caused problems with the Mellotron crucial to the track.

The US leg was capped off with a whirlwind stop at the first California Jam, April 6, 1974, which attracted to the Ontario Motor Speedway a crowd of a quarter million soon-to-be sunburned, who, in addition to the Sabs, got to see Earth, Wind & Fire, Rare Earth, The Eagles, Seals & Croft and Black Oak Arkansas, who would tag along as Sabbath played UK dates in May. Headliners for the event were Deep Purple and Emerson, Lake and Palmer, ELP's name held back until late in the game for suspense purposes. The headliners played for 90 minutes apiece, while Sabbath put in a 70-minute set. Sabbath had actually pulled out, over ELP's and Purple's carping over who was going to close the show. But Tony changed his mind, at the insistence of Spock Wall, and the guys were quickly on a plane, not having rehearsed and not having played a gig in weeks.

Organizer of Cal Jam, Don Branker, had this to say when asked by the author why he had put British hard rock bands like Deep Purple and Black Sabbath at the top of his bill.

"At the time, rock had been going through a change, a massive change, as more or less the British acts were coming back again. Our music here in America had sunk to the point of country rock. You had The Eagles, more folk like James Taylor, Carole King, but then comes this sound. Led Zeppelin, of course, lead it. Then came Deep Purple and Black Sabbath and it just fit for our audience. What we needed, in order to draw a crowd of a quarter of a million people, we needed an audience that would go through Hell and high water, if you will, to get to the event.

So by putting the English bands on it and some of the younger acts on it, it drove a crowd of 250,000 people there. And that was at their peak, too, by the way. If you look back in time, both of them, that was their high. Of course Ozzy's come back in more ways than one."

"Also on the show was Emerson, Lake and Palmer. There were three English acts on the show, but the real draw was Deep Purple and Black Sabbath. And their strength was amongst the youngsters—when I say youngsters, I'm talking about your 18-25-year-olds. They were primarily English-oriented here in America; they loved that sound. They didn't want the country sound, they didn't want the folk sound. They wanted that hard-driving music that Sabbath and Purple gave them."

"The English had dominated album sales with Uriah Heep, T Rex, Zeppelin and of course Sabbath and Purple and ELP," continues Branker. "That's really what we're talking about is album sales, not The Carpenters or those types with singles sales. Then the transition came as all of a sudden American bands started rocking harder with Nugent, Aerosmith of course, Heart and Foreigner. Those bands mostly had their first albums out at that point. But it's hard to capture that hard rock sound on vinyl that you can capture live, where it's not pre-mixed, it's not sweetened. It's the rawness of what heavy metal is about. It's taking those melodic chords, distorting them, turning up an amp from ten to 11 and making it distort even more so the kids not only hear it but they feel it."

"It was the most incredibly well-organized gig that I've seen," said Ozzy in July of '75. "There were no pigs, no busts; everything had a backup system to it so there were no delays. The PA was the biggest that I'd ever seen; you could probably hear it in the next state. It was the first gig that we played in a few months, and I got so high from it all. Going on stage and seeing people as far as the eye could see, just an ocean of people. I can't completely explain the feeling I got from it all."

Grossing $2M (advance tickets were $10), nonetheless not much profit was to be had by the promoters, although TV rights and a simulcast were part of the deal. It is said that the biggest glitch on the day was when 100,000 cardboard sun visors were dropped from a helicopter, with most being carried by the wind away from where the crowd stood baking in the hot California sun. Traffic was hell, with cars being abandoned on the freeway (over 700 were later towed), even though once weary walkers got to the event, the parking lot was half empty. As well, approximately 30,000 fans knocked down fencing and crashed the event. Still, the paid attendance figure of 168,000 beat out Woodstock, Altamont and Watkins Glen, even though those festivals had much bigger crowd counts in the aggregate. The second and last Cal Jam was to occur in 1978, and is better remembered, due to a double gatefold live album that was issued commemorating the event.

Curiously, the press in late '74 spoke of *Sabbath Bloody Sabbath*'s follow-up being delayed to make room for… the first Ozzy Osbourne solo album, provisionally titled *Am I Going Insane?*. But ultimately all was well with the band. After all, Ozzy's three mates were helpfully scheduled to appear on the record.

Rock journo legend Steven Rosen caught up with the band on tour in the States, where Ozzy confided in him, letting on that the Sabbath guys were "the biggest hypochondriacs you'd ever met in your life. We must have spent most of our earnings on doctor's fees. It was like, 'I've got a pain—go to bed for three days.' And all it was was fucking indigestion from eating too much Chinese food from the night before. Or, 'I've got cancer.' We'd say, 'Sure you have.' We always said, 'If I die, bury me in England.'"

"Bill Ward used to have a bag so full… I mean, it got to the point that we went on the road one time and he even had a snakebite kit. I said, 'Where the fuckin' hell are you ever going to see a snake? Where on this earth are you ever going to see one? Or are you going to fucking drive to a zoo or something?' He says, 'You never know because some of these snakes run pretty fast when you're driving across the desert.' I mean, if the snake ever bit him, the snake doesn't have a fucking chance. We used to call him Dr. Bill and Valiums Forever. If you had anything wrong with you, you'd just go and see Bill. He was fucking full of them—he had things for everything. I mean when he came up with that snakebite kit, it was like the ultimate. I'd never seen one of those things. He had a big old razor like your dad might have, and I said, 'What if it bites you up the ass, Bill?' He said, 'Somebody's going to have to suck the poison out.' I said, 'Don't come to me, man. Find a new friend to help you.'"

On a more serious note, addressing how Sabbath got to become who they became, Ozzy told Steven, "We got sick and tired of all the bullshit. Love your brother and flower power forever. We brought things down to reality. Our songs had real things behind them, which I think people wanted at the time. We didn't go out to say that we were the best musical or technical band in the world. We were just ornery backstreet guys who learned to play guitars, drums and sing. Suburban rock. Slum rock. We used to jam and play a few gigs together. We wrote original music and it worked. I had gone to school with Tony and I was working in a semiprofessional group with Geezer called Rare Breed. Then we all formed and met and we chose Black Sabbath as a name. I mean, we didn't plan it and expect it to make such a profit as it did. It's just one of those great things in life. We tried to put music over in a different angle. It had an evil sound, a heavy doom sound. And then there were all these fucking witches and freaks phoning us, wanting us to play at black masses and all this crap."

After a break in the schedule, November saw the band hit Australia, where a wee act by the name of AC/DC would back the mighty Sabs. Recalls Tony, "The first time they ever played with us was in Australia, and I thought it was some young kid on the guitar. I thought it was a schoolboy. 'Bloody 'ell, he's good for like a nine-year-old,' you know. I looked up, because I hadn't seen him before, and I just looked on the stage, because it was an outdoor show, and I saw this kid with a satchel on his back. Bloody 'ell, he only looks about nine. From where I was standing. But of course when you get closer you realize he wasn't. But they were good, a good rock band. They were all a bit wild, I think. They did actually come on tour with us in Europe, and ooh, they were big drinkers, all of them. We both got a bit outrageous, sometimes, I suppose."

"I have extremely fond memories of Australia," regales Bill. "I did manage to see a little bit more than the other fellers did and that was just purely because I wanted to discover Australia. I went to several Aboriginal villages—and it's always imprinted on my mind—and I saw how the Aborigines lived, at least the Aborigines that I saw, and I was reminded of some of the living conditions that I've seen North American Indians living in, here in the United States. I visited some of the rainforests and I traveled through the northeast coast. I remember seeing miles and miles of incredible blue ocean; I mean literally hundreds of miles, no towns, hundreds and hundreds of miles of blue ocean and white sand. I thought it was just amazing, a little bit overwhelming actually."

"I remember stopping off at one shack in the road—I guess it was a bar or something—and man, I had the time of my life there. At that time obviously I was drinking alcoholically so it was nothing for me to drink the place out (laughs) and I was with one or two Australian gentlemen who could certainly drink too, so I had some good piss-ups. I stopped at some real hole-in-the-wall places, just some old trees outside and sandy roads and a scruffy old bar and you'd just go in there and spit on the floor and put your ass up to the bar. I would've drunk many, many, many schooners. I had a lot of fun down there."

"The band at that point were definitely in their hey-day in the sense that nobody had burnt out quite yet. I think I was pretty much on burn-out. As a matter of fact I think on one of my trips to Australia I'd already burnt out for the first time. I know I'd been in bed for about nine months; I think we had to cancel some tours. I'd got Hepatitis B and the doctors had told me that if I carried on drinking and using I'd be dead in another year anyway. So I was already on burn-out by the time I was about 23 or 24. I can remember coming into Australia and I was carrying a walking cane actually. I was still very weak, I'd lost a lot of weight and I was still very, very weak from the illness that I'd been going through. But I do remember other trips to Australia where I definitely drank ... there were some pretty crazy times, I mean all of us were pretty crazy back then, that's for sure."

"I was stripped off at one point and put in the fountain right in the middle of Sydney," adds Bill, prodded for stories. "We came out of a restaurant and I was stripped down, completely naked standing in the fountain. There's been many a time when I've walked back into the hotel with my underpants barely hanging on me (laughs) and covered in crap and shit and God knows what else. I know everybody would get a kick out of that, and I would ask for my key in the most polite way and people would look at me and go, 'Oh my God, who is this insane person?'"

"We were out playing one day, out having fun, and the cars ran out of gas so we drove them into the ocean and just let them float there, and then we hailed a cab and went back to the hotel. I remember things like that. I can remember passing out. I was just drunk on my ass, and I think I passed out in Ozzy's room, nude as usual—I spent a lot of time with no clothes on in those days, I do remember that much—but Ozzy apparently took me back to my room; he dragged me back to my room because he couldn't pick me up and I woke up out of this passed-out sleep covered in rug marks, all over my back and all over my chest and my arms. Man, that stung! He'd dragged me all the way down the corridors and put me back in my room; that's what I was told at least—I don't even remember him doing it. So I was a bit pissed with Oz because I was just in so much pain; I mean I had literally scars all over me from him dragging me down the hallway! I realized that he was out of his mind as well so he probably thought he was doing me a favour or something."

Album 6

Sabotage

"The mellow parts were the good vibe that gave you hope"

From agony and strife would come a record that many of Sabbath's maddest fans, this one included, consider the apex of the band's career. *Sabotage* (Sabbath felt their career had been sabotaged by bad management) would combine the frantic, ecstatic creativity of *Sabbath Bloody Sabbath* with a returning heft, the band proving beyond a doubt through two cerebral records in a row that they fully deserved to swim with sharks like Deep Purple and Led Zeppelin in any waters, on any given day.

Beginning with the cover art, what you see (and what has become an iconic image, if not all that impressive of one!), was not the way it was supposed to turn out. Assistant to Bill Ward, Graham Wright (with David Tangye, Graham has co-authored the excellent *How Black Was Our Sabbath: An Unauthorized View from the Crew*), was in on the initial stage of the design.

As Wright explains, "What it was, was that it was going to be a passage way or corridor in a castle or an old house, and they were going to be standing with black suits on, in front of full-length mirrors, four mirrors that were hanging from the wall, with stained-glass windows, very dark, with the image reversed like a Magritte. So it was their image being sabotaged. This was the whole idea for the album cover. And we all thought, oh, that would look great, sort of like a really old dingy corridor, like Dracula's castle type thing. And the record company said, 'Oh yeah, we love the idea; we'll organize a photo shoot.' And we ended up in a studio in the middle of London. And we're going, what the hell is going on here?! 'Oh, don't worry about it; we just want photographs of the band.' And they weren't wearing suits. It was taken out of my hands. Because I was the drum tech. And then you've got management and the record company. They just pushed me to one side and it was just a disaster. After that, I just said hey, I'm not getting involved. But it was typical of that period."

"I remember myself and my drum roadie, who is an incredible artist, we did the design for the album cover," reiterates Bill. "Working on that was a lot of fun except for one thing. We forgot to let the guys know what to wear, so when we showed up for the shoot, it was a total fucking disaster. That's why we ended up with this very odd looking Black Sabbath. But I love the idea of the mirror. So yes, one thing we hadn't done was look at how the band might have to look. So when we showed up, we just kind of came in and we hadn't focused on wardrobe or anything, which was important. So in that particular shot, you'll notice that Ozzy's wearing a long cloak. Okay, well, he has no underpants on. I'm wearing his underpants, his checkered underpants. Because when we showed up for the session, I didn't have any underpants. I borrowed the red tights from my wife, who was at the shoot, because I hadn't thought what to wear either. So I had a pair of my wife's red tights on, Ozzy's underpants and my black leather jacket which was with me for years. I think Tony looks like he's just come from the office. I think the shot's hilarious, to be honest with you."

"I think it was going to be like in a castle, and they were all going to have the same clothes on," says David Tangye, Ozzy's personal assistant and close friend at the time. "Bill has got a pair of his wife Mysti's tights on, and he had to borrow Ozzy's underpants, because he never used to wear underpants. Ozzy had the kimono on, and they always used to say the homo in the kimono (laughs). It wasn't meant to be like that. Graham's idea—he's quite a prolific artist, Graham, and he's had stuff shown in America and all over—but his idea was more like a gothic image with the back reflection. They're sort of standing with their backs to a mirror and the mirror shows the front view. I don't know the whole total idea. But it certainly worked, because it's one of the most talked about album covers they ever did (laughs)."

But as it would turn out, beyond the cock-up job on the jacket, the worst thing about putting together this poison-penned opus of a record was having to deal with the band's collapsing business. Meehan and the guys were in a mammoth legal battle, and the paperwork was spilling into the studio, maddening for four working class lads cursed with a voracious, all-encompassing creative streak, even if it was half fuelled by drugs and booze.

"That was probably the hardest record, the bleakest," begins Geezer, "because we were in the studio and we were having lawyers come in. We were leaving the management at the time and he was suing us, we were suing him. He was trying to stop us from recording and freezing all our money. It was really bad times to go through. We used to turn up at the studio to go and write a song, and there would be like three lawyers waiting for us to put subpoenas on us, stuff like that. It took us about ten months to do the album because of all the interruptions we were having. But yes, the hardest would have been *Sabotage* but maybe also *Never Say Die*, and the most fun were the first three albums and *Sabbath Bloody Sabbath*."

It can't be stressed enough that even though *Sabotage* is seen by Sabbath fans the world over as a creative masterpiece (with a lesser portion calling it their best album), the band is still, 30 years later and to a man, so clouded by the tortuous assembly of it, that most gravitate to the similar *Sabbath Bloody Sabbath* as the creative pinnacle, Ozzy going so far as to call that album the band's last.

"I think we changed, purely because of the system, the people surrounding us, the things we were involved with," adds Tony. "We started going through things we knew nothing about, the legal sides of things, all these hassles with management, stuff we really didn't want to be involved with. But we were involved in it. And I think that really put a blunt end to what we were doing. Because suddenly here we are, musicians, or supposedly musicians, and then we needed to become businesspeople, which we weren't. And try to work out, bloody 'ell, what do we do now? Here we are having lawyer's meetings, and turning up in court and all this sort of stuff, swearing affidavits, getting sued left, right and center. It was a part of our lives we had never seen before, and I think it really interfered with our music. I remember when we were doing the album, we were bloody getting writs in the studio, and then we were having to attend court because we were obviously going against Meehan. So it became very hard for us. We were seeing the other side of life we had never seen, so it was not a nice time, really. And I think that changed us, to a point, because we were thinking more about how we were going to get out of this problem, than what we were supposed to be doing."

At this point it was Ward who took it upon himself to try deal with the monies, taking on a role that, curiously, quite often wound up the domain of drummers. "Bill did, yeah," laughs Tony. "We let Bill sort of start (laughs)... everybody had a part in the band, and Bill's part was to sort out the money, go down to the bank, get the money, pay all the crew and pay each other and stuff like that, the general running of everything. But it went to his head (laughs). He started dressing up in suits and going down to the bank with his briefcase. It was another Bill! He really took it to another level (laughs), Bill. But it was funny. We had some bloody laughs over it. But everybody tried to do their part, and Bill worked hard and tried to do what he could. But of course Bill got, in them days, as time went on, more into the alcohol, and became an alcoholic, in the end. It's very hard to talk to an alcoholic, even though he's your best friend. When he's drunk, it's very difficult."

"I think he was doing it simply because he was the only one who could be bothered at the time," says Geezer. "I can't really remember much about it. Yeah, he'd try and go get some money out of the bank for us, and phone up Warner Bros. and all that kind of thing."

"Yes, I know that I spoke to a lot of lawyers," confirms Bill on his new role. "I worked real close with Spock. Spock took care of the stage and all of our equipment and our sound, even in the studio; he was like a major player. But there were still problems and lots of things going on and I just tried to fill in the holes really."

Asked whether he had a natural affinity for numbers, Bill figures, "Well, no, Geezer is the smart guy in our band, as far as I'm concerned. He knows that kind of stuff. He's real savvy with the numbers. No, I just had an instinct about... as I've said, it was more like I was a mother hen than anything else—I still am."

"We spent a lot of time at it," adds Graham. "I was driving Bill and Geezer down to London to what they call The Inns of Court, to see the lawyers and barristers because they were in litigation. So there were quite a few weeks of that. They were trying to sort out their business problems. And that's a stressful time for any band, particularly in those days. Because they had worked so hard. They got ripped off. It's been well documented. Sure, they carried on, but I think there was a bitterness there towards management. It's like anything: 'Oh, why did we sign this and why did we go with this person?' 'It was your idea.' 'No, it was your idea.' All that stuff comes into it. Meehan was a businessman. He was in it to get as much out of it as he could for himself. That breed of person, they're ruthless. There's no loyalty in business. Bands are made up of artists. I mean, it's the same old story. Jim Simpson was sort of like a local promoter, from Birmingham. He was a nice guy. Once the band took off, especially in America, I think he was just out of his league. And then Patrick Meehan jumped in and said, 'Hey, come with me; I'm the big shot.'"

"There is just nothing that you can do," says Geezer, on the subject of watching Bill's drinking getting worse during this period. "If you try to do something with them then you just get abused by them anyway. I am not a qualified person to get somebody out of a drug or alcoholic situation. It is a specialist subject because if you try to do it then you just get abused. Plus, we were not exactly teetotalers either. But Tony and I didn't do it in the same excess that they did. I used to drink and do quite a lot of drugs. Drugs didn't really agree with me. Eventually, I didn't like the way they made me feel. I couldn't do them even if I wanted to because they made me feel horrible. Boozing gave me terrible hangovers so it wasn't fun anymore. I can drink socially. I go out and drink once or twice a month but I don't have to do it everyday. I never got into the situation like Ozzy or Bill did where they woke up in morning and had a bottle of vodka for breakfast. I could just never get into that—not that I ever wanted to. I didn't see how you could get through an entire day drunk. I got to the peak of the drug thing and the booze thing and said so what? I went back to the way I was before it. It's like the old saying, 'Drugs don't work anymore.'"

David Tangye explains the movement from Meehan and the imploding World Wide Artists, to Mark Forster, who has since died. "I only ever met Patrick maybe once or twice. It was when I was working with Necromandus that I sort of met him. I wasn't actually working for Black Sabbath. But he just seemed to be a manager, a London guy. It seemed that he had plenty of money and he was just sort of guiding them through. You just tipped your hat basically; you never really got involved when you're in the road crew. You just go about your own business. Mark Forster was there when I was sort of doing it. Mark was sort of managing them, tour manager/tour accountant. Mark was a lovely fellow; he was a great guy for them. He was very, very well-respected in the music industry, and I think he did a lot for them in America, because he had a lot of contacts. He'd been around the block a few times. He was good for them in America."

"At the time, after they'd finished with Patrick Meehan, which is like '74, it was like they were in freefall. They were just sort of gearing up to manage themselves. I think they talked about different managers and different people coming in and things like that, but there was no management at that time. When Mark Forster was actually brought in, they said we'll manage ourselves, we'll do our own sort of deal. Because they had all the court cases. Mark came out with them about March of '76. They just took control again of themselves and Mark just sort of helped them along, basically, helped them in America. And of course they had big accountants in America looking after the business side. That was how it happened. The Patrick Meehan thing had rolled on a while. I don't think they lost out a lot; I don't really know. You couldn't really put a comment on it because you don't want to say anything that could be contentious. What I put in the book, those were the actual figures of what happened. That was out of the press. But they were quite happy to juggle all the management themselves and talk to the record companies themselves and do all that. And as I say, Mark did sterling work, great work."

"All I know was that with *Sabotage*, it seemed the band were at their best, I think, because they were under pressure. And they were a bit pissed-off at the way things were going for them management-wise. And as I say, if you read some of the lyrics, that's the way it is, that's what they are singing about. I just think they work best under those sorts of conditions. Because it all sounded demonic at the end of it, didn't it?"

Ozzy, speaking with Scene magazine's Cliff Michalski back in 1975 just before the release of *Sabotage*, summed up the band's management hassles, also offering a characterization of the new record. "After we did a tour of the East Coast last July, the band just took a three-month vacation from everything; we just stopped to reassess our whole situation. We don't have a manager as such now; it's changed into a sort of family-type of operation to run things. We were tangled up with the political things, getting rid of our management. The band wasn't stopped from recording, but it was the wisest thing to lay back until the political things straightened themselves out. It's all a lot of rubbish to me, but we couldn't avoid it."

"We just wanted to reduce the whole operation to more manageable proportions," continued Oz. "It got to the stage where people were coming up to us saying, 'Hi, I work for you' and I didn't have the foggiest idea where. I mean, we got pissed-off because of all these managers treating us like products instead of human beings. I was beginning to feel like a prostitute, a musical prostitute. Forcing us to go on tour all the time was affecting us physically. We were ill; if we let people down, I'm sorry. It got to the stage where we had to rely on drugs, uppers, just to keep going, just to be able to get on stage. We played music that's false. The energy should come from the music, not from some artificial substance. You can only go so long; you just start going through the motions after awhile."

"That's why we had to cut some of them short," continues Osbourne. "The management seems to think that we're Superman; they don't give a shit about our lives. When I'm dead, they'll go and manage someone else. The only times these agents and managers would speak to us was when they wanted us to do something, and then they'd make it sound like they were the ones doing us a favour, that 'We're going to make you rich' line. I don't care about being rich; I just want enough to support my family, to live comfortably. I mean, it's like when people go, 'Yay, Black Sabbath,' the managers care about us. But when they go, 'Boo, Black Sabbath,' they don't want to know. If they could earn bread by gassing people, they'd be right there on the controls."

"*Sabotage* still emphasizes hard rock," added Oz, getting 'round to the album. "Sabbath couldn't be anything but hard rock. I like to feel my spine curl from our music, from its power. On *Sabbath Bloody Sabbath*, we experimented a hell of a lot with different sounds, orchestra backings. The new ones vary, but we've also tried to keep it as basic as possible. There's various keyboards on most of the tracks; we've hired a keyboard player, Gerald Woodruffe, to reproduce them on tour."

Black Sabbath's sixth album, *Sabotage* would be recorded at Morgan Studios in February and March of 1975, and issued on July 28th of that year, produced, essentially by Tony and engineer Mike Butcher, with Robin Black also engineering and David Harris serving as tape operator. Previous to arriving at Morgan (same studio used for *Sabbath Bloody Sabbath*), writing and rehearsal took place at Fields Farm, Bishampton, near Worcester as well as Ozzy's house in Staffordshire. Despite the reasonable-sounding gestation period, because of all the legal hassles, Ozzy quipped that the album took "4000 years."

Anything but a "basic" album, *Sabotage* opened explosively with "Hole in the Sky," a dense, purposeful doom classic that pounded the daylights out of anything from the competition circa '75. Previously not thought possible, Tony's tone had gotten even larger, placed over a looming, surging swing from Geezer and Bill, while Ozzy is forced into another high and dramatic vocal. Indeed, as one walks through this harrowing, chemically-induced record, it begins to come clear through the paisley murk that *Sabotage* would mark the finest vocal performance of Ozzy's career, with a certain savage anger in his voice cutting through the heroism of the ornate musical backdrop. Still, despite the bevy of deft production touches all over the album, Tony is adamant that they had made a rock album this time, versus *Sabbath Bloody Sabbath*, which he says, somewhat hyperbolically, was not.

"'Hole in the Sky' is great to play," offers Bill. "It's a tough one for a drummer because you want to push ahead but you have to lay back. That one is really behind the beat. So that one is kind of tricky. You've got to drive it hard but you've got to keep relaxed on the track, otherwise you'll blow the track."

Indeed Bill has to frame the song with a sort of heavy metal swing beat, and one played slowly. Up top, he's hitting crash cymbal quarter notes. Come chorus time, we get some of Bill's uniquely "orchestral" or "ensemble" drumming. For a guitar solo, Tony sits a fair ways back in the mix, using two tracks, one left and one right, to harmonize with himself.

Adds Geezer, "'Hole in the Sky' was just about the environment, pollution, just the way the whole western world was going at the time." Did scientists even know about the hole in the ozone or anything at that point? "I don't think they had discovered it yet. Or it was a brand-new concept anyway. I must have known something, otherwise I wouldn't have called it that (laughs), unless it was a coincidence."

Geezer might be pushing a little hard with the environmental angle. An analysis of this visionary and effortlessly flowing bank of words reveals a song that is more about escape, an "Into the Void" sentiment as it were, with travel through the hole in the sky, toward Heaven, also sounding like a metaphor for blowing one's mind, embarking on some kind of drug trip. But in keeping with Butler's pessimism, this isn't Friday night fun, rather grave dismay at the corruption rife in the world. The closing sentiment, about living off the profits of crime, feels like an admission that the band's bosses are criminals, and that by extension, the entire music business is rotten and that the band may as well consider themselves implicated as well.

Says Graham Wright on the writing arrangement, "The lyrics were all Geezer's, apart from the one Ozzy wanted. Geezer would never talk about them, to me, anyway. Or to anybody, really. He just brought them down and Ozzy would sing them. Geezer did a lot of lyrics, but he thought, 'Well, I've written them down; you decide what you think they're about.'"

"Oz was always sitting down with Geezer, going back and forth with different things," adds Bill, intimating that Ozzy was more involved than we think. "I mean, popular conception is right, that Tony wrote all the parts and that Geezer wrote all the lyrics. You're pretty much right there. There were lyrics and titles that were added, either by myself or by Ozzy and musically there were things that happened as well, where Geezer would introduce ideas, or myself or Oz. When I talk about this particular issue, if Ozzy had not been the singer, then lyrically I'm sure these things wouldn't have happened, because he is just incredibly... For me, if I had to write some stuff for Ozzy, which I have done, he's incredibly almost clay-like."

"It's very easy to take Ozzy," continues Ward, "because he's larger-than-life and really able to present some really neat things, that you probably couldn't present to another singer. We're all creators of our own music, wherever my attitudes might be, would interact between Terry and Tony. Although singers are really, really important and that's what makes the whole thing go 'round. That's why I like to call Black Sabbath a phenomenon and not a band. Because the phenomenon does allow for that kind of interaction. What happens is, when us four get together, things like 'Paranoid' happen, because Tony feeds off it the same way, or Geezer will get lyrically inspired by something. Sometimes Oz would just come out with a word, and it would totally spark a whole thing; he does it to this day. He just comes out with one single word, and if you're listening, it will inspire a complete song."

"Hole in the Sky" lurches, brilliantly and memorably, to an abrupt end. Once the shock wears off, Tony can be heard playing a barely audible, torridly exotic bit of acoustic guitar (Geezer: "The heavy parts were always sort of the bad vibe and the mellow parts were the good vibe that gave you hope."), before the heavy metal riff of all riffs announces the arrival of "Symptom of the Universe." Tony's 49-second acoustic respite is titled "Don't Start (Too Late)," inspired by tape op David Harris' exasperation with the band ploughing into their takes before he's gotten himself prepared. So that's David saying "don't start" and the band chuckling "too late." The piece finds Tony harmonizing with himself, left and right like his solo on the previous track. The piece is essentially melodically complex modern classical, but in keeping with the atmosphere of the song before it and the song to come, unsettling and "heavy," despite being mere acoustic guitar.

Concerning the "Symptom of the Universe" riff, sure there's "Smoke on the Water" and even "Iron Man" in terms of stark simplicity and hook, but "Symptom of the Universe" most purely gets at the crux of why doom darkens the heart so inexorably. Indeed Yngwie Malmsteen has quipped that Iommi's invocation of the flat fifth on this song would have got him burned at the stake a couple hundred years ago. Again, once the song percolates to a rumbled chug due to Geezer's and Bill's rhythm section violence, Osbourne is sent high up his register, twisting in the wind as he delivers Butler's poetic fragments of hippie wisdoms.

"That was me," says Geezer, with respect to the lyrics, which are essentially a more spiritual telling of the same flight-to-the-sky narrative of "Hole in the Sky," albeit exotic and even Wiccan. "Although Ozzy would come out with a vocal line off the top of his head, and the first thing he comes out with, that is what he usually sticks with. He has a great knack of being able to do that. That's the way I had to work. I had to fit in all that stuff. It does get frustrating because sometimes you have a thing in your head of what you want to say but then you have to do it in so many syllables, that is the hard part. You have to take what you want to say in less syllables than if you were just writing stuff down."

"Well again, there is the fact that we actually show up with jazz parts," comments Bill on this track's completely unexpected dispersal into jam territory late in the track. "And that goes back to our roots where there were some jazz influences in our playing. But back then, as we do right now, the songs are a little bit unpredictable. So we never quite know. We try to make it a bit unusual for the listener. 'Symptom of the Universe' was one of those songs. That's the other thing. We had so many people participate in so many different areas of the work. When one would leave off, another one would pick up and move it forward."

"It was just the appropriate thing to do," explains Bill, with respect to the involved drum fills he gets to perform on this song. "Tony and Geezer just hammered it out, and as soon as Ozzy's voice got on there and we got closer, it was just the natural thing to do. So I'm not aware that I had any preconceived notions. I just played it; I just played against wherever we were at the time. God, I love that song, but physically it's a tough song. Sometimes I think, without sounding aged and decrepit, the physical energy that came from some of those songs was absolutely incredible. When you're 20 years old, it's just like that's being pushed out of you; 22, 23, you can handle that because physically you're in pretty good shape, or your supposed to be in pretty good shape. When you're playing it past 50 years old, even though we're all fit and my health is really good, I'm still going to feel that song. I'm still going to feel 'Symptom of the Universe' physically, at age 53. Because the watermark or the benchmark that I set when I was 24, that's a lot of energy. And to perform at that level, you know, I'm going to perform as a 53-year-old, not as a 23-year-old."

Says Geezer with typical bluntness when he's looking for the short answer, "'Symptom of the Universe' is about love; that's the symptom, whatever that means. I don't know; I was probably smashed out of me brains at the time." Despite that dismissal, Geezer proves himself at the height of his lyrical prowess, really, for two records straight now, Butler writing not only longer lyrics, but ones that work both poetically and philosophically. Both the "Symptom" and "Hole in the Sky" lyrics prove that songs like "A National Acrobat" and "Spiral Architect," with compactness, intensity, exotic imagery and messages with substance, were no fluke.

And yes, Bill is accurate when he speaks of showing up with "jazz parts." The starkly surprising jam at the end of 'Symptom' rides a strange hippie terrain, with a little bit of beat generation that borrows from the blues, cocktail jazz and even Tex Mex, with Bill playing bongos and claves. In this section, which follows first upon a geometric riff from Tony at two minutes and then a joyous and floating jam, Tony is again featured, only with two coffee house-styled acoustic tracks. It's further testimony to the otherworldliness of an album that, as it unfolds, is going to get weird very quickly, menacingly weird, relentlessly weird, and even meanly weird through the middle of the second side.

Side one of *Sabotage* ends with a ten-minute monster called "Megalomania," which is this record's "In My Time of Dying," no light comparison, given that Sabbath's up-market rivals Led Zeppelin, four months before the launch of *Sabotage*, had issued an album this writer considers the greatest record of all time, *Physical Graffiti*. Not to slight Sabbath, at various times when prompted for such lists, I have rated *Sabotage* the greatest record of all time, and to be sure, at this level, we can just call it a tie (and if you want to tip to the Sabs, they manage the feat with one record instead of a double).

But yes, "Megalomania" is an evil epic of torrid, emotional movements. It opens like a schooner adrift with all dead or dying, slowly lifting off on a heavy Iommi riff somewhat similar in speed and structure to the "Symptom" one. As the song progresses, different melodies unfold, and the record's sturdy production values reveal tricky little details of tone and tenacity. Other features include more of Bill's slow "ensemble" playing, reverse vocal echo, funereal keyboards, surprise honky tonk piano, cowbell and atmosphere built from cymbals played with mallets. Once the song settles into a mid-paced groove, Ozzy harmonizes with a much lower version of himself, and adding to the party is tambourine and some melodically complex licks from Geezer. Come solo time, Tony characteristically offers two opposing tracks in the left and right channels, but heavily treated this time. The closing section is textured with all sorts of echo effect on Ozzy's anguished cries, which accompany an ascending Mellotron wash, backward cymbal effects, jamming drums from Bill, and brief stabs of additional soloing from Tony.

"We were going through a very tricky time, with getting ripped-off and stuff by tricky people," says Bill, affirming that "Megalomania" and "The Writ" revolved lyrically around the band's legal woes. Of course Geezer (and Ozzy—Oz is often credited with much of this one) hides the detail well, and what emerges are songs where you can taste the torment, a torment powerful enough to convey a sense of universality, especially when couched in Geezer's luxuriant poetics. Despite the many ways Ozzy sings of torment, dashed dreams and being pushed to insanity, expertly, as the track progresses, there are flashes of hope, intermittently, which increase toward a sense of triumph and freedom by the end of the trip.

"They are intertwined actually both of those songs," adds Bill. "'Megalomania' was about greed or coveting; that's at least what I interpret from the song. And then 'The Writ' is kind of like the coveter or the greedy person or whatever, the end result was 'The Writ,' if you like. They are kind of in the same family. I don't know if there's a big difference there. They are very different songs musically. Fantastic guitars, and I think the band sounded pretty hot on both of those songs. I liked Tony's solo in 'Megalomania,' and I enjoyed very much putting a very straight beat to it. It was like one of the only times I got the opportunity to do a very straight beat for a number of bars (laughs). So that was kind of cool."

"Like 'Killing Yourself to Live,' that was also written about management and record company people in general," offers Geezer. "It was so long because we couldn't figure out how to end the song. We just kept coming up with parts that were going to be new songs, but then we figured they would fit so we used them."

Curiously, despite the tour de force of light and shade exercised all over "Megalomania," and indeed almost all of *Sabotage*'s tracks, back in '75, Tony didn't quite see it that way.

Speaking with Mick Houghton from Circus, Iommi figured, "It's more of a basic raw album really in the same way that all the albums up to *Master of Reality* were, but we've taken a lot more care in the way that this one is produced. We spent a lot of time on *Vol 4* and *Sabbath Bloody Sabbath*, but they were moving away from a oneness of approach. *Vol 4* was such a complete change; we felt we had jumped an album really. It didn't follow suit because we had tried to go too far and again *Sabbath Bloody Sabbath* was a continuation from it. We could've gone on into more technical things and fulfill a lot the band is capable of achieving and which we don't necessarily do on stage either. But we decided we had reached the limit as far as we wanted to go. We felt we wanted to get back to a more basic thing. We'll pick up again and develop from *Sabbath Bloody Sabbath*, but that will come later when we are more ready for it."

Parse his words, and it's interesting what Tony is saying. There had been a palpable loss of confidence in the Sabbath camp at this point, to go along with a fading faith in humanity as it applies to the music business. Iommi is pretty much admitting that the band was trying to make an album that fans could understand, and that when the time is right, they'll get back onto what he was considering a whole different trajectory.

"I've always regarded it as important that people should pick up on the words," continued Iommi. "They're not just functional. The lyrics are about things that have happened to us, or dreams, or stages that we've been through. They're true for a lot of people who are actually experiencing them or have yet to go through them. They've felt whatever emotion, depression or whatever, and can relate the words to how they feel. Younger kids especially can latch onto what there is and realize that there is somebody else who's been through it. With *Sabbath Bloody Sabbath*, everything was said—on the whole it summed up everything we had done over the years. This album is like starting again—like the music, the lyrics aren't so technical."

"I don't read science fiction—well, some people may call it science fiction—but I believe Lobsang Rampa's writings about astral traveling in the next life. I believe there is a next life. It's easy to be skeptical but I understand a lot and get a lot out of reading his books. Geezer, who wrote most of the songs in the past, was into this kind of thing long before me, and I think the influence is in some of those songs. I don't write the words, but I know the wavelength Geezer is on. In fact, the whole group communicates on a very close level. Like, we have what you could almost call a third eye. We can sense with each other what is going to happen. We've had actual experiences. One, I remember, Geezer was asleep and he must have astral traveled. I was stuck in the lift. He dreamt this and when I woke him up, he said, 'I'm glad it's you, because I just dreamt you were stuck in the lift.' These are quite regular occurrences. They used to frighten me at first until I got used to it."

Noted Ozzy at the time, speaking with Harry Doherty, "There's one thing that everybody has got to understand about Black Sabbath's lyrics. They're not downer lyrics. They're just telling everybody where it's at. That's all it is. People must think we sleep off the rafters with wings on our backs every night, taking reds and drinking wine. We're just people. We see a lot and we write about what we see. We have a couple of songs about people getting stoned, but so have a lot of people. It's a heavy, doomy thing but it's what we see. A love thing wouldn't go with the style of music we play. It's like going to see *Frankenstein* with *The Sound of Music* soundtrack behind it. It wouldn't go. The way we write goes with the way we play. We're not telling everybody to jump off the cliff, and if anybody ever did, I don't know what I'd do. If that happened, I'd believe that I was the devil."

"Sabbath is one of the greatest experiences of my life," continues Oz, adding to the debate about the band's evolving sound. "We're stronger now than we ever were as musicians: it has progressed a lot. We have got a lot of ideas that we could put out, but it's a thing that once you take the plunge, you've done it. It's got to be a change drastically or a gradual change. Whatever the change, it's going to affect you one way or another. The longer you leave change the more chance you have of survival. If you go 'whack,' it's a big gamble."

"*Sabotage* was over a year in the making and the band have no intention of ever spending as long in the studio on future releases again. In the end, I felt like calling it *Crossroads* and having Meg Richardson star on it. Every time there was a session we used to call it chapter 99—'Will Black Sabbath complete the album this time?' It was like a bizarre nightmare sometimes, but other times it was fun, especially the times when we started throwing custard pies at each other. At the end of it, I was very confused because I had heard so much of it so I had to leave it alone for some time. When I heard it again, at first hearing I hated it. I realized that because of the constant work on it, I had built this barrier in my head but I'm really satisfied with it now. It's not that bad considering that we were all going through a lot of hassle with our own heads, like 'Where can we go from here?' 'What are we going to do to be better than the last one?'"

Again, the idea there is that nothing kills the joy of making music deader than lawyers showing up and serving you papers.

In closing, Ozzy figures, "To me, *Sabotage* does beat the last album, but I still have a liking for the last one. The last album was our first album really because it was the first time we had got into the actual studio production thing and it takes a couple of albums to get into that. You go through all the experiments of banging dustbin lids and running herds of cattle through the studio to find out what it sounds like."

Recap: Tony thinks *Sabbath Bloody Sabbath* isn't a rock album, but Ozzy likes it so much, he calls it the band's first record.

Kicking off side two of the album was "Thrill of It All," which begins way down on a noticeable downer rock downer. Before long though, the band pick up with a second, brighter more hopeful structure, Tony soloing, as usual, with two different performances sent to the left and right channels. Then the doom invades hard and hard-hearted—Tony's riff on this one is pure dark metal, its pregnant pauses more stillborn than anything. The percussion track is necessarily slow, and is punctuated with an echo effect.

"It's a Geezer title," notes Bill. "It's one of the songs where, musically everybody got it but sometimes you have to sit back two months later, and realize what the lyrics were." Geezer: "I think I was just reading a book about the 1920s and one of the titles was *The Thrill of It All*, and it's cool, that title." Still, there are some brilliant sentiments here, all couched in religion as Geezer wonders why the world is such a shambles, if Jesus can possibly still believe in man, if life is merely a transaction, something to be bought and sold.

Late in the track, the band break into a sort of relaxed and happy hard rock buttressed by synthesizers, the sum total of this one sounding like something that would have fit handily on *Sabbath Bloody Sabbath*. "I was a handclap," laughs David Tangye. "Bill had us into the studio clapping—myself, Graham and Bill's brother Jim. So that's my energy in there." Unfortunately the sabotage that was happening by way of the band's management problems extended to the recording of this track. Engineer David Harris had mistakenly wiped the original master and the band had to record the song again. Rather than get all upset about it, the guys actually credited him on the album with: "Tape Operator and sabateur – David Harris."

"Supertzar" is next, and for this one, Sabbath create a Luciferian bridge between classical music and metal that presages the naturalist and folk preoccupations of pagan black metal bands such as Tyr, Primordial and Therion. "Supertzar" sounds almost fascist, at minimum apocalyptic, rapturous, certainly Wagnerian. One pictures this choir in uniform, marching to Bill's military snare and bombastic percussion appointments. Indeed there was so much pomp and circumstance on the track, when Ozzy walked into the studio and saw the English Chamber Choir, he thought he was in the wrong place and turned around and walked out.

"That was a big production," explains Bill, proceeding to sing it. "Tony had the lick; that's all we had. And again, we were at Monmouth, at the farm there. And that lick kept coming up and coming up and coming up, and we thought man, we all knew something had to be done with that lick but we couldn't move on from there. And Tony, somehow, some way, found out what would be the next indicated chord, and was able to take us from that original lead lick and push it into a different area. And as soon as he did that, everybody knew that... that lick drove me crazy, and everybody was just saying 'Man, I'm hoping it can go somewhere,' and as soon as it moved into the change, all of us were able to just come into it. I had a field day. I put vibes on there, tympanis, snare drum… we had chimes, we had the English Chamber Choir. Plus there's these very professional harp players. There's all kinds of instruments that we placed on there. That was another one, speaking of drumming, where we had to be absolutely accurate. That's one of Geezer's titles. Primarily studio-built. We just kept adding more things to it and it just grew. And that was our opening theme for our shows after that."

As for working with a choir, Bill explains that, "It was a bit unusual at that time actually putting a big choir sound with the rock 'n' roll feel. Some of the bands were doing it. I'm not saying by any means that Sabbath was unique, but it was a little bit unusual. And the choir loved it. The lady who played the harp, I think she was from the London Philharmonic Orchestra, and she was fucking great, man. And we had an arranger come in—Will Malone I believe his name was—and Will put it all together really nice. But we knew where we wanted it to go. We were singing for them like a choir, all the low parts. It just completely made the song huge. But it was the right thing to do. I could hear the choir there, and it's like well, are we going to not say anything? Are we all going to keep our heads down or go, 'I think a choir would sound really good on there?' Is somebody going to speak up and say, 'Let's put a fucking choir on there?'"

"When they brought in the choir, it was quite funny," recalls Graham. "They were shocked, sort of, yeah (laughs). I mean it was just like a session choir. They all piled in, took over the studio, did their bit and off they went."

"Yeah, when Will came in, it was really strange," agrees Graham's writing partner David Tangye. "They'd come in the studio, set the gear up, and that was it, just do the bit, and they would be off (laughs). It wouldn't take long at all, a couple of hours maybe and that would be it (laughs). There would be more time spent tuning up and blowing the spittle out of the instruments, and they would just sort of do it. But yes, Will Malone, they called him. They would have an idea of what they wanted but I don't think there would be any score. Tony and Geezer would say, 'Well, this is what we want.'"

Indeed "Supertzar" is a production tour de force, with complex choral washes, a type of Gregorian chanting, acoustic guitar, harp, bell parts, tambourine, polite but driving military snare work, and then quite sinister and geometric riffing from Tony. In fact in the original demo, Tony had cooked up the choir parts on a Mellotron. As for the harp, Tony asked for it because he had one at home and thought it would be a nice addition. He had had a simple part in mind, but once he heard what a professional could do with the instrument, he was instantly sold. The relentless and ascending choral parts, along with the harp, underscore the spiritual themes all over the record, especially "Hole in the Sky," "Symptom of the Universe," "The Thrill of It All" and even "Don't Start (Too Late)" though the latter, like "Supertzar," is an instrumental, soundtrack to a wake, as it were.

While working on the track in Brussels, Bill had had what was later diagnosed as a mild heart attack, no doubt exacerbated by his self-professed alcoholism. Ozzy had been instrumental in taking the bull by the horns and getting a doctor on the case quickly, Bill having crawled to his room in the middle of the night. A month's rest was prescribed, with Bill worrying that if he didn't get his act together quickly, he would be replaced.

Next up on side two of *Sabotage* was another oddity, "Am I Going Insane (Radio)" hearkening back to the preceding album with its overt melody and synthesizer flourishes. Unwittingly, Ozzy had added hugely to the "Paranoid" sentiment (indeed the first line name-checks the song), finishing the job five years later with "Crazy Train," establishing a caricature that's his for life, this idea of a regular, not too bright geezer driven mad by his emotional unfitness for stardom, or at least touring—even "Who Are You" is in possession of a certain pathos in this respect.

Musically, the song features a stop/start pattern from Bill (sixteenth notes on the high hat, along with some military rolls and even a disco beat), while Ozzy sings a weirdly foppish and Shakespearean vocal melody over a soundtrack that devolves into tormented laughing and then crying. Additionally, Bill gets to play a lot of fills, and there's some tambourine, backward cymbals and echoing toms. Tony delivers a highly treated harmony solo followed by a lick with a sitar effect. Ozzy harmonizes with himself during both the verses and choruses.

"'Am I Going Insane' was Ozzy's song," notes David Tangye. "He did all that. He had his Moog. I don't know if you've been watching The Osbournes. I've been watching it a little bit. I can't get away from it, to be honest with you. It's still a little bit close to home for me (laughs). But he had the old Moog; he'd bought this synthesizer and he used to muck about with that in the studio in his house. And he actually came with that, 'Am I Going Insane (Radio),' which was radio rental, which was Cockney rhyming slang for mental. But that was down to Ozzy, that one."

Graham explains further: "The whole thing about that thing in brackets, radio. In Birmingham at that time, there used to be a shop called Radio Rental. And because of the rhyming slang, if you thought somebody was mental, you would say, 'Oh, they're radio rental.' Even if you knew somebody in the pub who was a nutcase, you'd say, 'Oh, he's radio, he is.' Radio rental, which rhymes with mental. It's English rhyming slang."

"I think 'Am I Going Insane' is kind of the blueprint for a lot of Oz stuff to come," says Bill, "which had never happened, you know the kind of stuff Oz did with Blizzard of Ozz, in the early days. Again, it was an Ozzy song. I think he came down again to Fields Farm and we got the roughs down there, and of course, he followed the song all the way through, did a fantastic job. The laughing on that, that's a friend of ours, from Australia, Adrian. The crying is Ozzy's daughter Jessica and we slowed it right down, and it was horrible. Because, I mean, everybody knew Jessica, and she was just this beautiful, beautiful kid and then when we slowed it down and it was like 'Oh God!' and we'd be getting high, and flipping out behind it and it was like, 'Oh, don't do that.'"

There's a spot of mystery surrounding this part however. First off, Jessica would have been three years old at the time, plus Ozzy vaguely talks about experimenting with it but only getting the *idea* from a tape of Jessica crying. Engineer Mike Butcher has also said that the crying originated from an unidentified cassette that was hanging around the studio. Then again, this could all be the same tape.

"We tended to sort of always do stuff at rehearsals, with Ozzy," remarks Tony, on interacting with Oz on a creative level. "We would always jam around as a band and Ozzy would sort of join in. He'd sort of (laughs) come in and out of the room. He'd sort of sing for a bit, then he'd go to make a cup of tea and bring tea and biscuits back for everybody or something, while we're writing the songs. So it's just different, different ways of working, really. Then he'd sort of take the... we'd do a take of the song, then Ozzy would take it into his room and you'd hear him wailing away there for a few hours, coming up with ideas."

Sabotage ends with a clang, "The Writ" being one of the band's under-heralded classics. The song revisits the sparseness and sluggishness of "Black Sabbath," the guys bravely writing and executing a plod, nightmarish boiling cauldron sounds adding to the madness. As with "Megalomania," it's almost detrimental to the enjoyment of the track when one finds out the lyric is rooted in the band's management troubles—everything else about it is so unearthly. But Ozzy delivers the song's spitting venom with manic savagery, and one quickly forgets the inspiration that resulted in the lyric, and to be sure, Sabbath again make sure to create something universal, with any detail worn to a bloody nub.

"That was written about our management at the time and how we were just all fed up with everything," affirms Butler, "recording with a room full of lawyers. Ozzy came up with those lyrics and I thought they were really good. But it was just this whole situation with everybody suing everybody else. We just wanted out of it."

As with "Black Sabbath," or for that matter "War Pigs," "Symptom of the Universe" and "Megalomania," Sabbath mix it up later in the track, adding segues and secret passageways. As they'd exercised on the preceding album, they dovetail in acoustic guitars with a sleight of hand that has the listener not watching the clock waiting for the next headbang. It's a trip, a journey, and we're all along for the developing, doomy story and lurching demise thereof. Additional ear candy includes judicious use of backward cymbal effects—in fact, the trick is central to the verse beat. There's also wah-wah added to Geezer's bass and bell percussion. In the first of the numerous prog-like switchbacks, Ozzy's vocals are heavily harmonized. The particular break with Bill hitting snare on one and three features one of the doomiest riffs Tony would ever conjure. The listener is rewarded, after the softest music on the album, by a return to this passage for the song's lurching, apocalyptic fade.

"No, I loved that!" says Bill, on the challenge of playing as slowly and simply as he has to on "The Writ." "God, I enjoyed that; the less the better. Because you can really… for me, that's what metal is about. Doing a slow song really loud, you just put the one down; you just put the bass drum where it has to go. You don't need a lot. You can use the air and you can use dynamics and that is where the song is, you know? Sometimes just not even playing can bring out an incredible sound."

Early copies of *Sabotage* included at the end of "The Writ," a 23-second joke song, recorded at low level, called "Blow on a Jug." Bill calls this one of his and Ozzy's "family songs," just something tossed off for light relief when in the mood. That's Bill playing piano and Ozzy and Bill both singing, if you can call it that. "That was just an outro," says David Tangye. "They used to muck about. It wasn't intentional. Daft stuff. There was a lot of comedy with Black Sabbath. It wasn't doom and gloom. It was more fun and games, down home. They didn't live that part really. It was more of a laugh than anything else."

With respect to chart placement, *Sabotage* saw further slippage for this band soon to be deemed out of steam. The record rose to #7 at home in the UK, where it stayed for seven weeks, but stumbled to a mere #28 in the US, eventually, way up into 1997, going gold for sales above 500,000 copies—it is the earliest Black Sabbath album not to have reached platinum status. No singles were issued until five months after release of the full-length when in February of '76, "Am I Going Insane (Radio)" came out, backed with "Hole in the Sky"—unsurprisingly, this weird, strangely irritating song failed to chart in either key territory. But look around the rest of the album, and there is absolutely nothing that bears any of the necessary characteristics of a single.

Iconic UK music industry scenester Mick Farren wasn't buying the value of Black Sabbath. His review of *Sabotage* for the NME reads in part, "I think it was Lester Bangs who put forward the proposition that people who went to Black Sabbath concerts derived their pleasure from ingesting massive amounts of downers and simply let the noise of the band vibrate their chest cavities, thus bypassing the ear altogether. The problem with this thesis is that it hardly holds true for Black Sabbath's records. You can scarcely achieve this kind of effect on the average home stereo without facing instant eviction."

"There simply can't be enough hermits and mountain dwellers to put this unpleasant record at #9 in the charts. At this point the fact has to be faced that Black Sabbath are simply low consciousness music. (At this point the ingratiating critic slips in a disclaimer). There is nothing essentially wrong with a low consciousness. It's simply that I find it hard to relate to. I don't have one. Neither do my knuckles trail on the ground when I walk. Little Richard used to call rock and roll the healing music. Daily Mirror columnists like to call a tune 'infectious.' This has to be atrophy music.

It's heavy metal that's so far into its half life that decay is almost complete. The snap and fire of Jimi, the MC5 and even the early Who has been transformed by Sabbath into a ponderous, rolling *thing* that crushes all in its monomaniac path. Is there no handsome young scientist who will come and save us in the nick of time? Just as religoid chorales and tired shock tactics fail to disguise the essentially brutal thud-thud structures, the five cent psychiatry in the lyrics fails to boost them to even B movie stature."

It's no wonder the guys thought it was the world against them, reflecting that thousands of people love them but then again, thousands of people hate them. At the same time Sabbath was at war with the critics, Ozzy was openly discussing in interviews the fact that the band would have to leave the UK to escape the taxman. In truth, it was likely as much to get away from Patrick Meehan and Wilf Pine and Don Arden. But where to run? As much as the band had made its bread and butter in the US, Ozzy openly expressed his fear of the place, how crazy and violent the band's fans were as well as how rotten the wider pop culture of the place was, even how slutty the women were. In short, America moved too fast for the Sabbath guys, resulting in the need to up the dosages of their various medications.

The high drama with Patrick Meehan resulted in a two-LP compilation also being issued in early 1976. *We Sold Our Souls for Rock 'n' Roll* would creep to the lower rungs of both the US (#48) and UK charts (#35, for a five-week visit), but its main claim to fame is the ghoulish gatefold image, that of a decadent society lady in a coffin clutching a big shining cross. All of the material was previously released with all but two tracks hailing from the band's first four albums. As was the case with *Paranoid, We Sold Our Soul* proved the immense power of hit singles to make wallets flop open. Unfortunately, one has to come to the conclusion that this record appealed to a lot of what one might call the casual Sabbath fan, with its eventual double platinum status (albeit each of its two records gets counted) trumping the certification of the previous three Sabbath albums, *Vol 4*, *Sabbath Bloody Sabbath* and *Sabotage*, each, of course, studio albums of all new material. If you wonder why records like this come out, well, that's graphic evidence.

"We won't have any more *We Sold Our Souls for Rock 'n' Roll* to contend with," groused Tony at the time, telling Steve Rosen that the band had finished ridding themselves of Meehan as manager. "We didn't even know they were going to put that out and if we had we would have used different tracks as well as new mixes. The first thing we knew of it, we were playing in England and suddenly we heard it was out."

Back on the tour trail, the Sabs played all of *Sabotage*'s Taurean side one and none of its Aquarian side two. "Hole in the Sky" opened the shows with "Sabbra Cadabra" closing them out, altered lyrics provided for amusement. "Rock 'n' Roll Doctor" from the forthcoming *Technical Ecstasy* was also boogied about, in roughed-in form.

The tour opened in July of '75 in America, a couple of weeks before the release of the album. Back-ups included southern raunchers Ruby Starr & Grey Ghost, along with the Leslie West Band, Lynyrd Skynyrd, Mahogany Rush, Peter Frampton and Kiss. The band's August 5th date in Asbury Park, NJ (Fire Ballet supporting!), was recorded for a King Biscuit Flower Hour radio broadcast.

Back in the UK, in October of '75, Sabbath played with Bandy Legs, precursor to Quartz, a band that Tony would produce. Up into the '80s, Quartz would also cough up one Geoff Nicholls to the Sabbath camp, as replacement for Gerald Woodruffe. O'er the straight to mainland Europe, Sabbath played shows supported by ZZ Top, Streetwalkers and Chapman/ Whitney's. A short jaunt back to the States in December of '75 was followed by more UK dates in January of '76—these were make-up dates from cancelled shows in November, due to Ozzy injuring himself in a motorcycle accident.

Recalls David Tangye, "The *Sabotage* tour had a massive big cross and it had like reflective crosses stuck on it, mirror crosses. Les Martin, Geezer's roadie, his dad made a big coffin to put this in (laughs). When the roadies cleared the show for the night, it used to come to bits. It was massive, in like two parts and then it fit into the coffin. It was all part of the effect. Oh yeah, that's right, yes. With all the lights on it. I don't know what happened to that. You see, a lot of this stuff, it went into storage and they get pulled to bits at times. You go in another time and something is missing and the lights are gone and that's gone; they get used in other things."

"They tried everything, including mirror balls," continues Tangye. "It wasn't as hi-tech as it is now. And they had the World War II footage in the background, Adolph Hitler and all that. Just one second, no, that might have been *Sabbath Bloody Sabbath*. Because for *Sabotage* they had the shell, the big fibreglass shell behind Bill, which was designed to throw the sound out from Bill's drums and stop the feedback from Tony's amps on the stage. It was like a double-edged thing."

Did it work? "Yeah, it did actually. It was a bloody nightmare. The roadies hated it because it was more to carry about (laughs). They got some company from Huddersfield or something like that to build this shell. You'll see it in a few of the pictures. And for *Technical Ecstasy*, Bill had the big drum riser and he had lights and strobe machines and they cost a fortune to make; it was done at a studio in L.A. Bill liked a lot of drums and the flowers. He always had loads and loads of flowers around his kit, red and white carnations. He liked the risers; he was into the risers. I'm trying to think… the first riser he had was a funny reflective material. Like, if you put a clear light on it, it used to reflect different colours, a rainbow effect—Mother of Pearl, that's it. That was his first riser. Because prior to that, it was just a little riser on the stage, nailed down eight-by-four foot sheets. But then when they got to America, everything had to be bigger and better. Because if you're playing at Madison Square Garden, you needed a big riser anyway. The band's got to look big, haven't they? And then in the '80s, it just went mad, didn't it?

"I liked the shell," laughs Bill, when asked about his favourite Sabbath prop of all time. "I thought the shell idea was a great idea, because it acoustically held in my drum sound. I just built it purely to enhance the sound onstage. We were looking for different ways to grab the sound of the drums. But it was a pain in the ass to the roadies (laughs). They hated me, and it became like a joke, Bill's shell. You know the book that David Tangye and Graham Wright had written, and I mean, the comments from those guys. Because they were just so dry with their humour. So I got a lot of laughs. But in practicality, it really worked well for me. Except for that it was a crap idea when it came to the auditoriums with the audiences that wrapped around, because they couldn't see me. I think some things really worked well. I like the effects we used to have in the song 'Black Sabbath.' There's only one band I've seen that ever do effects really, really good, and we ain't it, you know? And so, for me, I always found that Black Sabbath is better just standing up and playing. I don't think it needs a lot of effects. Just get up there and play our balls off and that's it. The band that I saw do it and has continued to do it is Kiss. Kiss are the band, quickly followed by Pink Floyd, but they're in a class of their own. But I've often said, why even bother at all? Why even bother putting anything up there?"

"When Bill came up with the shells, we all laughed and thought it was bloody ridiculous," adds Tony, "and quite honestly, I thought it was good. It was good for sound, for acoustics, because it bounced back the sound of the drums, which otherwise would just disappear behind the stage. So I thought that was a good idea. I don't even know if it was intended as that, but it worked really well."

Bill's assistant Graham, explains the flowers strapped to Bill's kit—quite an eerie, funereal effect really. "What it was was, throughout all the time I worked for Bill, after I finished setting up his kit, I always used to tie flowers to the drum kit and then throw them into the audience after the show. And to be honest, on the rider, there were always so many bunches of flowers. There'd be like six large bunches of flowers. And to be honest, it was any old flowers we could get (laughs). But carnations tend to last the longest. It was more often than not that we would end up with carnations. And as soon as the band went offstage and the lights came up, I would throw the broken sticks into the front rows and I'd rip the old flowers off and throw them, usually at the girls."

Perhaps foreshadowing the band's waning status as the early '70s became the late '70s—after all, *Sabotage* was going to stall at gold—the NME's Harry Doherty couldn't find much good to say about the band's Hammersmith Odeon stand in the fall of '75.

"Sure enough, they're a heavy rock band, with all the brain-shattering chords to match. But not one of those monotonous riffs went as close as tickling my spine. Sabbath's rock has gone stale. Every riff sounded like a variation of their classic track, 'Paranoid.' Sabbath underrate the intelligence of their audiences. Their logic seems to be that three, four or five sharp notes strung together constitutes a mind-denting riff. At one stage in their history, it might have done. It certainly doesn't now. It is no longer special. Frankly, I found them boring."

"So why did those 3,000 enjoy Sabbath? Why did they create a sea of hands, shout and clap, demand more? The only conclusion I can come to is that they were shouting for the Sabbath of three or four years ago. And Sabbath tried to give them the band of three or four years ago, with the majority of the act consisting of old material. Those kids would have enjoyed themselves even if Ozzy had opened with strains of 'Summerlove Sensation.' I wouldn't be surprised, though, if some fans thought afterwards when the frenzy had died down, 'You know, that wasn't really very good.' It wasn't good at all. Sabbath were dull and repetitive. Tony Iommi's guitar solos were sub-standard, and he didn't look interested. Bill Ward's horrific drum solo was about as original as getting up in the morning. Ozzy was Ozzy."

"We were playing this baseball stadium in the States," said Ozzy in the press at the time, relating a road story from the tour. "We were in the middle of a huge field, and there's a high wire fence all 'round, with the kids outside. So I say to them, you know, come on, come inside, and suddenly they're all climbing over the fence and running towards us like a human stampede, and we're playing away, waiting for them to get up to us. But when they do, they don't stop! They just trample right over the stage, bust up all our equipment and rush away across the rest of the field and out of the stadium doors! 'Cos the police are after them, see..."

Ozzy also talked about his cross collection. "I've got a drawer full of them. I couldn't hazard to guess how many I've got. I got them all over the house. People throw them on the stage at me and I pick 'em up and save 'em. I've got some really beautiful ones thrown at me and they're very personal to me because I've communicated with somebody in the audience. Sometimes they throw a cross and I didn't see it and it didn't work. When I pick one up, I've picked up the vibe of the person who'd thrown it. I've got seven or eight to take back with me from this tour."

Things then got a little silly in this same *Sabotage* press tour interview, Ozzy remarking, "I've got bats living in my house. I live in a 300-year-old house and when I first moved in, there was two or three and now there's eight or nine. Also in the Greenwich, there are eight or nine stray black cats. I live in the middle of the country and they appeared from nowhere. It freaks me out, so I've got crucifixes all over the house." When asked what he would like etched on his gravestone, Ozzy answers: "I was just thinking about that the other day. I'd like to have a great stone made for me of me as a young man instead of an old man. I'm gonna have a gravestone made with a statue of me and the position that I'm in on the cover of *Vol 4*. I've got to find out what stone is my stone."

Bill talked to the press about his home life as well. "I live on this farm in the countryside. I love to hunt and ride across the fields. But Ozzy here, he's dangerous with guns. Ozzy goes hunting with John Bonham, you know, the drummer from Led Zep. Sometimes we bring our families to one of our homes and have a huge outdoor feast or cookout. One time Ozzy got carried away with his guns. Almost shot off everyone's head, he did—of course Ozzy was drunk at the time."

As Oz had mentioned earlier, Black Sabbath had hired Gerald "Jezz" Woodruffe as a keyboardist for the *Sabotage* tour. Tony figured that he'd like some rhythm behind his solos for once, plus there was an increasing number of Sabbath tunes being written where some sort of keyboard or synth accompaniment had become integral. Ozzy had always been against the idea, however, and Woodruffe got no respect, sometimes being visible on stage, sometimes hidden or off in a corner. As well, just to wind him up, sometimes the roadies would point the smoke machines at him.

Here Jezz charts his joining up with the boys. "Well, the drummer that was in my jazz trio, Mike Evans, who unfortunately got killed, was a very close friend of Bill Ward's. And when Sabbath were looking for a keyboard player in 1975, Mike Evans said to Bill, 'You should check Jezz out, because he can play anything.' So I got a phone call from Bill, and met him at a drum shop in Birmingham, went to Ozzy's house, would you believe, and played with the band, who were just there. Ozzy had this room on the side of his house that was a special place for rehearsing, like a studio, but there was no recording equipment. And I walk in there, and they were all there, luckily, just a kid off the street, really, and it was quite mind-blowing. But I thought, 'Right, I've got to do this' so I just ripped into the keyboards, and they said 'Okay, you're coming with us to America' and that was it."

"I was very honoured to hang about with the guys from Lynyrd Skynyrd," says Jezz, when asked to recount a high point of the odyssey. "Because they toured with us, God knows how many gigs. They were fantastic. That was brilliant and I used to hang about with those guys. They really had it, when they were doing 'Freebird' and stuff like that. I didn't know how we could go on after them, to be honest. Except that it was a different audience, a Sabbath audience. I don't think they were really on the wavelength for that Skynyrd stuff."

Jezz lays out the extent of the tour. "England, all of Europe, Norway, all of the north there, America. We were in America for months on end. I mean, I did the *Sabotage* tour. In fact, I had joined just after they finished the *Sabotage* album. So, three years basically of just constant touring, but most of it in America. Hundreds of gigs. But they had to do that, you know? They just had to keep going."

"Bill had a massive Slingerland kit, didn't he?" continues Jezz, on the subject of gear. "I remember that big shell behind his kit. It looked like a big oyster or clam shell. I just had masses of keyboards, because in those days you had to have a keyboard for each sound. And they were just all over the place. My Moogs were the key to doing the *Sabotage* songs. I had four Moog synthesizers and I spent hours programming those to get as near and as close a sound I liked as I could. But I think the most successful thing was a Fender Rhodes going through a fuzzbox. That sounded very much like the backing chords, the heavy riffs, if I got it right."

Surprisingly, Jezz confirms that the band had played "Am I Going Insane (Radio)" live. "Yeah, we did. And I used Ozzy's ARP 2600 to do that, the one that he actually has at home, that he's standing next to on The Osbournes from a few weeks ago. There's the one where he's trying to get the noises out of his synth. It's the same synth because I remember sticking the tour sticker on it where it is on that one; it's the same one. And it's worth a fortune now, because those old synths are just collectible. Otherwise, I used to try copy Tony's original guitar parts on keyboards, so he could do the solos and the riffs would keep going; I used to do a lot of that." In addition to the gear Jezz discusses above, he also had with him a Clavinet, a Wurlitzer and a Korg 800 DV.

Asked if he contributed backing vocals, Jezz says, "No, I can't sing. I sound like Ringo Starr."

As a trivia note, press in the day had Jezz talking about a matching white leather fringe jacket to Ozzy's, although, he said, it never got seen, given his position hidden from view. As well, Jezz had talked about his impending (but never appearing) solo album, *Variations on the Ascent of Man*, for which Ozzy was to guest vocal.

Finally on gear, Graham Wright says that, "Tony just played his Gibson SG and his John Birch guitars, and he played through Laney valve amps and Laney stacks. There wasn't the technology there is today. And Bill just played his... I think it was a Tama kit by then. No, it was all very basic really, compared to what they do with sounds these days."

A further UK leg of the *Sabotage* tour had to be postponed when Ozzy smacked himself up in a motorcycle accident, although December dates back in the States would go ahead, Sabbath playing with the likes of Aerosmith, Manfred Mann, Savoy Brown, and once more both Kiss and Ruby Starr, who would die in 1996 at the age of 44 of a brain tumour. The *Sabotage* tour, not a particularly long one, ended back in England with the rescheduled dates from November performed in January of 1976, the year that would mark a miserable downward slide for the band from which they would never recover.

Chaotic Japanese single sleeve.

Alternate Russian sleeve for *Sabbath Bloody Sabbath.*

Alternate sleeve for *Sabbath Bloody Sabbath.*

Rare two-colour, two-page newsprint ad for *Sabbath Bloody Sabbath* UK tour dates.

UK newsprint ad for *Vol 4* tour dates, supported by Badger and Birmingham baby band Necromandus, briefly mentored by Tony.

UK music weekly ad for short British tour, support courtesy of from Nutz (soon to be Rage).

BLACK SABBATH WORLD TOUR '76-77

OFFICIAL PROGRAMME

Front cover of *Technical Ecstasy* tour program.

Later period Warner Bros. promo photo. Stay classy, Birmingham.

Bill Ward in all his propulsive glory, 1978. © Rich Galbraith

Japanese issue of "Am I Going Insane (Radio)"/"Hole in the Sky."

Yugoslavian issue "Gypsy"/"She's Gone" single using much earlier photograph.

A couple of versions of singles produced to help make "Hard Road" a hit. Neither worked.

Geezer and Ozzy were the original headbangers, even though Robert Plant could shake his mane as well.
© Rich Galbraith.

Geezer Butler, fan of fashion. © Rich Galbraith.

Tony Iommi watching Eddie Van Halen. © Rich Galbraith.

Japanese single featuring title track from *Never Say Die,* backed with "She's Gone" from the previous album.

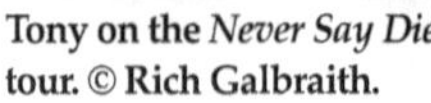

Tony on the *Never Say Die* tour. © Rich Galbraith.

Bill, November 20, The Myriad, Oklahoma City, Oklahoma. Suppert came from Van Halen. © Rich Galbraith.

Album 7

Technical Ecstasy

"Stupid, really"

Everybody's got their Sab favourites, but, as with other monumental greats like Zeppelin or Purple, once sick of the usual old rotters, the discerning fan digs deep into the dark horse albums, finding treasures along untrampled pathways. *Technical Ecstasy* is one of those potential treasures for the deep Sabbath fan, an album that is oddly, uneasily mainstream in its construction and lyrics, but somehow cloaked in a thick damp blanket of doom, a hacking flu the inevitable result. It is a record of corruption absorbed and then Oz-mosed through the pores, a corruption more sophisticated in its seduction than the shouting and pointing version represented by the overt horrors of records like *Sabbath Bloody Sabbath* or *Paranoid*. *Technical Ecstasy* will rot your brain if loved too obsessively.

Incongruously, the album was recorded in sunny Florida, temporarily lifting the spirits of a band desperate for a hit, reeling from drug and drink, increasingly at each other's throats (or smouldering, or at minimum vaguely aware of discomfort) over the workload of making yet another album.

"The album was written in England at Ridge Farm," explains Tony. "What we had done is that we had moved to this farm and we lived there for six weeks while we wrote the album, which was pretty quick for us. I remember when we had done it, we had all really liked it and we were playing it all live, and it sounded really good live, so basically when we went in the studio we had done the same thing; we played it live and recorded it. So it was pretty painless from that side of it."

The pain, like the record it would produce, was more insidious—it came from having to operate at manic warp-speed as Black Sabbath, any sense of personal identity or life outside the band strewn to the wind like the direction of the band's 1976 songs. Bill was not too bad, but Tony was over-worked. Ozzy had become increasingly surly, and to throw a wrench in, the presence of keyboardist Jezz Woodruffe deep into the writing also upset the familial, years-old balance, even if as consolating comfort, Woodruffe was at least from Birmingham. As well, Tony found it productive to have Jezz to collaborate with at this stage, Woodruffe taking Iommi's ideas and creating an underpinning of chords and chord changes that Tony could use as a framework on which to add the rest of the house.

Technical Ecstasy, now somewhat written, was carried away to be recorded at famed southern rock locale Criteria Studios. With none of the usual technical Criteria folk on board, the album came out self-produced and quite sonically satisfying in light of its successor *Never Say Die* and about half the starchy records from earlier in the catalogue. Much of the task, including mixing and mastering, fell to Tony who has often and vociferously made clear over the years that he resented doing as much work on that album as he was forced to. "Yeah, Criteria Studios was really great," recalls Tony. "It was a great atmosphere and I think we really had a good thing going. But I remember being stuck in the studio a majority of the time while everybody's out sunning themselves. But yes, I like that album."

"But, it wasn't that long at all, relatively quick," adds Tony. "It's just the old thing. You get to a lovely place and you sort of tend to take a bit longer. You tend to be on the beach during the day and working at night. But it was really great, I liked it. I remember trying a few different amps on that one. I used a transistor amp a lot which was very unusual for me. I think the engineer we were using almost went around the twist at the time. We were driving him up the wall. But definitely, I was left to do that album more or less on my own, so I did feel a bit left out on a limb with that one, yeah. I followed it all the way through."

Bill Ward also recalls the experience as basically enjoyable. "We were in Miami and we were having a great time (laughs). I might have been having too much of a good time. It was the first time we ever went to Criteria Studios. It seemed to be a time where we were attaching ourselves to a lot of experimenting, moving into new areas, seeing if there were things that could work, also going back to things we knew worked and we enjoyed, but at the same time saying let's stretch it here, let's go forward. For instance, 'It's Alright' is just this really soft song, a bit of a risk. But I liked the idea that it was a risk from where we were. But I can only remember good times recording that album."

Which included the following, according to Tony: 1) putting a pile of gorgonzola cheese under Bill's bed in the hotel room, which just got worse and worse without him noticing (Ward would never let the maids into his room); 2) dressing a very drunk Bill up as Hitler, his hair fashioned with gaffer tape, which had to be cut off, taking half his hair with it, and 3) messing up an Andy Gibb doll (the Bee Gees were there) to look like Bill—this even fooled Andy who said, "Bill's got a doll out too?!"

"Oh yes, we were down at Ridge Farms," explains David Tangye, charting the process from writing through to completion. "Actually, I think first off we went to a place called Glaspant in Wales, an absolute dump, this place. And everybody started scratching and itching saying, 'Well, we've got to get out of here.' So the band upsticks and they went to Ridge Farm Studio, down in Rusper, in Sussex. It wasn't a full-blown studio as it is now. Ozzy did his first two albums there, maybe the first three; I'm not quite sure. But they went down there to rehearse it all, and then of course took it over to Miami. A lot of the finishing off was done in Miami, and then I think Tony went to L.A. to do the final mix with Robin Black. Robin Black sort of co-produced on that, and Robin had worked with Jethro Tull; he used to do quite a lot of stuff with the Rolling Stone Mobile. I think they did some of the mix at Sounds Interchange in Toronto as well. But most of it was done in Miami and we were there for two or three months."

"It was a funny time for Black Sabbath, I think. They were going through a lot of changes in their personal lives. Tony really worked hard on that album. He was bringing new stuff in, and of course Gerald Woodruffe had come out. He had come to do the keyboards, which was excellent. Gerald is a brilliant musician. He injected a lot of creative stuff into that album, because he could play. And that's why it was so different from a lot of the other stuff they did in the past. A lot of the fans didn't like it (laughs), because there was more melody and strings. They did that track 'She's Gone,' and I can't remember the name of the company they brought in to do the strings. That was totally different for them. And of course they had Bill singing 'It's Alright.' But I love that album actually, and a lot of people have knocked it. As has been said over the years, Tony and Geezer were working on it hard and then of course Ozzy went in in the end and overdubbed everything, got his vocals down. It went well actually. We just had quite a bit of fun there, because there were a lot of people in the studio at the time. The Eagles were in there doing *Hotel California*."

"They were, yeah," adds Jezz. "The Eagles were in Studio 3 and Fleetwood Mac were in Studio 1. Micky Fleetwood used to call me into their studio to listen to what they were doing, which was nice. He was a great bloke; well, he still is, I suppose. I haven't seen him for years. But what really impressed me was the rows and rows of guitars in the other studio that belonged to Joe Walsh. There were about 30 vintage guitars and this one roadie, who had only two fingers on one hand was in charge of them all. And I thought, well, that's cool! (laughs)."

David comments further on the presence of Robin Black, who had also co-engineered *Sabotage*. "Robin was in there, like engineering, really, more engineering than producing. Because Tony and Geezer would probably do the majority of the production. I think Robin was down as the engineer. And of course Spock Wall would be assisting him as well. But Robin was a lovely fellow, a quiet fellow. And then Robin and Tony actually went to California to do the final mix, to do the mastering and that. Robin was quite involved with it. But the majority of the time, I looked after Ozzy and basically that was it. There were loads of different camps in Black Sabbath (laughs). Tony, Geezer, everyone had something to do. And of course when Ozzy was off, although he was busy working on the album, he still had his bits of time off. So we had our things to do. We weren't necessarily screwed to the floorboards in the studio. It was more an in-and-out type thing."

"I think they were just experimenting," reflects Tangye, on the tenor of the record at hand. "*Sabotage* was a really big turning point for Black Sabbath. 'The Writ,' 'Hole in the Sky,' absolutely brilliant. That was Sabbath at its best, really. Because that was when they were all... you had the management problems, writs were coming in, this, that and the other. There was loads and loads of light and shade on that album. I think they got a lot of aggression out with *Sabotage*. And *Technical Ecstasy* was a different thing altogether, because they had gone to Miami to do that. I mean, all the other albums, they'd either been in Record Plant or London basically, Morgan Studios. So for *Technical Ecstasy*, they went to a warm climate. And climate changes you; it gives you a different perspective. As I say, they had the ideas in England originally but they just expanded them, basically. And that was the end result, *Technical Ecstasy*."

Geezer's celebrated creativity extended to the album graphics this time out. "That was my idea," notes Butler. "I just gave them (noted UK album cover artists Hipgnosis) a rough thing of what I wanted and let them go at it. I wanted the sort of robots, but with an art deco feel."

"I thought it was a good title," adds Tony. "Geezer came up with that title, as he did with most. If you remember the cover, it has the two robots going past having sex—technical ecstasy (laughs)." Ecstasy technically speaking perhaps, but the communication within the cover art comes off as blind, machine-like, functional and mindlessly procreative at best, a perfect visual wrap for the hypnotic, fascinating sleepwalk enclosed.

"Geezer, that was his title," recalls Bill, in agreement. "I think we saw a couple of things, as far as the artwork goes. It was one of those situations where somebody magically was coming up with the artwork (laughs). And it kind of drifted past our eyes, so to speak. And everybody settled on the album cover. It was like, well, that makes some kind of sense. We were all attracted to it. I kind of liked it for about ten minutes (laughs). I think I'm used to it now. It's like, oh, okay. I pretty much went along with it because Geezer thought it was great. We influenced each other. If Geezer thought it was okay, then it was okay."

"Yeah, there was a title for that," confirms Aubrey Powell, co-chief of Hipgnosis along with the late Storm Thorgerson. "There's an interesting story about that, because what we always do is we do it photographically. But Storm and I realized we would never be able to reproduce robots that looked any good. You know, to have robots built, it would look something like out of *Dr. Who*. It just wouldn't… we didn't have the kind of money that, say, someone like Steven Spielberg would have or George Lucas would have for *Star Wars* (laughs). So what we did is photographed the whole thing in the background and everything to work out where the people would be. And then I went to George Hardie and said, listen, we need to have this illustrated. Because we simply can't do it photographically. So will you illustrate it for us? And he said okay. So he created those cartoon characters that you see on there. And it's a love between two robots passing on an escalator, basically. Which is why it's called *Technical Ecstasy*. That's what it is—it's a lust between two robots; that's the narrative."

"Anyway, I went to see the band, and I walked in there, and they were all there, at Tony Iommi's house. Except for Ozzy Osbourne. And I showed the band, and I kept thinking, where's Ozzy? When is he gonna come in? And suddenly there's a knock on the door, and this guy stumbles in with black glasses and black leather, as Ozzy does, and there's Ozzy. And he's obviously had a couple of drinks (laughs), and he started shouting at the other members of the band. And I'm a very laid-back kind of guy. Slightly taken aback. And then he said, 'Oh, you're deciding on the album cover.' And they had already chosen this idea. And I thought, where is this gonna go?"

"So he walked down the line and he pointed at the same picture.

They had the choice of about 12 different ideas, and he pointed at the picture of *Technical Ecstasy*, and he said, 'I'm having that one. That's the one we're having.' And I said, 'That's lucky, Ozzy, because everybody's chosen the same one.' And he looked at me like, who the fuck are you?! (laughs). And then they broke into this enormous fight. I mean, absolutely screaming at each other. And the manager turned around to me and said, 'I think we'd better go.' So I grabbed up the artwork and walked out the door. And I was quite shellshocked. And I said, 'Well, that's all a bit of a surprise. I wasn't expecting that kind of thing to go on.' And he said to me, 'I think it went rather well, actually.' I said, 'Really?' He said, 'Well, we got an album cover out of it.'"

"But this was about other band stuff. I never understood what it was about. I didn't want to get involved. It was quite aggressive and I was quite shocked. Because normally, when I would see people, Paul McCartney or whoever, we'd have very cool, laid-back sessions, chatting about art and life. This was, whoa, okay, this is another side of rock 'n' roll. It was just a funny moment."

For his part, Storm stressed that the image is more a representation of love at first sight, but that love at first sight between robots would occur differently with robots than with humans, and so they are squirting liquids at each other in public and at some distance. Storm also considered the fact that the female was represented by curves and the male by sharp angles to be a bit sexist.

Back to the music, *Technical Ecstasy* opens with a bold gallop of a rocker, a song that amounts to the album's pure metal moment, "Back Street Kids" discharging an immediate blast of uptempo precision metal that was almost too energetic for a band labouring up the road low on motor oil. "I love 'Back Street Kids;' that's so fun to play, man," offers Bill. "We were actually messing around with that one during rehearsals a couple of weeks back (this interview was conducted April 11, 2001), but it's very high vocally for Oz." Geezer had also noted that bringing this song to life in '01 wasn't exactly working out for the band, this blustery, hard-charging rocker joining "Symptom of the Universe," "Hole in the Sky" and "Sabbath Bloody Sabbath" as tracks off-limits late in Ozzy's career.

David Tangye, given his role as Ozzy's personal assistant at the time, offers a glimpse into the working methodology of the Oz-man.

"I'd say 'Back Street Kids' and 'Rock 'n' Roll Doctor' were good ones for him, in terms of a personal stamp. Because a lot of the stuff they didn't put together when we were in England. Sabbath used to come up with their songs… I mean, usually it was a big jam sort of thing and then record everything and then basically the words would come on top. Tony would come up with riffs and Ozzy would just sing anything that came into his head. And they would have it all recorded and played back maybe at the end of the day's rehearsal. And then Geezer would be thinking about it. And we'd just let them get on with that, because that was band stuff. That was their creative period. We didn't really have any time to sit in with them on that stuff. Words would come up; probably Geezer would come up with words and Ozzy... they were quite close and they worked together. Ozzy would have some good ideas. If you read a lot of rock journals, these newsletters that kids post, they say 'Ozzy had nothing to do with this and he didn't do that,' but he did, you know? (laughs). He was there, you know what I mean? And he wouldn't have survived, if he hadn't. And he did survive."

"But basically after *Technical Ecstasy*, that's when things were really going downhill for the band. It's like familiarity... they'd been together a long time. And when you start making money, I think you get different ideas that you want to do something else. Because I remember when I came back from Miami, we went back to Ozzy's house, and that's when he told me he wanted to get the guys from Necromandus, the band that I had looked after and managed before I started to work with Sabbath. He wanted to get these guys down. Not necessarily as a band that he wanted to put together. I think it was more of a band that he wanted to try some of his creative stuff out with. He was wanting to experiment, basically. I mean, he couldn't get away from Sabbath because he was still with the band. But I think it was more of an experiment, to see how he would work with other musicians. I mean, he's worked incredibly well with other musicians as time's got on (laughs). And they were all feeling sort of... they worked hard those few years. They'd never stopped really, if you think about it. Touring and recording and all the rest of it, and all the personal side they put up with, hassles they had with the management. I think they weathered the storm really well, actually (laughs)."

"I think Ozzy's idea was more down-to-earth solid rock like the first album; get in, get it done," says Tangye, noting Ozzy's dissatisfaction with Sabbath at this point. "When they did the first album, very little time was spent. And as the albums went on, it got more complicated. Of course, recording techniques changed as well. There was more stuff in the studio to play with. Tony would be experimenting with different stuff. But

I think Ozzy thought that basically keyboards and all this stuff... he wasn't really over-keen on having the keyboards. I got the impression at the time he wanted the four guys doing it, the guitar, bass, drums and vocals and that was it. Although they brought Gerald in to sort of fatten the sound out, if you like, I think Ozzy is more inclined to the earlier stuff."

Asked if Ozzy was insecure about his writing, David figures, "No, I honestly don't think so. I think he had problems with dyslexia, but that was never an issue. Ozzy would come up with some good words and great ideas. But Ozzy liked change. He liked to put his two pennies in. He wanted to say what he wanted to say and that was it. But I think generally, collectively, they got everything down that they wanted to get down, that they felt between them. Geezer was great; especially the first few albums. He came up with some great stuff that has stood the test of time. I suppose they were quite happy with each other. They wouldn't have kept going for so long and there wouldn't be these reunions (laughs). Those first seven or eight albums, there is some great stuff there."

"They were all quite involved," continues Tangye. "When they were in the rehearsals, Spock would be in there with the Revox tape and everything. That side of it, we wouldn't all be in there when they were rehearsing, of course, because it would just be a distraction. They were quite intense when they were working. And as I said, they would all have their two pennies. They would say, 'We should put this in.' There would be jam sessions, all banging away, putting in their own ideas. It's like building a house. You would put the foundation down, put bits in, take bits out. Tony would have a few ideas that he would put out and they would just build from there."

"But yes, they were totally involved with it. Even today. There'll never be another one. It's those four people. There are a lot of people who say Tony did this, Tony did that, but I think Black Sabbath will always be Black Sabbath. It's like seeing the Beatles. The Beatles would never be the same without those four guys. The name goes with the band. If the band had success with that name in the early days, you know, you can rehash it and change it, but… They were so close. They were brought up with each other and were all of the same mind. And I don't think you'll ever change that. But Tony did great to keep it all going, and he's had some great musicians with him over the years."

"I think they were really into it," adds Jezz, specifically answering as to Bill's and Geezer's involvement with the record. "At that time *Presence* came out by Led Zeppelin, and they couldn't understand that. They were going, 'Why is this #1?' And I was saying, 'This is unbelievable!' So they weren't on the same level musically as bands like Led Zeppelin. It was much more simple than that. None of them had any musical education. But I had, you see. I'd been sent away to public school, and I was in the school orchestra and I'd done theory and grades on woodwind instruments and piano and all the rest of it. So I had this big advantage, which they used. You know, they used me to help them get to that next edge further. So no, everybody at that point was putting in what they should be doing, apart from Ozzy. He was never there."

Asked where Ozzy was, Woodruffe laughs, "He was probably out with a shotgun shooting chickens. He just disappeared and nobody knew where he was. And he wasn't into it at all. We had to drag him into the studio. We had to push him onto the stage when we were touring. He just wanted to go home. At that stage in his life, I don't think he was interested in anything. He and Tony were really at loggerheads. But it was Tony's band. Well, as Tony was concerned, he'd taken over the role as head of the band. So that might be where the confusion was. He wasn't actually that in control of the music at that point. Tony was definitely in control of Black Sabbath, because Ozzy was not interested. Bill was taking care of business. He was always on the phone to L.A. sorting out deals and stuff. It was like that."

"Ozzy is just music—that's all he's ever done and that's all he knows," sums up Tangye. "The only thing that Ozzy knows is getting up on the stage and performing. He's very, very intense, or he was. Quite a complicated chap, you know what I mean? I just think he's like the rest of them. They had the time of their life, really. They were doing what they wanted to do and they had a lot of success. They had a lot of real fans, if you know what I mean. Because they were so involved in it and so sort of... it was all Black Sabbath; that's all it was. There wasn't anything else. And Ozzy just lived the role; he lived Black Sabbath and that was it. I suppose he was two people. He was John Osbourne and Ozzy Osbourne, like an alter ego. He was just enjoying himself, basically. I got on great with him. I don't see much of him now, but when we do meet up, we have a laugh. Ozzy is as you see him—that's him. There are no airs and graces about him. There are no back doors—that's him. He's in your face and that's him. He's a rock star and he's a singer in a heavy metal band (laughs)."

Back at *Technical Ecstasy*, things slow down with a deathly lurch for "You Won't Change Me." There's something a little obvious about this song. To its credit, Sabbath create a dirge that is as depressing as they've ever done, no small feat given the misery-ridden back catalogue—it's what they do best. But then again, the song is written somewhat conventionally, it is accessible and it's almost a ballad, if of a bludgeoning sort, Bill dropping bombs, the band bashing in resignation of an end to come. But you never quite feel the song could support a sour, head-scratching wig-out like those all over the late stages of songs from the last two records. Instead, the break is Beatle-esque. Tony however turns in not one but two ripping yet still sorrowful and bluesy solos, choosing a tone that just scrapes the heartstrings until they recoil.

"It's about just sticking to your principles," remarked Geezer on the uncharacteristically straightforward lyric. "And no matter what people try do to change you, nobody's going to be able to do it."

Jezz sings the melody to "You Won't Change Me," and says, "That's all keyboard patterns. You can spot them a mile off. They don't come from the guitar like that," intimating a big writing presence in the song. Beyond debate is the *Exorcist*-esque keyboard line Woodruffe puts into the track, adding to its creepy mystique—it's almost shocking to hear this song placed at the second position on the record.

"He was helpful, yeah," recalls Tony on the contentious issue of Jezz in the band. "Because I basically wanted somebody else to play with. Ozzy was going, 'Oh, we don't need a keyboard player.' But I just thought it would be helpful for me, for writing the songs, to bounce off somebody. Because it was always me that had to come up with the riffs. So I thought it would be a nice touch to widen our scope by using another sort of wider variety of sounds, with the keyboards. I think in the day, it was a lot of pressure, because there was a lot of responsibility and somebody had to come up with the ideas and somebody had to get it down, so I started getting more and more things put on me on the production side, and booking the studios and doing this and doing that. Because at certain stages, of course, we didn't have management and we were doing things ourselves. So I was supposedly supposed to know more than anybody else in the band about the studio, and it was left to me to book the studio and book the people involved in that. So that's what we did, really. I think it's good to have someone for the other members to turn to. I used to tend to be that one. If there was any problem then they used to come to me. Sometimes, it wasn't a good thing for me because I couldn't go out and get drunk when they did. Somebody had to stay straight to see that things happened correctly."

Tony also felt however, that this was a really fertile period for him with respect to his playing abilities. "I felt, sometimes on stage, as time went on, oh yeah, you feel like you can play anything. And I was playing things and I didn't even know what it was I was playing (laughs). It was becoming like second nature. Things were coming up and I couldn't remember what it was, so of course, I couldn't play them again. Things were getting better at one point, and I felt things stepping up, which is probably around *Technical Ecstasy*."

"It's Alright" is unarguably the most left field track on the album, a fully Beatle-esque ballad written by Bill and astonishingly, sung by Bill. "Actually I started that one some time before," notes Bill. "I wrote it at Field Farm, our first house in England; that's the house I shared with my second wife. And the guys would come down. That's where we used to rehearse as well; it turned into a rehearsal place. Oz would come down and write stuff of his own. It was a kind of commune-type place for awhile."

I asked Bill if it took some coaxing to get him out of his shell to do that song. "Yes, I was scared to death!" laughs Bill. "I had it in the house and the guys knew about the song and Ozzy kind of liked the song but it was like, 'Oh my God, am I going to play in Sabbath one of my own songs?' Because it's one thing being a co-writer and supporter and a semi-arranger, but then moving into your own material and being supported by your band mates, it's pretty scary. I mean, Tony was doing it with 'Laguna Sunrise,' but yes, you're right, he didn't have to sing them."

"Well, I liked it," adds Tony. "I thought it was really good. We tried to encourage Bill, yeah, you should record that. It was quite different for us. Bill wrote all the lyrics on that and the music, and I just wrote the solo part in the middle."

"I remember when we were in Miami, Bill never surfaced," says David, remembering the working dynamic of the drummer. "He was the only Englishmen to go to Miami and come back lighter than when he left (laughs). It was just how he was. He's a creature of the night, Bill. Fairly nocturnal. Because we were booked in the studio in the night-time, from six until six, we'd get back in the early morning and have a couple hours sleep, and then of course we're up around the pool. But whenever Bill came onto his veranda after his deep sleep, he used to get a big rapture of applause. And the other guests used to think, well, maybe it's his birthday. Because we used to sing 'Happy Birthday' and all sorts of things, just as a bit of a joke."

Bill pleads, of all things, sobriety. "What happened, in the weirdest way, when we were down in Florida, and there was a lot of cocaine use then, and I wasn't using (laughs). So I got to watch them. Some of them were pretty out of it, and I just couldn't hang in any more. I couldn't hang with the all-nighters, stoned with the blow. I used to isolate anyway, but I just didn't join in the big cocaine parties and things like that. Because by the time I was 25, I was burned-out. I had already had hepatitis. I guess at that time I was the band member most likely to fucking die before he was 30. So if there was ever an award like that, I was probably the strongest contender. Which is nothing to be proud of, but I just couldn't hang where the only talk's about what drugs we were going to do and things like that. It's almost like I became quieter; I just watched."

"Ozzy hated it right from the start, never wanted it on the album," notes Woodruffe, contrarily to the above, on Bill's big number, "It's Alright." "And when we just finished it and Bill had done the vocal, we were just getting ready to do another take, and Ozzy came into the studio and said, 'What's that fooking rubbish?!' And Bill went absolutely ballistic and trashed his drum kit. He'd just spent hours getting a drum sound and he just smashed the whole lot, the microphones, the whole lot. The whole studio was a wreck. And a few weeks later, they decided to put that song on the album. And a lot of Sabbath fans hated it. Because it was Ozzy's territory; it always had been. The fans thought that commerciality had invaded the band, and to be honest they were right. But I thought it was a good song. Bill heard it when he was cruising down the freeway, on FM radio, and he was thrilled to bits (laughs). He had his five minutes of... that."

Bill denies that there were any rows over "It's Alright" going on the album. "Oh, not all. To be honest with you, I was really reluctant for it to go on there. I felt really uncomfortable that "It's Alright" was going to go onto an album. I wasn't aware that I was pushing it or anything. I felt the opposite, like, 'This is a bit weird.'"

"Bill hasn't sang for years," Iommi told Steve Rosen at the time. "Bill and myself did this number a long time ago; we went in the studio and done it. This must have been four years ago; we put it down but then we just scrapped it. We decided to re-record it again in Miami and it came out differently."

As for Ozzy, he's on the record as saying he really liked it and pushed Bill to sing, Oz remembering that Bill was a singer in his pre-Sabbath band The Rest. As well, Ozzy was really losing interest at this time, plus drinking so much that he booked himself into rehab when he got home to England (which lasted about five minutes). This is also the time when he made himself a Blizzard of Oz shirt (one "z" at this point), and imagined what it would be like being a solo artist. He considers *Technical Ecstasy* to be "Tony's album," and recalls that at the time Tony was pushing for the guys to get more commercial, like Queen or like Foreigner, and that both Geezer and Bill quite liked these types of bands as well.

Side one of *Technical Ecstasy* closes with "Gypsy," one of the album's stronger tracks, one that played on Sabbath's key strengths, namely heaviness and unpredictability. Bill's opening rhythm is tribal and busy, but then Geezer and Tony place the simplest of chord patterns over it. Eventually the song collapses into a bold but simple and groovy hard rock, a third transition and then a (Queen-like) fourth and then a fifth to close out: five completely different passages stacked one after another, no chorus, no verse, the last being a dark jam that recalls the alchemy of old.

"I like 'Gypsy,'" remembers Tony. "We used more of a piano. I think with that album we used keyboards probably more than most. Gerald playing keyboards made it a bit easier for me because I could concentrate more on the guitar stuff instead of playing piano on bits here and there, you know?" Bill has said that he thought that "Gypsy" was first conceived at Strawberry Studios in London around Easter, and that Ozzy may have had a fair bit to do with it lyrically.

"'Gypsy' was just a throwaway lyric about meeting a gypsy. Stupid, really." The tone in Geezer's voice says so much more than the words themselves (I almost couldn't suppress my snicker), betraying the fact that the band could indeed write a throwaway lyric at this tired time, and not care. It also contains within its timbre the reminder that one shouldn't read too much into many of Geezer's seemingly deeper and more poetic lines. In many cases it was the drugs talking, and a deadpan, thoroughly honest Geezer will say as much.

"'All Moving Parts (Stand Still)' was one of my titles," recalls Bill with a laugh, zoning in on the opening track of the original vinyl's side two. "And it manages that; I think it was that literal. I just loved it; it was just really odd. The working title for that was 'Claret on the Blanket.' I think that might be new to everybody. And that referred to a very dysfunctional sexual thing. I'll just leave it at that right now (laughs)." Actually, that's one way of looking at it, with Bill having said at other times that it simply refers to the menstrual cycle. He's right about the motion of the song though, the track moving laboriously with shallow breaths—elephantine and clumsy and murky—signaled by Geezer's lobotomized disco funk of a bass riff, and the progressive herky jerk of the break section. Still, this was a rocker and at least a bit of an avant garde one, not so obvious or on the surface as, well, everything presented on the album thus far, save for "Gypsy."

Says Geezer, "'All Moving Parts (Stand Still),' I think it was about Margaret Thatcher at the time, something like that. It was about a woman that was... because at that time, well, there still hasn't been a woman President in America. It's about a woman who has to dress up as a man to become President, because that's how misogynistic American society is. Britain cancelled it out when Margaret Thatcher became Prime Minister—that was another coincidence. By the time the album came out, we had a woman Prime Minister." Not quite, with Margaret Thatcher having been elected May 4, 1979, but indeed The Iron Lady (!) had been the leader of the Conservative party since 1975.

"Aha! Now then, 'All Moving Parts,'" laughs Mr. Woodruffe. "That was really funny, because we were set up in an amazing manor house somewhere in Surrey, and Ozzy disappeared for a couple of hours. And he came back with an armful of marijuana plants that were about eight feet high (laughs). 'Where did you get those from?!' And he found a greenhouse just up the road, that was about 100 metres long that was full of these plants. I mean, how he found it, I don't know. So what he did then was, we had a log burner in the room where we were all sitting and he put the whole lot on the fire (laughs). And then the words to this song 'All Moving Parts (Stand Still)' started arriving."

Wow, and what do those words mean?

"Well, it means that Ozzy put lots of dope on the fire."

Next up we had "Rock 'n' Roll Doctor," perhaps the album's second least characteristic Sabbath track, Tony remarking that "we made it more into something with a honky-tonk feel, a piano thing, although it didn't start out that way." It is in fact both a boogie woogie song and a party rocker, although the idea of "party" was painted in typical Sabbath greys and deep blues. Essentially, Ozzy's anguished cries sound less like a celebration and more like a dance with the devil, the central character of the lament seeking a temporary respite from bone-wracked ills, a simple salve on the shakes. Bill offers the following comment. "'Rock 'n' Roll Doctor,' we did really fast. That one just kind of like came off. As a matter of fact, I think we started jamming it live, before we even knew that that was going to be a song. Because Tony would always do those long solos. And you know, we had half of our material right there (laughs), you know, for the next album. Because he would just be putting riff after riff together. And I think that's where 'Rock 'n' Doctor,' or part of it, might have stemmed from. The song was pretty good but it needed something on there, just to give it a bit of a honky-tonk feel, which is why there's the piano."

"I think 'Rock 'n' Roll Doctor' was to do with Ozzy," says Geezer. "I think he came up with that, either the lyrics or the title. It doesn't sound like anything I'd write."

As Jezz indicates, if that's the case, he didn't see any of it. "No, Geezer wrote all the lyrics; he always did. Nobody else ever had a part in that, you know? Right from the very start. Well, for the three years I was with them, I never saw anybody else put pen to paper. It was all Geezer. But musically, it was all a group effort. Do the riff and see what comes out. We were desperately short of songs anyway. We had to drag everything out of the bag. There wasn't anything left off."

Asked if there were any cool keyboard things he tried that didn't get used, Woodruffe says, "There was a lot that was pushed back into the mix, but I can't remember the details. But that's an interesting question."

I also asked Jezz to pinpoint a key Jezz moment on the album. "The piano in 'Rock 'n' Roll Doctor'—I like that. Me and Tony worked the riff out, and it was new to them; they didn't do stuff like that. You know, I've seen reviews saying that that album was one of the worst Sabbath albums they've ever done; I've seen a lot of feedback like that. And I actually think it was quite refreshingly different (laughs). In the end, it went platinum in the UK. It struggled to start with, but it got there."

Hard feelings begin to surface on this subject of Woodruffe's stamp on the album. "Well, that's a very difficult area, really, because my input into those songs is a tremendous amount. But you'll notice on the re-releases, I don't even think my name is on the covers. And this is... the truth of it is that I can't really tell you what the truth is because it's heavy business stuff, and I'm owed massively, but I ain't going into that."

It sounds similar to what went on a few years later between the Osbourne camp and Bob Daisley and Lee Kerslake.

"Ah well, at least they knew they were selling their stuff. They were paid. A bit. And it was straightforward. Sharon would say, 'You want to be on the album? We buy it off you and that's it.' That's the hard rock 'n' roll business. With me, back in the '70s, there was nothing, no agreement, anything. No paperwork, nothing. Because actually, to be honest, I never did it for the money anyway. I never have. I never did any of the stuff with Robert Plant for any other reason other than the fact that I desperately needed to do this for myself. Which is what I do now. But I was involved in virtually everything all the way through. I was heavily involved in the arrangements of all of them. I think it just says 'Additional Arrangements' by me somewhere."

Jezz denies this sentiment that Ozzy was resentful of keyboards. "It wasn't that as much. It was a massive clash of personalities between me and Ozzy, because of where we'd come from, our backgrounds. They were totally different. I was very fortunate. My dad was a band leader in the '40s, and after the Second World War he built up a retail music instrument business which was, you know, big-time. So I had a privileged lifestyle. Whereas Ozzy was struggling from the day he was born, really. And there was that real clash there of totally different backgrounds. Which didn't bother me, but it sure bothered him."

But things were much warmer with Tony. "It was me and him (laughs). In reality. And we had a very close bond for a long time. We actually both come from the same kind of background, music-wise. My dad used to play for me Django Reinhardt and Errol Garner, and that was my roots really, and Tony's roots were Joe Pass. And I used to go to his mansion in Leicestershire, this stately home place. And the only record he would ever play was Joe Pass; he was listening to it all the time. So we both have this in common, this sort of jazz thing. So when we started writing the album, it's not fair for anybody to say that it was his responsibility. In the public's eye, it was, because I didn't really exist. Because if I existed, I was going to cost them lots of money (laughs). That's the truth of that. So they kept me in the... well, behind the curtain, for the first American tour. Eventually I came onto the side of the stage, but was never ever really given a prominent part in the band. But it was the start of my career and I caught a lot of experience from that. So that's how I got paid, really."

On the subject of whether any of the Sabbath guys can play keyboards, Jezz says, "Not really. Well, that's subjective to me, because you know, people who I think can play keyboards are people like Oscar Peterson (laughs). But yeah, they can get a few chords. Tony can. In fact, Tony plays on the original 'Changes;' that's his piano playing." Adds Graham Wright,

"I think Tony was a bit more technical than Bill because he used to play accordion when he was a little kid, so he was much better using both hands."

Nearing the close of this album—a record that is with the world but without it—is a melancholy wisp of a ballad called "She's Gone" ("a big production thing," says Bill). Worlds away from "It's Alright," on this one it's not alright, except maybe for those flawless orchestrations courtesy of Mike Lewis. Says Jezz of his input on this one: "The intro to the strings, I think that's it. I worked closely with the guy who arranged the strings, so the beginning of the strings section, I really like that. It was done at Criteria Studios in Miami, and they brought in an orchestra to do it."

Closer "Dirty Women" was a particularly rousing piece, meandering depressively them blazing out with a free-burn of a riff from Tony, triumphant, the euphoric heavy metal high point of the record. But as Tony agrees, it is a strange topic for a Sabbath song. "Yes, well, Geezer was writing about more obvious things on this album, but 'Dirty Women,' that's the one we had a laugh about." Bill says that live, he "loved doing the end of that, with Tony. We do that big build-up with the double bass drums. There's a lot of nice stuff on that one."

Jezz chips in. "'Dirty Women,' that was completely mine; I wrote all of that, and you'll see no credit at all. I wrote it in the barn at Glaspant Mansion in Wales, which is where we did the first rehearsal for that album," with Geezer volunteering that "'Dirty Women' was about... every day we used to go past this red light district on the way to the studio. We were recording in Florida, and we would see all these prostitutes waiting for the clients, all these dirty old men. It was about that, basically."

"Dirty Women" will forever be paired with "Gypsy" on this record, given that they are both side-closers, both epic, complex and heavy, and both about evil women, a topic that is a heavy metal crutch, but one this band did pretty good to steer clear of o'er the years, (at least the Ozzy ones). Throw these into the mix, and what you had was an album that seemed all too deliberately to check off boxes, Sabbath filling out a form to apply for a place in a changing rock 'n' roll landscape, searching valiantly, bravely, but falling short through a compartmentalization of their ideas into digestible nuggets. Diminished was the imploding, exploding, dark star black hole progressive rock possibility of where a song might go, never to return. Lyrically Geezer behaved and played along. These songs were more "about something," and often that something was unremarkable.

With a few months' hindsight, Tony offered this summation upon *Technical Ecstasy* to Steve Rosen, over breakfast on Rosen's home turf, sunny California. "Personally I like *Ecstasy*. We got very involved with it, saw it all the way through. Most people that have heard it thought it was a big step from *Sabotage* and a lot of people say it's totally different from anything we've done before. I think it's probably the type of album you have to listen to a few times before you really get into it. I don't think it's sort of an instant thing."

"I think my technique is changing," continues Iommi. "My style of playing is changing. I'm getting more freedom in it and I know how I want to play; where before I was playing a lot of double notes and chords and maintaining the depth and not concentrating as much on my solos. I'd say things with Sabbath are better than they've ever been really, because the band are really coming out to fight this time. You know, in the past we've had all these various hang-ups, management things and all the rest of the junk, but it's like a new lease on life with this album. It's really been a thing where we've all got involved in it and got behind it."

Sabbath remained a main player on the concert circuit in 1976 and 1977, their legendary status intensifying. But slippage in the charts was the order of the day, with *Technical Ecstasy* rising only to #13 in the UK, for a six-week stay, and a paltry #51 in the US. "It's Alright" was launched as a single, backed with "Rock 'n' Roll Doctor" (the two happiest songs on this glum record), but this was not to be a replay of "Beth" and Kiss and Peter Criss a mere two months after that drummer-sung ballad put Kiss on the fast track to the top. *Technical Ecstasy* would go gold, but not until 1997.

Reflecting upon the record with Tony Stewart from the NME, Ozzy figured that getting *Technical Ecstasy* done was more of a relief than anything, after everything the band had been through—by this point they had been sued by both Patrick Meehan and their old pal Jim Simpson, who went about suing Meehan as well, settling with both parties.

"It had an effect on us in that it was very tiring and separated us from what we were here for. We were more tied up with sitting in solicitors' offices than in getting things together as a band. I just didn't want to know anything about that. I wanted to get it out of my head and carry on doing what I started out to do. Which is what I'm doing now. It's a nice progression we're now going through. It's like after a headache you feel good and so you want to get up and do something good. We are really pleased with the album. It's been a helluva tonic for the band."

"The pressures we were under were ridiculous," continued Oz. "We were flying here, there and everywhere. I felt like a tin of soup: a product. Whereas now I feel nearly human. I don't do any chemicals or anything. I don't get involved in any heavy situations. When I get strung-out I walk around with the dog and gun in the fields around where I live. I just think about a few things; get away from it all. For three-and-a-half, four years I didn't have a break from it at all in my head. I used to go on holiday, but I was still thinking about it. The only thing I can do now is go for a walk in the countryside and totally shut it off. It stops me going over the top. This album is like when the laxative has worked and you've just got it all out and you're all right again. It's like being constipated for two years and you've got rid of it. You've just got it out of your system. It's taken two years to get it all out and the crap we were going through has gone now."

A typical show on the *Technical Ecstasy* tour would open with the carnality of "Symptom of the Universe," the new songs introduced into the set being "All Moving Parts (Stand Still)," "Gypsy," "Dirty Women" and "Rock 'n' Roll Doctor." "Electric Funeral" was brought back from the old days, with "Hole in the Sky" and "Megalomania" from one record back now dropped, possibly in part to the energy they took to pull off vocally, indeed on the latter, Ozzy known to give in and drop down an octave on the highest bits.

"Boston, Kiss, everyone," reminisces David of tour mates for the *Technical Ecstasy* tour. "Everybody backed up Sabbath. But they used to do that purposely. We used to get Bob Seger, Ted Nugent, bands that were sort of breaking in America then. Because it was to sell the shows out, basically. You get people who come to see Black Sabbath, but they had also come to see Ted Nugent or whoever else was on the bill; everybody used to do that. There wasn't a great deal of interaction between Sabbath and support bands, but nine times out of ten you would stay in the same hotel as them anyway, so you're going to bump into them. And some of them would want to say hi (laughs). I remember Kiss being like that. A bit of a nightmare with them, actually, very, very obnoxious. I think at the time, there was a lot of money behind Kiss and I think they were just sort of going for it. And they were under the impression that it was their gig, although they were the support act as such. They were more like, 'Really, it should be Black Sabbath supporting us' and all this. I mean, if you think about Boston, they had an album high in the charts. So it was probably a contractually obliged gig; they did the deal to do the tour before the album was released type thing (laughs). All sorts of politics."

Bill pipes up on Boston. "Boston, I mean, Sib Hashian is still, to this very day, a good friend of mine. Obviously, Sib, when we get to Boston… Sib stays in contact with me all the time, Christmas cards, I watched his family grow. Sib was in the Nam, and Sib used to ride on our bus. Oz came onto our bus and then eventually Sib came onto our bus, and of course we were drinking heavy back then, but Sib used to tell us all the nightmare stories in the Nam. He went through a lot. Great drummer, great man, and he's doing really well right now. He's doing real well; he's an actor. Boston, theirs was a story, in the beginning, of a band that was completely and totally broke."

Other bands performing one-offs or only a handful of shows on the first leg of the tour, the American leg, included Target, Montrose, Dr. Hook, Black Oak Arkansas, Mother's Finest, Climax Blues Band, Heart, Moxy and Journey.

When the band rolled into L..A. to play Long Beach Arena, November 6th, Tony had as his guest Sharon Arden. Then 24, Sharon was of course the daughter of Don Arden, the strongman manager and promoter who tried to sign the band after Jim Simpson's reign, but losing out to Patrick Meehan. Six years earlier, Sharon was also with dad at the Marquee show in London where Arden had initially tried to sign Sabbath. Sharon would go on to manage and then marry Ozzy, with Osbourne starting his illustrious solo career on Don Arden's Jet Records label. But at this stage, Sharon's connection had been with Tony. Sharon and her brother David had been friendly with Patrick Meehan, and the three had all met up at a party at Meehan's house in the Spring of '74, all the while the friendship with Meehan kept from Don, a.k.a. "Mr. Big."

"Ozzy never drank before he went on stage," says David, asked about the potential for booze-addled wipe-outs. "He'd have a pint maybe, but he was always straight when he was on stage. There were odd gigs where the equipment gave us trouble. I remember a gig in Fort Bragg or one of the American bases. It was something to do with the stage. It was metal or something and I think the taxi was coming through the PA (laughs); used it like an aerial. It was never a clear run (laughs). There was the one in Germany, Ludwig's Arms or something; that was nuts. That was the GIs all jacked-up. You used to get the GIs and the locals in Germany; it was a mixture of GIs, Hells Angels, and disgruntled heavy metal fans, a recipe for disaster (laughs). But that's how these gigs used to go. I remember Tony would take forever and a day with his tuning up. Because he used such light strings, he had trouble keeping his guitar in tune. Because of the prosthesis he wore, he had lights strings. It was a bit of a chore for anyone listening. But Tony was like that. Tony wanted it right. If Tony wanted it right, he would have it right (laughs)."

After UK dates with hard-hitting A&M blues rock artists Nutz (soon to change their name to Rage), in April of 1977, a young, brash and bounding like kangaroos AC/DC hitched a ride on the Sabs' European jaunt.

David counters rumours that AC/DC stole these shows from the tiring veterans. "I don't think so, no. AC/DC was a great band, but two different bands altogether. I actually thought they complemented each other. I suppose some gigs… it's like any other night. You can have a good gig one night and then maybe a so-so one. It also depended on the equipment and how it runs. But I don't think there were any words spoken about blowing anybody off the stage. I remember the early tour with Yes; that was two totally different bands, different spectrums. Yes was very, very technical, and I just think that was a total mismatch. I think Yes were the headliner."

"But so I knew Bon Scott, yeah. I actually have Bon's backstage pass when they played at Langley. He gave me his pass. He was a lovely guy, Bon; he was great. That was a big shock. It was a big shock for the guys in the band as well. The thing about AC/DC was, the guys, Keith Evans, and the guys who worked for them, the road crew, they were all part of the Field Farm set, so we were all mates. It was like Keith and Terry Lee, who does Light and Sound Design now, we were all in each other's pocket, if you like, mucking around together. That's why it was a good tour, because we were all friends and the bands got on well."

"AC/DC, yeah, I used to know Bon and we used to go drinking together," laughs Bill, "after we'd finished doing a concert or whatever. We spent quite a bit of time together. He was just a really nice guy. We used to have some really good heart-to-hearts, chug on a few beers. I just liked the guy a lot. Sometimes we would rub shoulders, a few ego things from time to time. I mean, we've played with so many bands, and some of them have been our mates and some we didn't have a lot to do with."

One incident that got blown out of proportion had Geezer flicking open a switchblade comb. Malcolm Young warned him not to point that thing at him and the situation was quickly defused, although it was reported in the press that there had been a physical row over the situation.

David addresses the subject of unhinged fans. "Personally, no, I never had to deal with much of that. You'd always get weirdos at the gig and you'd have to deal with them. We used to get some people who took it to the extreme, but it was never really a problem. Really, with crew, in the later days when I was there, no. But they did have problems. Somebody jumped on stage and tried to knife Tony in Memphis. And David Hemmings who sadly isn't with us anymore had to disarm him, get the knife off him. We don't know if he was a Satanist or not. I think he was just a lunatic (laughs), high on drugs." (The incident of which David speaks took place on March 1, 1971, near the end of the *Paranoid* tour).

"Yeah, Frank Zappa," says Tangye fondly, recalling an event caught on tape and now part of bootleg lore, Frank Zappa introducing the band live on stage, December 6, 1976. "Frank, he was absolutely brilliant. I think it was the second time they played Madison Square Garden, and Frank came along to introduce the band. He was absolutely brilliant. We went for an after-show meal at the Time Life Building. Ozzy said to me, 'You like Frank Zappa? Would you like to work for him?' I said yeah (laughs). Frank was a big fan of Black Sabbath; he loved Sabbath. He told me that actually because I was sitting beside him. Elvis Presley was a big fan of Black Sabbath. We almost met him. He didn't show, but I think he was in his last days because he died about six months later. Mike, the Warner rep, said he was going to come to the gig, but he didn't, and we were very disappointed."

Asked about the condition of Ozzy's voice at this time, David says, "Yeah, he used to have problems with his voice. Sometimes he used to complain that some of the tunes were too high for him, that he couldn't hit the notes and all this. Tony would always say, 'Give him some honey! Give him some honey!' (laughs). I think 'Sabbath Bloody Sabbath' he always found difficult. 'Rock 'n' Roll Doctor' was the other one I think, yeah. I mean they got through it, like every band. Singers are singers, aren't they, with their idiosyncrasies? And it was difficult singing the things they did; there was a lot of light and shade. If you look at all their albums, I mean, there are ballads and then really heavy rock songs. It's hard to go from one to the other. It puts a strain on your vocal cords. It's different when you play guitar or drums, but a voice is so personal."

"I liked the *Technical Ecstasy* tour," adds Graham. "That was quite interesting, with the big chandelier above Bill, and the big 14-foot-wide drum riser on a stained glass pedestal. And they had like burning torches and some nice backdrops. We used to lower the big cross. We had cobwebs, and a snow machines for 'Snowblind.' There was supposed to be a live album. We recorded something at the Hammersmith Odeon, because I remember the mobile studio coming and parking outside. But they didn't use it. They weren't happy with it, the final result of it."

"We did do a live album," confirms Jezz. "I don't know whatever happened to that. Just after that tour, we went to Holland, to a studio called Real Light Studios and we had all the masters for a live album. We spent weeks and weeks trying to sort it out, but I don't know whether that ever came out or not. We were doing overdubs in the studio. I remember Bill was trying to sort out some of the drums where he'd messed up. So it was a serious project, but I don't know what happened to it. It would've been the first Sabbath live album, wouldn't it?" As an addendum, I had recently brought this up with both Geezer and Tony and neither professed any recollection of these sessions.

And that was it for Jezz Woodruffe's tenure with the Sabs. "Ozzy left, and the band didn't know what to do, so they just said, 'Well, that's it; it's all over,' and then they didn't come back to me. And I was off anyway; I was off to Europe and doing some stuff out there. It just fell apart when Ozzy went."

Jezz is referring to the on again/off again status of Osbourne in the band that would persist right up until preliminary work on 1980's *Heaven and Hell*. Few would notice, because Ozzy would be back for one final album, 1978's *Never Say Die*, so it looks essentially continuous up until the arrival of Ronnie James Dio. Indeed, there were no shows without Ozzy either.

The next significant move for Jezz was a fusion-y, funky, quirky keyboard-mad solo album in 1980 called *Opposite Directions*, which helped Jezz get his esteemed gig with Robert Plant. "Right. Well, after I left Sabbath, or the whole thing finished, my friend David Anderson, who was the bass player in Hawkwind, he had a studio on another Welsh mountain just up the road from me. So I decided to record my first solo album there in his studio. And that was put out by a small independent label called Graduate Records, who, at the same time was signing me, signed UB40. And the guy who worked for Graduate Records, Lord Williams, was a friend of Robert's. He knew Robert was looking for a keyboard player so he gave him a copy of *Opposite Directions*, and then Robert came to find me. And that's how it started."

At this point, David Tangye also relieves himself of his service to the band. "For *Never Say Die*, they went over to Sounds Interchange. I didn't go out for that; I finished after the European tour they did with AC/DC. I came back and there was nothing to do. And Mark Forster was there. I was working for the band then; I was actually working for Black Sabbath and actually on the payroll. Because previously I'd been working for Ozzy and Ozzy used to pay me. It was all up in the air a bit. It's a hard life."

In any event, Black Sabbath's seventh album, *Technical Ecstasy*, was to be no more than a bullet-pocked signpost on the road to misery, the band soon to follow up with a record that would be received with even less enthusiasm. As Geezer relates though, at the time, "the press were saying that we were a bunch of morons and couldn't play our instruments. That's how we were perceived and that's why the original band folded, because we just lost confidence in ourselves. We didn't think there was any future in the band and Ozzy had lost all his confidence. He believed in the press and the press, particularly in England, slagged us to death, particularly him. They didn't give him any credibility whatsoever as a singer or a front man. The British press were calling us dinosaurs in 1976. It was unbelievable. We started believing it though, and we were looking in different directions ourselves and not realizing we had the direction. The record company was that way as well. We'd go to a reception with them and they'd be playing the latest punk album or Bob Marley. They didn't give us any confidence whatsoever. We didn't believe we had any relevance."

Album 8

Never Say Die

"Like it was recorded underwater"

Black Sabbath limped through the latter half of 1977 a band in tatters. Eventually they were to get it together enough to cobble and bobble a record, but before that, Ozzy would be out of the band and back in, replaced for about three months by Dave Walker, from Savoy Brown and briefly Fleetwood Mac.

As Ozzy explained to the NME's Tony Stewart during his self-imposed exile, "I was drinking like a fish for two years. It was just getting worse and worse, off one thing and onto another. Finally I nearly ended up an alcoholic. We'd come offstage, for instance, and I'd just go straight to the bar. Perhaps I'd meet one of the band there, but I wouldn't drink for the sake of having a good time. I'd just drink to get out of the way. And that's when you've got to say to yourself, 'Hey man, there's something wrong.' You're just going through the day, just to get on the stage for an hour to do your gig, just to go home, get stoned and go to bed. The next day's the same. There was no excitement. I would have been dead in two or three years if I'd carried on. I know I would. And I don't think anything's worth giving your life up for."

"I realize I've let a lot of people down," continued Oz, "because it's never going to be the same again for the people who liked Sabbath then. We haven't left on bad terms. But who knows—it may turn out that way, because time has a weird way of eroding a friendship. I wouldn't say the band screwed me up. But there were a lot of personality clashes. We all thought we were tin gods. But at the end of the day it just turned 'round and kicked us in the teeth. I just want a simple life for a while. I just want to be an ordinary, everyday, run-of-the-mill guy. Inside I ain't a tin god. I ain't a tin of beans walking around. And that's what I began to feel like: a product. 'Buy Ozzy Osbourne and he'll clean your carpet faster than anything else.' I'll do it again, but I'll do it comfortably. I won't ever let myself be prostituted again."

A bootleg exists documenting the band's one live performance with Dave Walker, on the BBC Midlands Look! Hear! show, January 6th, 1978, where Sabbath performed "War Pigs" and an early version of "Junior's Eyes," on which the vocals alternate between highly stylized bluesy (hoary almost) and somewhat Dio-esque come chorus time. The lyrics are sporadic, slurred and mostly unintelligible: "Louie Louie" has got nothing on this guy. Bill drummed with his arm in a cast after slamming it in a door, due to frustration—it still flares up into arthritis to this day. Walker, who the band had known since the early '60s and his Birmingham band The Redcaps, had moved from San Francisco to London to consort with the guys, even writing lyrics for the sketchy new songs. By the end of January, all would agree that the match was bad.

"Brummie solidarity is exactly what it was," agrees Walker, when asked by Dmitry Epstein if that might explain why he, a lifelong bluesman, would join up with the Sabs. "Actually Tony Iommi, for whom I have great regard was helpful in my joining Savoy Brown in 1971. Tony and Black Sabbath were represented at the time by Chrysalis Agency, I believe, and Savoy Brown worked out of that office also. Basically, Tony had a word with Harry Simmonds, Kim's manager, on my behalf."

Asked if any of his vocal melodies turned up on the eventual album he could have been part of, Walker shrugs. "I have no idea, having never heard the album. And I didn't know Geezer was supposed to be the main lyricist. I was the only one writing lyrics, as I recall."

Then came the end of this curious experiment. "I showed up for rehearsal. As I walked in, the band announced that they were going to the local pub for a meeting and that I was to wait until they got back. When they did, Bill Ward spoke for the band and said, and I quote, 'We're still here and you're not.' That was it. I had been in the US for a year and my marriage had broke down, and then after Mistress and my failure with Black Sabbath, I returned to the US from Great Britain and basically became a shiftless hippie for a few years, working on ranches and doing a lot of manual jobs—construction, kitchen work, etc. In fact, I don't think you can call yourself a 'blues' singer if you haven't had a few dishwashing jobs!"

Back in Birmingham, in the interim, Tony would produce, quite capably, the debut album by Quartz (formerly Bandy Legs), who would relinquish one Geoff Nicholls to the Sabbath camp, soon to be the band's second hidden keyboardist, then major writer, then briefly, full-fledged member, then hidden keyboardist again. "Well, I sort of remember some of it," says Tony, of producing 1977's *Quartz*, reissued in '79 in unique paper bag packaging as *Deleted*. "It was something they asked me to do, so I had a go at it. It was interesting. I thought they had some good songs. Quite straightforward, basically. I had done sort of the same format as we do with the Sabbath stuff, really, same sort of recording. Because that's all I knew. Since then, of course, now I've learnt a bit more and I do things differently. But then, I operated the same way I did with Sabbath."

"We teamed up with Albert Chapman as our manager, and Albert Chapman is a close friend of Tony's," recalls Quartz drummer Malcolm Cope. "We just all built on that. We used to rehearse every week, changing our style of music and the type of music we wanted to write. Tony was coming to our rehearsals and spending hours and hours with us, and giving his input into where he thought some of the songs should be, one thing or another, and we went and recorded the first album. I thought it was a bit too clinical, to be honest with you. I think we were all a little bit nervous in what we were doing. And Tony was very precise in what he was doing. A lot of the songs on there, we'd rehearsed and played them many times, but when we'd come to record them, we changed them as we were recording them. And it's not quite the same, as opposed to when you're really familiar with what you're doing."

Playing gigs with Sabbath, Cope says that he could sense the coming resurgence of heavy music in Britain. "Yes, we noticed it. One of the big surprises for us was when we started touring with Sabbath, and all of a sudden the kids were coming out of the woodwork. You weren't seeing the type of kids the way they were dressed particularly on the streets, but all of a sudden you'd get to a gig, and it's a fantastic following as a gig. You know, we're talking about 4000, 5000 seaters. All of a sudden you're seeing all these kids that are quite young. That was a major attraction, to get into this mould of music and to see this following, this fan base—it was marvelous."

The Quartz guys had watched Sabbath, first-hand, arrive at the stature they had when Quartz was opening their shows, first as Bandy Legs. "Yes, well, they used to play this nightclub called the Rumrunner," recalls guitarist Mick Hopkins, "and they'd just get up and do bluesy type things. They were managed by Jim Simpson who was also a blues man. He played in jazz and blues bands and he used to play trumpet, I believe. And he took them under his wing, and then eventually they changed to heavy metal. That's when they started travelling the world, then. I used to see all of them in the really early days. I mean, where I am now, a place called Great Barr, is four miles from Aston where they were all born, sort of thing. I used to see Ozzy, used to see Geezer Butler and Geezer's nephew, Peter, and Tony. When I was playing sort of rock 'n' roll in the '60s, Tony was in a group called The Chevrolets."

"We had some great times with them," chuckles Mick. "Because of knowing them and having known them for years, it was just like being with your pals. Ozzy had this thing about... you know the toilets from years ago, where there was a plastic thing at the end of a chain to flush it? Ozzy would paint that black, or he'd paint the toilet seat black and just wait for somebody to go to the toilet. But I copped him out on one thing. I'd buy these sweets, candies as you call them there, and they kept disappearing. I'd think, I've only just had one or two and it's like there's quite a few gone. So I thought, you know, I'm gonna find out who's doing it. Because nobody's admitted to doing anything. So I went out and found a joke shop and I got the sweets that colour your mouth. And so I wrapped them in the other wrappers that were there, put them all back together, and left them there. Who should have a blue one but Ozzy? Of course, he said it wasn't him. What?! Have a look in the mirror!"

Most coincidentally, Quartz was on Don Arden's Jet Records label and now Don Arden was finally managing Black Sabbath. Tony had gotten fed up with having no real management, so he had a chat with Don about coming on board. Don would only do so if Ozzy was back in the band and so relations were patched up with Osbourne, even if the reunion was not to last.

"When we first met Don, I was only about 17," explains Malcolm, painting a bit of a picture of Mr. Big. "What can I say? He dominates the room whenever you're there. And everybody that works for him was quite... I wouldn't say frightened of him, but they had a lot of respect and made sure if they were in his presence that they spoke to him in the appropriate manner. I mean, I was first involved with Don when he was with Tin Pan Alley, when he had a company called Galaxy Entertainments and he was looking after bands like The Move and Amen Corner. And then he brought Wilf Pine in to be his bodyguard. Wilf was the guy who went to go collect all the money from the late payers and all that. Wilf took us on as Copperfield, and Wilf actually came from the Isle of Wight, so we went north and lived on the Isle of Wight for a while and rehearsed on the Isle of Wight under Wilf's umbrella, if you like."

"Wilf, to us, was a nice chap," chuckles Mick Hopkins, adding to the portrait of what was a bit of a team. "But he was Don Arden's bodyguard, and if anybody crossed his path, was a bit naughty, he could show them a thing or two—about being naughty (laughs). But to us, he was great. No problem. But I mean, it's somebody who, if you're in trouble and you have Wilf on your side, he will give you a lot of comfort; you know, you'll be looked after. That's what he used to do, and he managed Copperfield and another group I was in. But Don Arden... I never got on with Don, just the way he was, or Sharon Arden. I don't know, it's just strange. But they certainly knew what they were doing, and could promote people, but they also did a few dirty deeds on some bands."

Back to Sabbath, as it would turn out, the image seared into the minds of all involved in the making of *Never Say Die* was the biting cold of trying to stitch the damned thing together in—of all places—Toronto, Ontario.

"That was quite strange," begins Graham Wright, "because they had actually been to the studio in Toronto in the summer. And being there in the summer, 'Oh, great place, lovely Toronto,' in the summer. It is a great place in the summer. Lots of leaves outside, and it's warm (laughs). And the only time they could get the studio was in the winter. And at that time it was flavour of the month, Sounds Interchange. It was like, hey, what a great studio, being up in Toronto. The Stones had recorded there. Entering their rehearsals for that, that was when Ozzy left and Dave Walker had come in. And when Ozzy had left at that time, he had actually got together some old friends from Necromandus, and this was when Blizzard of Ozz began. Even then, Ozzy was thinking about his own thing. You've got to always remember that, that when he got the sack, it was like I can go on and do my own thing."

"But we went off to Toronto," continues Wright. "They were still rehearsing basically, and we took over this old cinema, in Toronto, and they could have it during the day, because they showed movies during the night. So we went into this cinema on the stage and they were rehearsing during the day and then going into the studio on the night and putting stuff down. And it was freezing cold and it was snowing and the blizzards were hitting. You know what Toronto is like in the winter (laughs), especially a bad winter, and there was one. We all stayed in this apartment block, just around the corner from The Gasworks on Yonge Street. It wasn't the best place to be, because they were used to going to Criteria in Miami, and L.A. (laughs)."

"My God, that was when Ozzy left the band," recalls a wincing Butler. "And just as we'd gotten the studio all booked and everything, he decided to come back to the band. So we had to scrap everything that we'd done and start all over again. So we got to Toronto, and because the studio was booked from like 2:00 in the afternoon, we had to start rehearsals from 8:00 o'clock in the morning so we could write the songs before we could record them (laughs). And so we hired some old cinema somewhere and we had to be out of there by like 12:00 so they could start showing the movies. And the cold got to me. It went into me ears, and I was like deaf for about three months after that. So everything sounded like it was recorded underwater."

"It wasn't very good," says Geezer, of the material put together with Dave Walker. "It wasn't us anyway. I mean the *Never Say Die* album wasn't very good anyway. It was sort of thrown together at the last minute, and that's why it's so bad. There's some good stuff on *Sabotage* and *Technical Ecstasy*, but *Never Say Die*, I just don't like that album."

"Oh, it was terrible, yeah!" continues Graham, remembering the infamous theater. "I remember we were trying to rehearse, and there was this old lady with this Hoover, Hoovering the aisles of this thing (laughs). It didn't last long, but it seemed like it was a long time. They were only rehearsing in there for like ten days or something. And writing too, because there was a shortage of material. I remember Geezer going to see Elvis Costello and the Distractions at the El Mocambo. I was really pissed-off I didn't go, and he saw me the next day and said, 'Hey, I bumped into a mate of yours, Bruce Thomas!' And I go, 'Bruce Thomas?!' I knew him from school days because he came from the same hometown, Stockton-on-Tees. And he was the bass player in Elvis' band. Because Geezer was talking to him after the show. 'Is Graham Wright working with you?' (laughs). Anyway, they left right after the show, so I didn't see him. We went to The Gasworks, saw local bands. It was quite funny, because Ozzy and Tony, we would go into The Gasworks on the odd night off and just sit there and have beers and nobody used to bother them (laughs). I mean, they used to walk up and down Yonge Street and nobody used to bother them."

"I remember it being really cold in Toronto," adds Bill. "Some things were conceived in other places but probably the strongest memory I have is that we were really struggling for material. We had lots of things, but I know that I was kind of dismembered. I guess we were all cold and dismayed. It's difficult for me to talk about where everybody else was. I don't like to do the dirty laundry type of deal. We saw Rush there. We were in the studio, and Rush were in there and we would go over to their studio and say hello, screw around a little bit. And I think they came to our studio. But that was about it, really. We would literally just pick up our crates of Molson (laughs), put them in the back of the station wagon, go back to our rooms. I forget where we were staying. It was like a bunch of apartments. And we would go there and get drunk and try to work on the homework of the day, the stuff that we had put down in the theater."

"Being at home was strange because we'd never been at home," explains Tony, referring to the despondent break before gearing up to make this record happen. "We were always out touring. Nothing was happening with the writing; it had dried up. And a lot of other things—drugs was probably a part of it. When it first started happening, was with *Never Say Die*. Before we recorded that album, Ozzy left. We brought another singer in for a short while, wrote some more songs, and then Ozzy wanted to come back. We used to play moodies with each other, like a spoiled kid, you know? So you'd have to pamper everybody and it got silly. I see it with a lot of these other bands, like Guns N' Roses or whomever. They go through the same stages that we went through then. Two days before we were due to go into the studio, Ozzy wanted to come back. Okay, Ozzy came back. We all went to Toronto for six, seven weeks. And Ozzy wouldn't sing any of the stuff we wrote with this other guy, because I think he felt like, well, I'm not involved in it. He was a bit jealous, I suppose. I don't know."

"So what are we going to do now?" continues Tony. "Here we are, we're due to start recording in two days, and we've got nothing, no material. So we go into a cinema at 9:00 in the morning, freezing cold it was, and started trying to write material to record in the evening. Which was a bloody joke! Some of the stuff, when I listen to it now, sounds really disjointed. Because it was done too quick. We never had time to analyze it. I never want to do that again. That was a nightmare! It was done in the morning, and that night we were recording. So we did that with Ozzy, and recorded that album. And then of course, it was the next period when it came to moving to L.A. We lived there for like 11 months, to write an album. And nothing happened. It was drugs, sex and rock 'n' roll, as they say. We did an eight-month tour on *Never Say Die*, which was great. But problems were setting in with the band."

"I don't know if I'm a medium for some outside force," said Ozzy, playing up the band's image in the press back in 1978. "It sounds crazy, but in '74, '75, when it really got intense, I sat down and thought about whether or not we were influenced by an outside force. Whatever it is, frankly, I hope it's not what I think—Satan."

"There's a little bit of each year involved in our new album," said Oz, of *Never Say Die*. "It's a subtle combination of the changes we've gone through musically and in our personal lives. We've got more involved technically. The first album was done on an ordinary eight-track machine and it took us only two days to record. Now we use a 24-track machine and it drives us mental. We play games with the machines. It's quite fun for a while, but I don't really care for the studio. I just like to go in and do it. All I am is a ham, to be blunt. I'm not the world's greatest singer. I'm just a front man with a band. I just get up there and play good, raunchy music and kick my ass around the stage."

Lamented Oz on the perennially lamentable tour grind, "It was getting too serious, so after *Technical Ecstasy*, we decided to wind it down a bit, just to give our heads a rest. The heaviness of it all got so intense for me that I just had to take a break. I was drinking and generally abusing myself, just being an animal, and it was destroying me, killing my ability to do anything. I didn't want to destroy myself or my family. Now I've really got it together on a good level and I really love what I'm doing. We take our time about what we're doing; before, you'd get people screaming at you on the phone about commitments. 'You've got to get this out; you've got to do that.' What's the point of doing anything if you're not satisfied with it?"

"The fans would be very surprised to see the way we live. I don't live in a castle with Count Dracula as a doorman. My house is a small little cottage. I have three children, two boys and a girl, and a wife that's raving mad. All wives are raving mad. Living with me leaves something to be desired. I'm absolutely mad. I change with the wind, always have. Dr. Jekyll and Mr. Hyde a thousand times a day. But I don't change for the bad—basically, I'm a gentle person. I do crazy things to make people laugh because if people are laughing, then they're not going to be aggressive. Keep them happy and they won't pull a gun, or pull the trigger. Where I grew up, if you weren't good at fighting you were stabbed into the ground and victimized, but I hated that, and felt that the best way to get out of it was to be funny and make them laugh."

"I suppose it was a progression from that to the band," continued Osbourne, armchair philosopher. "Keep a lot of people happy, let them get rid of their aggression in a hall, and they're not going to be outside mugging some old lady for her purse. When I make the peace signs at concerts, it's like waving at someone, knowing they're with you. I'm like a front man for positive things. If I see any fights, I stop the show instantly; I walk off. I don't want anyone to get harmed. We all realize that we have a big responsibility. I've never said this before, but I'm afraid of people really, because people can hurt in very subtle, evil ways. The challenge of my life is to try and win them over. When we began, we had nothing. I was walking around in rags. My mother never had a nickel, my father was working constantly, we were like the street's tramps. But I had all these dreams. If you're sitting on a gutter and you've got nothing, your ass is hanging out and your mother cries because she doesn't have any food to feed you, you write hard words because that's the way you've been reared. You're a hard person from the word go. We got success from that. We got out of that and now I'm living in a very nice house in the countryside, breathing fresh air. I live a relatively happy life but it's such a cost to have happiness in this world. I don't believe there's anyone in this world that's 100% happy."

"I'm 29-years-old now. I saw what happened to the flower power generation, how a bunch of people got an innocent, beautiful thing going, and the big machine made money out of it. Made it filthy dirty and horrible and destroyed it. Then, when we came in, at the end of the disaster, we got 'em going again. We were telling them the truth, what was happening, and if you've been stoned on acid for five years, you need something to hold onto."

Never Say Die was pulled from the freezer on September 28, 1978, and eventually limped up the charts, to a spirited six-week #12 placement in the UK, but a lowly #69 in the States, even if eventual gold status was its hopeful lot. The album was wrapped in pretty cool but weirdly uneasy and uncommunicative Hipgnosis-generated cover art (much like *Technical Ecstasy*), featuring two completely covered-up fighter pilots. Faint images were painted into the clouds, sort of like Blue Öyster Cult's *Mirrors*. Two of these might represent the ghosts of the shot down, and two more "mechanical" ones are difficult to make out. Sabbath had been asked to choose between this particular cover art and the famous doctors shot that wound up being used three years later for Rainbow's *Difficult to Cure*. Some copies list the songs on the back in shuffled order, an oft-used convention of the day, while others list them in the correct order.

Explains Hipgnosis' Aubrey Powell, "We were given a title for *Never Say Die*, and then to be honest with you, at the time, we were very into, there was another partner with the company at that time named Peter

Christopherson who was very much into fetish imagery, and we were talking about fetishism and stuff like that, and we talked about kamikaze pilots saying 'Never say die.' And so the idea came, well, why don't we create two pilots, and put masks on them that we make up, in a rather suffocating way? And put them in front of an old Second World War plane. And it's got that kind of emptiness to it, and put in the sky… If you look at the sky on the album cover, it's got slightly traced-out figures of wartime pilots and things like that. And it was intended to be a sort of a homage, I suppose, to kamikaze pilots of the Second World War, in our own way."

"Plus it had the overtone of an S&M vibe, especially with the very suffocating masks," continues Powell. "They're not pilot masks. They're masks we had made. We had them made up. So again, if you buy that book, *Hipgnosis Portraits*, you see a great shot in there, in black and white, of one of the masks really close up. I have all the original artwork."

And for the draftsman-like renderings on the inner sleeves, Powell once again tapped George Hardie. "Yeah, that's right, again, George. We were like family, all together. Hipgnosis worked as an art studio, I'd say similar to Andy Warhol's Factory. We were a bit like that. Storm and I came up with the ideas, we worked with a lot of assistants and a lot of people around us, who could do things better than we could, so we would call upon them to do things for us. And George Hardie was one of them. With both covers, they've both got line drawings, and the one with *Never Say Die* has an industrial turbine engine and jet engine and stuff like that. And *Technical Ecstasy*, the high heels for the female figure. They were just nice bits of imagery that go with the covers, simply a graphic. You know, Hipgnosis reinvented itself weekly. We just thought out of the box all the time. What is it that people are not expecting? What can we do? What do *we* like? We worked for *us*. We were terribly selfish. Storm and I would think, what do *we* want to do?"

Past the austere wrapper, *Never Say Die* kicks off on a hopeful note with the record's title track, a happy, melodic, bashing hard rocker, Tony turning in a spirited and spiraling solo as the song smashes to a close. The cheerful effect is created by the exclusive use of major chords in the verse, although typically stormy minor chords are introduced come chorus time. Ozzy's sing-songy vocal melody further brightens the verse, one built of hanging chords that bear a similarity to those of Thin Lizzy's "Get Out of Here." Also keeping the song afloat is the virtual suspension of bass drum for long periods of time, Bill finding jazz despite a driving 4/4 beat. Ward's bass drum can be heard distinctly on the big drops punctuated by crash cymbals, but he's either using his foot lightly or not at all for long stretches. The song ends in what feels like a faux-dramatic flourish. Tony tears into a gritty solo, Geezer throws in some super-high bass notes and then there's seven whacks before an amusing low octave "Never say die" summation, punctuated by a big wind-up from Bill.

Instantly, one's attention is drawn to the garagey, distorted, midrange-heavy, ambient sound of the record, production that is vaguely Zeppelin-esque, circa perhaps a combination of *IV*, *Houses of the Holy* and *Presence*. There's also a similarity, especially in the drums, to the Mack/Musicland sound of Sweet's *Give Us a Wink*. Geezer's lyric is chock full of enigma, although one senses a coherence with past themes, this idea of looking to the future, hoping things can be saved before it's too late. People usually remember the innocuous and comparatively somber chorus, but miss some of the great lines in here, no help from Ozzy however, who makes them somewhat unintelligible.

"Yeah, I liked that one," volunteers Bill. "It was made well. And it did reach the British charts. I remember we came up with the title for that. Ozzy and I were in the conservatory in Monmouth, when we came up with that title. He was saying 'die' and I was going 'never,' or whatever (laughs); one of those kinds of deals." The idea was to find something that summed up the band's ten years together, in light of the upcoming anniversary.

Indeed "Never Say Die" did make the charts, hitting #21 in the UK as a pre-LP single four months before the launch of the album. The track, backed with "She's Gone" from *Technical Ecstasy*, was the first single Sabbath had put in the charts since "Iron Man" and "Paranoid" a lifetime earlier. The band would repeat with "A Hard Road" (backed with "Symptom of the Universe"), issued in conjunction with the album's launch in September. Of note, the "Never Say Die" single would feature a graphic of the Geezer-designed "Henry" the dancing devil which would crop up on Sabbath artwork repeatedly over the ensuing years.

"It was about... I don't think it was about anything," says Geezer quite amusingly, with respect to "Never Say Die." "I think it was just trying to be up for once instead of always been miserable and down. We were gunning for anything we could come out with at that time. Like, desperate."

One could almost position "Never Say Die" as the band's answer to punk. The sentiment was tough, even political, the playing a pile of noise, and Tony's chords pinned the listener against the wall.

"The Sex Pistols were great, but then you got all these other bands that couldn't play," sneers Geezer, reflecting on the punk explosion in the UK, which was framed neatly by *Technical Ecstasy* at the onset and *Never Say Die* at its death. "Sid Vicious slashing himself and everything; it just became a bit of a joke then. So I think a lot of the kids who went onto heavy metal in the '80s started in punk, and realized there's better things than punk and started listening to metal again. But the punk thing, the lyrics were really angry and everything. I'm talking about the Sex Pistols; I wasn't really into The Clash or The Damned or anything, but I really liked the Sex Pistols. *Never Mind the Bollocks* is a great metal album with great metal riffs, it really is. And the lyrics were just so angry and off the wall at the time. I mean they really did have an impact at the time. So I think it took a long time to come up with anything as heavy or as angry as the punk thing. I think once the Sex Pistols were gone out of the way there wasn't really any band to come up and match them as far as punk guys. They did it all."

"And you know, a lot of the original punk bands loved Sabbath. It's weird. It's just the thing in the press—they didn't get it. The press hated metal, full stop, or anything that sounded like Sabbath. But as soon as punk came around, they were like the press darlings. I mean I met Johnny Rotten and he's an Alice Cooper fan. See, punk came from London and New York, which is where the press is. And I know half of them were all alcoholics. They'd go out on tour; they'd only go for the drink. They'd go to the nearest bar and there'd be a punk band playing, so that's what was happening. But a lot of them just could not play and that was the whole thing. Like, people's music they used to try and say, but it was 90% crap as far as I'm concerned. But the good stuff was brilliant. The Ramones supported us on one tour, and they were getting bottled off every night. The kids hated them going on with us, and we had to let them go in the end for their own health's sake. There were bottles… this one place we played, they picked up a whole row of seats, the kids, and threw them at The Ramones. And The Ramones just kept playing the same song all night; it was great. They're great guys, but eventually you go, 'We can't keep doing this every night.'"

Back to *Never Say Die*, "Johnny Blade" is announced by a dramatic and thespian synthesizer pattern from Don Airey, none other than the synth player on "Mr. Crowley," early *Blizzard of Ozz* hit extraordinaire. Airey of course would join Ozzy in his solo band and then years later settle in as Deep Purple's keyboardist following the death of Jon Lord.

As introduction, Don had been sent the workings of four proposed songs for the album. Airey was hesitant to get involved as he knew all too well about the band's reputation but turned out pleasantly surprised at how agreeable and polite the guys were. He worked with the band for two days and was offered to come along on the forthcoming US tour, but he had to bow out because he had just joined Rainbow.

Back to "Johnny Blade," Bill trundles in with one of his trusty single roll snare patterns and it's off to the races, the band creating a caterwaul of a rocker briefly fired by melodic respites, one of which is the twangy chorus. Later the song takes a Sabbatherian left path turn, Tony breaking out one of his tuneful yet doomy he-man riffs. Airey throws in a few percolating and novel licks, his performance on the album reminiscent of Tony Carey's on Rainbow's *Rising* album. Eventually, the song collapses into a groovy jam, with Tony driving it with one of his freight train-styled solos. But it is Bill's drumming that dominates, Ward captured loudly like Bonham.

"'Johnny Blade,' was, I think, partly about Bill's brother," notes Geezer. "He used to be a bit of a tear-away, a bit of a hooligan, when he was a teenager. He used to be in gangs and things like that." Adds Bill, "I remember distinctly Tony coming up with this incredible lick, and I immediately copped to it and I put down a four-stroke roll. It was freezing cold in that theater, absolutely freezing—I've never felt such cold. But yes, as soon as Tony started playing that, it just felt to me like wow, we're back in 1964 or 1965 (laughs). It was just that kind of rock, that kind of playing, midnight music or whatever."

"And I knew exactly where to go with the drums, to that particular type of playing; it just matched so well. Because Tony and I had played together and had done a lot of bands when we were 15, 16 years old. So we had the playing experience where we had played, kind of cover tunes from the early '60s bands or even bands from the '50s. We were brought up with that influence. So when I heard 'Johnny Blade,' I recognized that had something that was almost an influence from the '50s. And I know that conceptually, Ozzy and I started messing around with the idea of 'Johnny Blade.' I got hooked with the song and took it back up to the apartment. I got some things worked up and I called up Oz and said, 'Come on up; let's have some brews' and he liked the idea. I knew that was a song already. It was just a weird character. I thought it was a really nice song. I had done some nice fills, Don Airey had played the keyboards on that particular track, plus Geez brought everything together with the final lyrics."

"My brother, for awhile, was a bit of a, like Teddy Boy, you know?" says Bill, answering to Geezer's assessment of the lyric. "I'm just trying to think of the American equivalent, possibly like a Zoot suit? So he would wear a Zoot suit and the chain, with these little razor blades, with the open edge—they called them flick blades back then. So my brother had a lot of that image about him, and it was a very popular time. People had slicked-back hair and everybody dug Elvis, so he had a lot of influence. My brother turned me onto a lot of rock 'n' roll, and he was very influential in my life. And yeah, Geezer knew my brother real well. Oh, God yeah, they got on great."

"'Junior's Eyes,' I wrote that about Ozzy's father," says Geezer with respect to the record's third, melancholy, mournful, boldly good third track. "His father had just died. It was all about his dad. Ozzy was devastated at the time."

"'Junior's Eyes' was really, really sad," adds Bill. "Ozzy's father died during these sessions. Of course, that was Jack. Jack gave us all the original crosses. We all loved Jack. We all knew each other's parents and we all interacted. But Ozzy was off the wall, totally. And we came up with 'Junior's Eyes' and Oz loved it. We actually did the preproduction work on that at Field Farm. Field Farm was where my wife and I lived—my second wife and I actually lived in the house and we built a little studio in there. We didn't know, but when we left, other bands started using the studio. It was kind of a party house. We had some of the guys from AC/DC living in the house. Judas Priest used to go down there and rehearse as well. So the house actually gave birth to some new songs. Ozzy did both of his songs, 'Am I Going Insane' and 'Who Are You,' two of my favourite songs (laughs), he did both of those at Field Farm, initially, the preproduction."

"The guy who took care of everything in the band, Richard Wall—we call him Spock for short—he actually dug up some stuff he had recorded of me, at Field Farm from way back. Black Sabbath actually recorded there at one point as well. We did all the early work for 'Junior's Eyes' and some other tracks. But Spock sent me a cassette tape of some of the early songs that I did, including 'It's Alright.' So I'm sure there's stuff floating around. But yes, Jack was great. We were there at the funeral; everybody was there for the funeral. We were in different places. I'm not sure what studio we ended up in but we were definitely in London doing the finishing touches to *Never Say Die*. So in-between there, there was a death."

"Junior's Eyes" creeps into existence on a psychedelic and funky bass line, a Bill Ward lope, and an even more psychedelic squall of noise from Tony, who takes a back seat as colourist, making heavy use of wah-wah effect. Once the chorus hits, the clouds open for a comforting but sorrowful unfurling of melody. It is Bill Ward and his big stout-of-heart fills that really imbue the song with passion, not to mention Ozzy's anguished vocal.

"'A Hard Road' was just about being on the road, in general," cites Geezer about the next one, a panoramic shuffle, trundling but somehow stately and melodic, a creative success and yet somewhat aggravating, especially come chorus time given a vocal melody that is a bit wearying (note the backward cymbal effect come solo time). Interestingly, both Geezer and Tony sing back-up vocals on this one. Tony chuckles that his backing vocal performance on that song would be his first and last—finally it was his turn to get laughed out of the room by the other guys in the band.

"Tony's solo in 'Hard Road,' I totally dug it," enthuses Bill. "We have a live version of 'Hard Road,' and I don't know where it is now. It's off one of these recent... *Past Lives*, I think it is? And man, that sounds incredible! It's just so powerful. I'm like, holy cow! Because we used to do that live too."

Indeed the song ends with voices darting in from all angles and at all frequencies, the whole band ganging up for the close of this hopeful song, Geezer writing an inspirational lyric of the world going around, people falling down and getting back up. It's vintage Butler, with an eye to the future, Geezer massaging in with motion gentle reminders that we all should clean up our act.

Side two opens with what is, essentially, *Never Say Die*'s most conventional heavy rocker. "Shock Waves" possesses no soft breaks save for a few acoustic guitar strums massaged in like we're back at *Sabbath Bloody Sabbath*. Again, Bill bashes the song into fit-as-a-fiddle shape, his drums pounded and recorded brutishly like Bonham while he turns in a performance touched by the spirit of Keith Moon, dead exactly three weeks before the album came out. Tony's solo is particularly carnal. Geezer's lyric, about the point of death, embodies a battle between good and evil typical of the man's more religion-based lyrics. Still, it's a little straightforward, lacking the unearthly patina of the man's many freaky poems.

"Air Dance" is a poignant dark paean on the subject of old age, similar in theme to one half of Rush's "Losing It," Geezer imagining an old woman time-traveling to her dance-filled youth. Musically, "Air

Dance" is a daring track, a sort of jazzy, progressive rock ballad stabbed by ugly guitar licks from Tony, chopped by jerking rhythms. Late in the sequence, it's hit with a baffling bit of Goblin-esque/Kraut-like fusion rock that really drove home the point that Sabbath had lost their marbles. Raised some eyebrows with this one, they did. "Well, yeah, definitely," agrees Bill. "It was almost like a modern jazz quartet on that one. We were definitely bordering on some jazz feels."

As a kid listening to this album, I subconsciously had paired "Over to You" with "A Hard Road," both being these languished, smeared and smudged walls of sound, heavy of a manner (me and my buddies gave the Sabs this one grudgingly), but melodic and a little under-written. Note the incongruous Liberace-like piano runs from Don Airey, placed atop a point-counterpoint prog rock section that serves somewhat as a chorus.

Says Geezer, "'Over to You,' I stole that from a Roald Dahl book I was reading at the time, called *Over to You*. The song wasn't about what the book was about, but I liked the title of it." Adds Bill, "We had a bit of a problem there, trying to get a melody. I did a ghost melody on that, to see if I could help it along a little bit. I mean, keep in mind, we were going through a major loss at the time. You know, we were scheduled to tour. In fact, I think that I may have been the last man out, on those sessions."

Despite the backing track's lazy churn, the lyric Geezer puts to it is a poisonous indictment of society, a crystallization of the communiqués the Sabs had laid out for their pessimistic, outcast fans since the days of "War Pigs" and "Paranoid." One of those is about strife from outside and above and one is about strife from within. The almost resigned, morally-void torment of "Over to You" is the result of both dualities.

Kraut-rock returns with a vengeance for the worst jazz song ever written, "Breakout." Mercifully short, this one is loaded up with non-Sabbath-specific instruments, including horn arrangements by Will Malone and prominent sax soloing, overtop a steady and hypnotic beat from Bill that again demonstrates a certain Mack-ness of tonality. Geezer has said that the sax was added upon Tony's suggestion because Ozzy wasn't around to lay on a vocal. When Ozzy finally showed up and heard the sax on it, he apparently turned tail and walked back out. Come closing time, "Breakout" breaks down, degenerating into a free jazz skronk worthy of *Trout Mask Replica*.

Ozzy's attitude was getting to Geezer. "I was getting more and more uncomfortable having to write lyrics anyway. The *Never Say Die* album had me writing lyric after lyric after lyric and Ozzy wouldn't even read them in the end. I was really getting frustrated having to come up with Ozzy's lyrics and then he would not read them. I was really pissed-off."

A question to Bill as to Tony's resentment over his having to lead the band and write all the music over the course of the last two Sabbath albums leads to a comment on "Breakout."

"Oh God, well he's a workhorse anyway. You know, Tony always has been the worker. You know, I hope Osbourne don't get pissed off or Geezer don't get pissed off. But yeah, Tony put in an incredible amount of work. I mean everybody had their own different ideas and stuff. But it's like, okay, what's acceptable and what isn't acceptable? So there would be a lot of sitting around, waiting to see what Tony might be able to bring out. I can remember the big band thing on there, 'Breakout.' Now, that particular riff, Tony was playing around with it, and he'd been playing around with it for a couple years. And every time he played it, I would rush into the room and say, 'Let's do something with that!' And it would go by the wayside until eventually he found another part to go with it (laughs) and he said, 'What do think of this?' And I thought, oh my God, this is incredible, something has to be done with it." Something did get done with it, and what you end up with is an interesting sound collage that is the wackiest thing Sabbath had done or would ever do. Sure, "Breakout" is reviled, but always with a bit of a chuckle and a shake of one's mullet. I mean, this sure as hell wasn't a case of the guys trying to write a radio single.

Never Say Die closes with what just might be the best track from either this record or the one previous, "Swinging the Chain" packing a wallop that sort of embodies all the doom and anguish of Sabbath's situation at this tiring turning point. Tony's riff is sinister but, well, it swings. His guitar tone is buried, covered with cinder blocks and rebar. Bill is brought about to sing that track, and his world-worn voice is dragged and ragged beyond recognition against the sweet McCartney-esque pipes behind "It's Alright."

Explains Graham, when asked why Bill's doing another vocal: "Well, again, it was Bill trying to help Ozzy out, if you know what I mean. Bill was like the mother hen of the band. He was trying to keep it all together all the time, Bill was. So in singing a song, he thought, 'I'm helping out, we're getting stuff down, I've got some ideas.' With songs like 'Johnny Blade,' he was almost like trying to go back to the old days. It's just the way it was at the time. 'Never say die, come on, we don't want to split this up, we want to carry on.' It was hard for them."

"The studio was a bit awkward, because when we got there, it was so dead," continues Wright. "So they wanted to liven it up and I had to go to get loads of sheets of plywood and put plywood on the floors and up against the walls to try to sort of brighten the sound up, because they didn't like the sound in there. And because they were having financial problems as well, they couldn't like just cancel it. They'd booked it! They weren't happy with the studio, they weren't happy with the weather, and it was a kind of forced album. Everything seemed to be going wrong for them at that time, which was a real shame, because they were really trying hard amongst themselves, to get back together and produce an album. It was basically that they made a mistake by going to Toronto. They should have gone somewhere warmer, like back to Miami. But see, there were distractions in Miami and in L.A. that they were trying to avoid. A band like Sabbath, you go to Miami, you've got every coke dealer in the world trying to give them coke. And that's the problem, especially in those days. And L.A. is the same. You've got the whole Sunset Strip scenario. And we'd rehearse in Wales because they were away from all that. At the end of the day, they were so down to earth; they were great guys, that if they could get away from the distractions, they'd be fine."

"You know, that was a really difficult album, because Oz was going through a lot of stuff then," says Bill, backing up Graham's assessment of the situation. "On that particular album, I put my drum tracks down, but I was also trying to be as helpful as I could in the vocal area, and trying to come up with ideas. And some of them worked and some of them didn't. Oz had been having a difficult time; there were some problems in his family. Things were pretty rough for him. As I say, I did lay some ghost vocals on 'Over to You' and I did backup vocals on 'Hard Road' and a couple of other things as well. But I did a ghost vocal and Oz came in and he liked it, so he came in and just went over my track."

"It was Bill Ward at the time," laughs Bill o'er his chain-smoker of a vocal on "Swinging the Chain." "I wish I could still sing like that, actually. I listen to it sometimes, and I go, my God, the range on it was just unbelievable. There are a lot of high notes there. It's like, wow. I just like what Tony and Geezer had put together. I thought oh man, I could get behind this, you know? And I like the big jazz thing we put on the front, 'Breakout.' I know that that came under some comments, but I thought it was fucking great. I remember I was trying to finish the last verses on 'Swinging the Chain' and I knew that the very next morning... we'd finished about 3 AM and we had to get up at 6 AM to catch a flight to the

East Coast of the United States, because we had a gig that night. So we were balls to the wall on that album."

Additional in the surprises department, "Swinging the Chain" includes loads of harmonica, supporting and soloing, torrid waves of new Iommi riffs late in the tale and a bunch of seemingly impromptu gang vocals. Plus there's an elevated section where Bill sings like Robert Plant losing his voice. All told, this is a brilliant, crushing, non-obvious rocker that proved Sabbath still could write well away from the norm. Tony's solo sounds like a noisy cross between Jimmy Page and Brian May. There are voices in this song that sound like no Sabbath member I know, but apparently Ozzy is added somewhere in the fade.

"Well, Bill wrote 'Swinging the Chain;' I think it was about Hitler or something. He knows what that's about," is Geezer's curt assessment.

Bill answers this charge—sort of. "Well, there was definitely a reference to Adolph Hitler, in the sense that, you know, at the time, vandalism was pretty rampant. So I did make a reference about vandalism, and Adolph Hitler being the biggest vandal of all. Because he really went to town on that. I just liked the title, 'Swinging the Chain.' When we were doing that at Monmouth Valley, in Wales, my all-time favourite place to be, my brother came in. And we had been to the pub and kind of drunk and everything, and Tony was playing that first riff (sings it), and my brother came into the room, and he was almost like swinging a chain, but there was no chain; it was invisible, and he was kind of getting down and rocking to it (sings it). So he was almost like dancing to it, that kind of feel, as if he had a chain in his hand. So I think that's where the title came from."

When Ozzy showed up in Toronto to do the record, the band had little in the can. Three songs had been worked up with Dave Walker, namely "Junior's Eyes," "Over to You" and this album closer, "Swinging the Chain." Ozzy had refused to sing any of Dave Walker's lyrics (he also refused to put a vocal to "Breakout"), and so we know that the former two got rewritten. But it's possible that Bill sings "Swinging the Chain" to avoid having to do a rewrite of lyrics that were at least a collaboration with Walker. Whatever the circumstance, the song gets a simple group credit, as does every song on the album. As well, perhaps Ozzy's refusal to sing any of the songs worked up when Walker was in the band was not because of lyrics per se, but just because he wanted to start fresh. Still, all the material done then, at least musically, had to be used and was used, given the writer's block Tony was experiencing at the time.

All told, "Swinging the Chain" was a momentous way to end what was to be Sabbath's last album with Oz, the God-given original Black Sabbath rocking hard but almost laboriously, definitely elliptically, with folks cast into unlikely roles. Bill in particular proves himself to be the secret artist in the band, stepping up and presaging the beauty that would present itself all over his three precious solo albums spread across the ensuing decades.

"It was going in different directions," muses Ward, upon the state of the band in 1978. "All of us were growing, all of us were still being influenced. So there was a departure from those first three records and a departure from each album thereafter. A lot of it was based on our own push/pull feels of what each individual liked. Towards the very end we allowed more jazz to come on our records than ever before. In hindsight we'd almost given ourselves permission to really just play what came, with less regard for having to maintain whatever we were in the early '70s and more about who we were on that given day. I mean, listen to Terry's bass on 'Junior's Eyes.' That's a full-on jazz riff; it's like a jazz song. We were developing, coming into our own as musicians—we were always developing."

As for how *Never Say Die* reflected a mirror back at what was going on in music at the time, "I thought that punk enhanced our music," figures Bill. "I don't really have any comments about disco, although I found myself being pissed off my ass and dancing to disco music, which if there had been a camera there it could have been quite amusing. But the focus was still on whatever we were. Like Tony would have a lick and it's like what are we going to do with that lick? Everybody knew it was good, but where's that lick going to go? What's going to happen to it?"

"What we were on those first three or four albums always existed throughout our career, but we became more honest with ourselves and allowed ourselves to step out into places which were unknown. I'm so happy that we did the vibraphone and the tubular bells and the choir on 'Supertzar.' I'm glad that Rick Wakeman played such incredible keyboards. I'm glad we did 'Spiral Architect' with all that orchestrated sound and when we did 'Junior's Eyes,' I'm glad that we went in and grew as jazz players. We'd all had a taste of that growing up as kids, Tony with Django Reinhardt, and me being brought up on Krupa, Baker and Hughie Flint."

Surprisingly, the esteemed Trouser Press, thoughtful champions of new wave at the time, were quite happy with *Never Say Die*, Jon Young writing, "I can hear all you 'critics' rattling off what you think are

Sabbath's faults. Those aren't faults; that's just the way they are! So what if the sound is muddy and you can't understand a lot of the words. Yes, I would like Bill Ward's drums to be louder, too. But Black Sabbath don't want it to sound good—if they did, it would, right? By making *Never Say Die* murky, it's just like being at the show where the instruments run together and the speakers get all hummy and it's just too much! So turn it up, and if you're too wimpy for 135dB, go back to your John Denver records. And don't accuse the Sabs of stealing; you have to admit that nobody can thunder like Black Sabbath."

"The only times I don't much like *Never Say Die* are when Sabbath forsake their lethal style. 'Johnny Blade' opens with a synthesizer, which is kind of a sissy instrument. 'Air Dance' has a break that reminds me of jazz. Gross, of course. 'Breakout' is instrumental, which is bad because that's what jazz is, and it even uses horns. Nevertheless, Sabbath are in good shape overall. They're just as deadly as they ever were, you know? There aren't too many bands who would do a song about death itself ('Shock Wave') and fewer still who could make it come to life. I mean, when you hear it, you'll just want to die."

Sabbath's *Never Say Die* tour is one of those that has been continually battered by headbanging historians as a bit of a disaster, in large part due to the contrast between the bitter infighting and boozing Sabs on one hand, mounting their "ten year anniversary" tour, and Sabbath's back-up band for a huge stretch of it, four firecrackers from California collectively called Van Halen. Heating up the crowd o'er every crease and corner of a detailed UK jaunt, and then kicking ass back in the States for interminable months on end, Van Halen were on fire, out to prove what became obvious every night, that these guys were shooting stars about to magically flare.

"I thought when they came out, they were really very good," says Tony. "But the problem was, you see, they were going on before us, and it was all new to them. And they were picking up stuff from our show. So we would do a drum solo, guitar solo and all that, and the way that Ozzy would say things, it was gradually getting put into their show. Which made it very awkward. It did cause problems, because they were on the road with us for eight months. It was sort of like our show being played twice (laughs). The same sort of chat in the middle and the same sort of antics, and then they started getting bigger drum risers and more of this and more of that. Which was great, I mean, they were all learning, and they were good players, great band. And I got very close to Eddie. We used to sit in my room and talk a lot over things. And I just got annoyed one night, and I said to Eddie, 'Eddie, are you going to play a couple numbers off our new album tomorrow?' And he says, 'Hey, man, you know...' and of course, 'Come on, let's go in my room' and we had a chat. And he said 'Look, you know, we grew up with you guys and we look to you as our influence' and whatnot, and what can you say, you know? I said, 'That's great, you know, but you can't do the same things as we're doing on the same show. When you get your own show, fine.' But they were fine, that was great. I'm glad they did what they did."

Geezer strongly concurs. "I liked them as a band, but it was like their first major tour and they ripped off everything from us (laughs). I mean, it was unbelievable. The difference from the first night, in Sheffield, England, where they just went on and did like, the Van Halen show, and by the time they got to America with us, they were doing all Ozzy's peace signs. Everything Ozzy was doing, David Lee Roth was doing. Eddie Van Halen was doing his long guitar solo because Tony was. In those days, Tony used to do like a 20-, 30-minute guitar solo. So Eddie Van Halen started doing that. I used to use a wah-wah pedal on my bass, so their bass player went out and got a wah-wah pedal. And they were doing all that before we went on. So they were doing the Sabbath show before Sabbath went on. And Tony had a go at Eddie one night (laughs), and he's going to beat the hell out of him (laughs), but he just told him to stop copying him, basically. And Eddie sort of agreed and didn't do it. But David Lee Roth still carried on ripping Ozzy off." Amusingly, Ozzy didn't mind telling the press at the time that Van Halen were so good, they ought to be headlining the tour.

"Oh, they were just having a ball!" was Graham Wright's assessment of Diamond Dave & Co. "They used to be the house band at Gazzarri's on the strip. And they just started to break the club circuit in America, and then they released that Kinks song. And then they came over to England and supported Sabbath. It was just this young band full of energy. Yeah, they were just loving every minute of it."

Bill gets the final word on Ed and the guys, and he's pretty kind about it… "Well, I knew they were influenced in the early days, but they were still in the old format, if you like, drum solo, guitar solo, bass solo. In other words, all the other bands that had come before—Zeppelin, you name it—we were all doing that same type of show. And Van Halen probably were one of the last bands to arrive and still do that. And I think on a slightly different issue, yeah, Van Halen, in the very early days, tended to watch the show and pick up a few things (laughs). But they quickly—I mean, more credit to Van Halen—I think they're such an incredible band; they moved on and formed their own pathway."

Bill figures the *Never Say Die* tour was the first one where he started using oxygen onstage. "During the real hot gigs I was starting to get tired out. Oddly enough, I don't use oxygen anymore (laughs). My health is a lot better—that's why. But back then, I was still drinking, and to get through a show… we were playing for up to two hours, and we were still playing a lot of the fast stuff and it was a hardcore show, back then at least. And so the energy I was using up... sometimes, I would just burn out onstage. I would be like 'Man, I can't even breathe, it's so hot.' So I would get a couple of hits of oxygen which would really help me to just breathe through it."

I asked Bill about his philosophy with respect to his drum solo. "Well, it was popular to do drum solos in the late '60s, because, obviously, Ginger Baker had forged the way, so to speak. So we'd all do drum solos. It was like, that's how a gig was in the late '60s and the early '70s. Stage shows were much different because they would feature the artist, Jimi Hendrix and Mitch Mitchell. All these drummers performed drum solos. So naturally we would feature Tony, obviously, and then I would do my solo. I would have a solo for 15, maybe 20 minutes. I knew different parts that I was going to go do, but a lot was left open for change or for anything that might interest me—improvisation."

"One of the things that might be good to mention at this point is that playing night after night as we did back then, it could become monotonous. So one of the great things Sabbath did was to leave out an area of about 30 to 40 minutes sometimes of improvisation. So we never quite knew what we were going to do. So we would show up in front of 30, 40, 50,000 people, not knowing what we were going to do. And it really does give us a great sense of freedom, to be able to do that, knowing where we were going but at the same time not quite knowing. Because that way surprises would happen and things would come out that we totally didn't plan."

"That was the great thing about doing the live show. There wasn't any kind of set order, if you like, as we do now. When we play Black Sabbath now, it's bam bam bam bam and that's it. It's like a set order, everybody knows what's going to happen, la di dah. And unfortunately, I think the kids know what's going to happen as well (laughs). And I say unfortunately, only because, you know, I want to think about the people who come to the shows. I think they've been very patient. I don't want to continually come to the stage and just play the same things over and over again. It's like a rip-off, almost. And so talking about Van Halen, because Al would do his solos and Eddie would do his solos, they were probably one of the last great bands to still emulate what the bands of the '60s and the early '70s had been doing."

Asked if he ever choreographed his drum solo with lights or effects, Bill chuckles, "No, we never put those things together. Yeah, that's intelligent stuff. This is primeval. Sabbath, you know; we don't think in those terms."

Given his vantage point, I asked Graham Wright to tell me a bit about the engine room of the band, the man from which you've just heard, Bill Ward, and how he did what he did live. "When I first started working for Bill, he was unorthodox. He had this totally hodgepodge kit, all different makes. Even his toms, there were different sizes, although they did range from the highest to the lowest. But it was all different colours, bits of Gretsch kits, bits of Ludwig, bits of Slingerland. His mates ran a drum shop in Birmingham called Drumland and we arranged to get this white Slingerland kit sent over from the States with the hardware not attached to it. So I spent a couple of weeks on the top floor of Fields Farm, where I used to live and I built the kit around Bill, this white Slingerland kit. He used to come over and I'd fit the hardware to the tom toms and I built it around him so it fit like a glove, basically. So it was good fun as well, and Bill got a good feel from that. It was nice to bring these shells out of the box and do all the fittings, so we were getting involved in the kit. So I built that around him and he used it for a couple of years. And then he changed to a Tama kit, a silver/grey Tama kit he used up to *Heaven and Hell*."

"He had gongs, one of those big Chinese things," continues Wright. "He used it in his drum solo. He always did a drum solo (laughs). I used to sit behind him. He had oxygen as well. I was always feeding him with these oxygen bottles and his water as well. He always had a big bottle of oxygen there. He was a hard player, Bill was. The whole kit used to be bolted down to the riser. I mean, everything was bolted down to the riser so it couldn't move. If he did lose his temper, he couldn't trash it anyway, because nothing would move. He could play double bass drums, but that was mainly for drum solos. He used to have Remo Emperor skins because they were the heaviest, hardest skins, so he hardly broke skins. If you broke a skin on the snare drum, he'd change it. He didn't like cleaning his cymbals, because he reckoned they would lose tone."

"Plus he had tympanis, but that was mainly for studio work. He even had tubular bells. He didn't use them that much; he messed around a bit. On *Sabotage* there were backwards cymbals used, 'ssssst' sounds; on the recording, just reverse the sounds. But Bill was a bit of an unorthodox drummer. He wasn't a time man. But again, the whole Sabbath sound... I mean, them four guys together just produced this brilliant sound. For the *Never Say Die* tour, he used the old drum riser from *Technical Ecstasy* but I painted it white. We just had a backdrop with those pilots' heads. There wasn't much going on. Dry ice."

No keyboardist either. Jezz was gone, Don Airey only did the album, and this is before Geoff Nicholls' long employment.

"Sabbath were a good-natured bunch to work with, I can honestly say that," muses Graham in closing. "They are good people. There wasn't the scandal. Yeah, there was the drug-taking, there were binges. But it wasn't like all the time. Never heroin, just coke, pot and booze, and to be honest, there wasn't much pot (laughs). It was more drink than anything. But even then, it wasn't like a lot of bands. There's a lot of myth that goes on about things."

And all this stuff above Bill taking over the business end of things… was he actually quite capable of doing that? "No! No, he wasn't (laughs). But he tried. Oh, he tried, he did. He was concerned and he tried. When you're talking with top lawyers from London and record company executives, you're going to be out of your depths. But he tried, and he was trying to keep his finger on the pulse and he was concerned and he just wanted the best for everybody. And you know what? I think the top people at Warner Bros., Joe Smith and that, when they met the guys, they actually liked them, you know?"

But the time was ripe for a makeover. Black Sabbath's last album of the '70s, and the band's last album with Ozzy (until the *13* reunion record), *Never Say Die* was not representative of a band going out with a bang and Geezer, for one, knows as much.

"The only time we really lost faith in it was *Never Say Die*," reflects Butler. "I think we were just going through the numbers on that album. And the press, they never forgave us for them missing out on us. The press is like… they made all the punk bands massive in England, and we were told that we were a dinosaur band and all this kind of thing. We'd only been going for like five years or something and they were calling us too old. And we were all 24, 25. And they were saying we were all past it and it was time to let the young kids take over now."

So the press was down on Sabbath, and nor were they getting respect from their label, who was suddenly becoming really tight with the dollars. Plus it was obvious Ozzy wanted out and on top of it all, everybody was worn-out, drinking too much and smoking a lot of dope, especially in Toronto.

"We seemed to be on tour endlessly, and if we weren't on tour, then we'd be in the recording studio," continues Geezer. "So we were totally wholly isolated from the rest of the world. Our little thing just moved from country to country and we could have been anywhere, because it was the same rooms, same hotel room or being in a studio room. So it seemed for four or five years like this little band of people going around the world and never going out *into* it. And we didn't really take much note of other things that were going on."

But 40 years on from *Never Say Die*, have no fear, Black Sabbath's legacy is assured, and the lion's share of the credit goes to what the band accomplished across their first eight albums.

"It *is* great," agrees Geezer, "as so many bands tell us that these days. But in the 1970s the music press hated us and the record company wasn't really into us either. They were when we were selling millions of albums, but when we were not selling as much in the late '70s, the record companies didn't want to know us anymore. After all of these years of being put down as a non-entity, we were being noted as major influences to hard rock and heavy metal bands and that is great."

"And people listen to the lyrics and they know that there is always something uplifting at the end of them," reflects Geezer in closing. "I think it's just people who are trying to score points with themselves, like local politicians or local churchmen, who complain. We haven't really had that much trouble from people these days. Usually it's a local politician that wants to score some votes by saying something negative against metal in general. We don't get that these days. The fans know much better. And thanks to them for keeping us here. Thanks for being with us for all of these years. It has been great. They really are the best fans that anyone could ever wish for. They've been with us since day one. They have been fighting for us and they are so loyal. It is incredible. We are so blessed to have them."

Discography

Black Sabbath

(Vertigo VO 6, February 13, 1970)

Side 1: 1. Black Sabbath (6:22) 2. The Wizard (4:25) 3. Behind the Wall of Sleep (3:37) 4. N.I.B. (6:07)

Side 2: 1. Evil Woman (3:27) 2. Sleeping Village (3:46) 3. Warning (10:33)

Notes: North American issue substitutes "Wicked World" for "Evil Woman" (a Crow cover). '96 Castle remaster includes both tracks. Original and very rare pressing has gatefold in black, text in grey; second pressing is white with black print. Some pressings have the intro to "Behind the Wall of Sleep" designated as "Wasp," the intro to "N.I.B." called "Bassically" and the intro to "Sleeping Village" called "A Bit of Finger."

Paranoid

(Vertigo 6360 011, September 18, 1970)

Side 1: 1. War Pigs (7:55) 2. Paranoid (2:50) 3. Planet Caravan (4:30) 4. Iron Man (6:00)

Side 2: 1. Electric Funeral (4:50) 2. Hand of Doom (7:10) 3. Rat Salad (2:30) 4. Fairies Wear Boots (6:15)

Notes: "War Pigs" includes "Luke's Wall" and "Fairies Wear Boots" includes "Jack the Stripper"—depending where you look, it's not clear with respect to either's intro or outro status.

Master of Reality

(Vertigo 6360 050, July 21, 1971)

Side 1: 1. Sweet Leaf (5:02) 2. After Forever (5:25) 3. Embryo (0:30) 4. Children of the Grave (5:15)

Side 2: 1. Orchid (2:00) 2. Lord of This World (4:55) 3. Solitude (5:02) 4. Into the Void (6:12)

Notes: Some versions list "Solitude" as 8:08 with "Into the Void" as 3:08, with no blank band in-between them. "Solitude" is in fact 5:02 with "Into the Void" clocking in at 6:12. "Embryo" is also erroneously timed on some issues. Original pressing was housed in "flip-top" box with poster. Some issues of *Master of Reality* include the following "extra song" shenanigans:

1) "After Forever" listed as "After Forever (including The Elegy);" 2) "Children of the Grave" being followed by "The Haunting" (0:45); 3) a named segment called "Step Up" (0:30) between "Orchid" and "Lord of This World," and 4) a listing for "Death Mask" (3:08) before "Into the Void."

Vol 4

(Vertigo 6360 071, September 25, 1972)

Side 1: 1. Wheels of Confusion (8:00) 2. Tomorrow's Dream (3:08) 3. Changes (4:41) 4. FX (1:41) 5. Supernaut (4:43)

Side 2: 1. Snowblind (5:28) 2. Cornucopia (4:52) 3. Laguna Sunrise (2:50) 4. St. Vitus Dance (2:25) 5. Under the Sun (5:52)

Notes: On some copies (and as with previous albums, only in some locations) outro to "Wheels of Confusion" is called "The Straightener;" outro to "Under the Sun" is called "Every Day Comes and Goes." Original pressing with four-page stitched-in insert. Other later pressings with back-shot live shot only.

Sabbath Bloody Sabbath

(WWA WWA 005, December 1, 1973)

Side 1: 1. Sabbath Bloody Sabbath (5:35) 2. A National Acrobat (6:20) 3. Fluff (4:10) 5. Sabbra Cadabra (5:55)

Side 2: 1. Killing Yourself to Live (5:35) 2. Who Are You (4:10) 3. Looking for Today (5:00) 4. Spiral Architect (4:40)

Notes: Some versions feature "Killing Yourself to Live" with the subtitles "You Think that I'm Crazy" and "I Don't Know if I'm Up or Down," but these are rare. Lyric sleeve in some issues, lyric insert in others. Original pressing was gatefold with psychedelic naked-in-bedroom band shot.

Sabotage

(NEMS 9119 001, July 28, 1975)

Side 1: 1. Hole in the Sky (4:01) 2. Don't Start (Too Late) (0:49) 3. Symptom of the Universe (6:29) 4. Megalomania (9:46)

Side 2: 1. The Thrill of It All (5:55) 2. Supertzar (3:42) 3. Am I Going Insane (Radio) (4:13) 4. The Writ (8:17)

Notes: Some pressings include a quiet 0:23 joke song called "Blow on a Jug" tacked on at the end of "The Writ," but not designated in print as being there. *Sabotage* features the most basic packaging of all the Ozzy-era Sabbath albums, i.e. no gates, inner sleeves, inserts or other goodies.

Technical Ecstasy

(Vertigo 9102 750, September 25, 1976)

Side 1: 1. Back Street Kids (3:46) 2. You Won't Change Me (6:34) 3. It's Alright (3:58) 4. Gypsy (5:10)

Side 2: 1. All Moving Parts (Stand Still) (4:59) 2. Rock 'n' Roll Doctor (3:25) 3. She's Gone (4:51) 4. Dirty Women (7:15)

Notes: Lyric sleeve in some issues, lyric insert in others.

Never Say Die

(Vertigo 9102 751, September 28, 1978)

Side 1: 1. Never Say Die (3:47) 2. Johnny Blade (6:27) 3. Junior's Eyes (6:41) 4. A Hard Road (6:03)

Side 2: 1. Shock Wave (5:13) 2. Air Dance (5:15) 3. Over to You (5:21) 4. Breakout (2:36) 5. Swinging the Chain (4:18)

Notes: "Schematics" sleeve included, but not lyrics. Technically there is an exclamation mark in the title (as demonstrated on the cover but rarely elsewhere), but it has standardized over time without it.

Interviews with the Author

Allom, Tom. 2009.

Anderson, Ian. September 28, 2001.

Atkins, Al, June 1998.

Atkins, Al, February 17, 2006.

Atkins, Al, 2009.

Branker, Don. 2009.

Butler, Geezer. May 20, 1997.

Butler, Geezer. November 1998.

Butler, Geezer. April 10, 2001.

Butler, Geezer. June 14, 2004.

Butler, Geezer. April 29, 2005.

Butler, Geezer. May 16, 2005.

Butler, Geezer. August 4, 2005.

Butler, Geezer. January 8, 2007.

Butler, Geezer. August 13, 2008.

Cefalu, Ernie. 2009.

Cope, Malcolm. January 7, 2015.

Hopkins, Mick. December 9, 2014.

Iommi, Tony. November 1998.

Iommi, Tony. October 17, 2000.

Iommi, Tony. November 10, 2004.

Iommi, Tony. February 21, 2005.

Iommi, Tony. September 1, 2005.

Iommi, Tony. 2007.

Iommi, Tony. March 26, 2009.

Osbourne, Ozzy. November 5, 1997.

Osbourne, Ozzy. November 1998.

Osbourne, Ozzy. October 5, 2001.

Powell, Aubrey. July 14, 2016.

Simpson, Jim. 2009.

Tangye, David. October 25, 2004.

Tsangarides, Chris, February 16, 2006.

Tsangarides, Chris, 2009.

Wakeman, Rick. May 7, 2004.

Ward, Bill. July 28, 1997.

Ward, Bill. November 1998.

Ward, Bill. April 11, 2001.

Ward, Bill. June 2, 2002.

Ward, Bill. November 13, 2003.

Ward, Bill. June 14, 2004.

Ward, Bill. March 29, 2005.

Ward, Bill. 2009.

Ward, Bill. May 1, 2015.

Woodruffe, Jezz. October 20, 2004.

Wright, Graham. October 29, 2004.

Wyper, Olav. 2009.

Additional Citations

Bronson, Howard. Black Sabbath: No Downer Group. 1972.

Circus. Raw Rock from Birmingham England. 1971. Circus Enterprises Corporation, 747 Third Avenue, New York, NY 10017.

Circus. 'Snowbird' – Black Sabbath Tumbles into Mantovani's Orchestra Pit by Michele Hush. October 1972. Circus Enterprises Corporation, 747 Third Avenue, New York, NY 10017

Circus. Why Black Sabbath Hates America by Barbara Graustark. Vol. 7, No. 5, February 1973. Circus Enterprises Corporation, 747 Third Avenue, New York, NY 10017.

Circus. 'Sabbath Bloody Sabbath'—Black Sabbath Hits a Happy Note by Kathleen Stein. March 1974, Vol. 8, No. 6. Circus Enterprises Corporation, 747 Third Avenue, New York, NY 10017.

Circus. Sabbath's *Sabotage* by Mick Houghton. October 1974, No. 119. Circus Enterprises Corporation, 747 Third Avenue, New York, NY 10017.

Circus. Black Sabbath's Ozzy Osbourne: "I've Got Bats and Eight or Nine Stray Black Cats" by Scott Cohen. No. 122, November 1975. Circus Enterprises Corporation, 115 East 57th St., New York, NY 10022.

Circus Raves. Black Sabbath by Barbara Graustark. Vol. 1, No. 1, January 1974. Canadian APAG House Publications Ltd., 1330 Michaud, Drummondville, QC, Canada.

Circus Raves. Black Sabbath's Bill Ward Reveals the Black Brotherhood by Kathi Stein and Robbie Granit. Vol. 1, No. 5, July 1974. Canadian APAG House Publications Ltd., 1330 Michaud, Drummondville, QC, Canada.

Classic Rock Revisited. Interviews with Geezer Butler, Tony Iommi and Bill Ward by Jeb Wright. classicrockrevisited.com.

Creem. Black Sabbath Don't Scare Nobody by Ed Kelleher. Volume 3, Number 7, December 1971.

Creem. *Sabbath Bloody Sabbath* record review by Wayne Robbins. April 1974.

Creem. Close-Up: Metal. An Exciting Interview with Black Sabbath by Sharon Liveten. September 1985. Cambray Publishing, Inc., 210 South Woodward Avenue, Suite 209, Birmingham, MI 48011.

Discoveries. "Sabbath Bloody Sabbath": The Enduring Riff-Rock of Black Sabbath by Paul Gabriel. Issue 97, June 1996. P.O. Box 1050, Dubuque, IA 52004-1050.

Dmme.net. Interview with Dave Walker by Dmitry Epstein. May 2008.

Dunn, Sam. Interviews with Geezer Butler, Jim Simpson, Bill Ward and Olav Wyper. 2009.

Guitar Player. Interview with Tony Iommi by Steven Rosen. October 1974.

High Times. The Wizdom of Oz by Chris Simunek. No. 283, March 1999. Trans-High Corporation, 235 Park Avenue South, 5th Floor, New York, NY 10003.

Hit Parader. Black Sabbath – Laying Off. 1972. Charlton Publications, Charlton Bldg., Derby, CT 06418.

Let It Rock. *Vol 4* record review by Max Bell. December 1972.

Live Wire. The Great and Powerful Oz! by Mike Smith. Vol. 7, No. 9, September 1997. J.Q. Adams Productions, Inc. 28 West 25th. St., New York, NY 10010.

Logan, Nick. Black Sabbath: Simple and Basic. 1971.

Melody Maker. Black Sabbath: Paranoid by Harry Doherty. October 11, 1975.

Melody Maker. Black Sabbath: Hammersmith Odeon by Harry Doherty. November 1, 1975.

Metal Maniacs. Black Sabbath: Forefathers Reunite by Peter Moses. Feb. '93. The Sterling/Mcfadden Partnership, 355 Lexington Avenue, New York, New York 10017.

Mix. Classic Tracks: Black Sabbath's "Paranoid" by Russell H. Tice. January 1, 1999.

New Musical Express, The. To Knock or Not to Knock the Rock by Keith Altham. April 14, 1973.

New Musical Express, The. Black Sabbath: Sabbath Days of Rest by Keith Altham. September 1, 1973.

New Musical Express, The. *Sabotage* record review by Mick Farren. October 11, 1975.

New Musical Express, The. Ozzy Osbourne: I Got Sensitive Didn't I by Tony Stewart. October 23, 1976.

New Musical Express, The. Ozzy Osbourne: Beyond Black Sabbath by Tony Stewart. December 3, 1977.

Ram. Observe the Sabbath by Kate Phillips. No. 20, December 5, 1975. Ram, Box 281, P.O. Broadway, N.S.W., 2007, Australia.

Rolling Stone. *Black Sabbath* record review by Lester Bangs. 1970.

Rolling Stone. Cream on Ice. May 13, 1971. 625 Third Street, San Francisco CA, 94107.

Rolling Stone. How Black Was My Sabbath by Robin Green. No. 94, October 28, 1971. 625 Third Street, San Francisco CA, 94107.

Rosen, Steven. Interview with Ozzy Osbourne. 1974.

Scene. Black Sabbath, 1975 by Cliff Michalski. Vol. 6, No. 29, July 24 – 31, 1975. Toledo, Ohio.

Sounds. Black Sabbath: Technical Knock-Out by Steve Rosen. January 22, 1977.

Southern Cross. Interview – Tony Iommi, by various fan club members. Issue 19, March 1997. Black Sabbath Fan Club PO Box 177, Crewe, CW2 7SZ, England.

Trouser Press. *Never Say Die* record review by Jon Young. December 1978.

Vintage Guitar. The Masters of Reality Return by Lisa Sharken. Vol. 13, No. 4, January 1999. PO Box 7301, Bismarck, ND 58507.

Webb, Julie. Black Sabbath: Gradual Change and Live Gigs. 1973.

Zimmerman, Deane. Interview with Ozzy Osbourne. 1978.

Zoo World. *Vol 4* record review by Jim Esposito. November 25, 1972.

Credits

Front cover photo of Ozzy Osbourne and back cover photo of Tony Iommi and Bill Ward © Rich Galbraith, who also kindly provided the live photography in the two tipped-in colour sections.

The graphic design and layout of this book is by Eduardo Rodriguez, who can be reached at eduardobwbk@gmail.com. Pleasure working with the guy—he's done about 25 for me now.

John Chronis, a buddy of mine who has helped out with some of my previous books, has once again turned his eagle eye to copy editing for me.

Mohammed Osama is an inspirational friend of mine and a huge Sabbath fan that has encouraged me for years to get my original Sabbath book back into circulation in some form. He's helped with research and articles to get me going and I thank him for his positive attitude, scholarship and friendship.

About the Author

At approximately 7900 (with over 7000 appearing in his books), Martin has unofficially written more record reviews than anybody in the history of music writing across all genres. Additionally, Martin has penned approximately 77 books on hard rock, heavy metal, classic rock and record collecting. He was Editor In Chief of the now retired Brave Words & Bloody Knuckles, Canada's foremost metal publication for 14 years, and has also contributed to Revolver, Guitar World, Goldmine, Record Collector, bravewords.com, lollipop.com and hardradio.com, with many record label band bios and liner notes to his credit as well. Additionally, Martin has been a regular contractor to Banger Films, having worked for two years as researcher on the award-wining documentary *Rush: Beyond the Lighted Stage*, on the writing and research team for the 11-episode *Metal Evolution* and on the ten-episode *Rock Icons*, both for VH1 Classic. Additionally, Martin is the writer of the original metal genre chart used in *Metal: A Headbanger's Journey* and throughout the *Metal Evolution* episodes. Martin currently resides in Toronto and can be reached through martinp@inforamp.net or www.martinpopoff.com.

Martin Popoff
A Complete Bibliography

Sabotage! Black Sabbath in the Seventies (2018)

Welcome to My Nightmare: 50 Years of Alice Cooper (2018)

Judas Priest: Decade of Domination (2018)

Popoff Archive – 6: American Power Metal (2018)

Popoff Archive – 5: European Power Metal (2018)

The Sun Goes Down: Thin Lizzy 1977-83 (2018)

The Clash: All the Albums, All the Songs (2018)

Led Zeppelin: All the Albums, All the Songs (2017)

AC/DC: Album by Album (2017)

Lights Out: Surviving the '70s with UFO (2017)

Tornado of Souls: Thrash's Titanic Clash (2017)

Caught in a Mosh: The Golden Era of Thrash (2017)

Rush: Album by Album (2017)

Beer Drinkers and Hell Raisers: The Rise of Motörhead (2017)

Metal Collector: Gathered Tales from Headbangers (2017)

Hit the Lights: The Birth of Thrash (2017)

Popoff Archive – 4: Classic Rock (2017)

Popoff Archive – 3: Hair Metal (2017)

From Dublin to Jailbreak: Thin Lizzy 1969-76 (2016)

Popoff Archive – 2: Progressive Rock (2016)

Popoff Archive – 1: Doom Metal (2016)

Rock the Nation: Montrose, Gamma and Ronnie Redefined (2016)

Punk Tees: The Punk Revolution in 125 T-Shirts (2016)

Metal Heart: Aiming High with Accept (2016)

Ramones at 40 (2016)

Time and a Word: The Yes Story (2016)

Kickstart My Heart: A Mötley Crüe Day-by-Day (2015)

This Means War: The Sunset Years of the NWOBHM (2015)

Wheels of Steel: The Explosive Early Years of the NWOBHM (2015)

Swords And Tequila: Riot's Classic First Decade (2015)

Who Invented Heavy Metal? (2015)

Sail Away: Whitesnake's Fantastic Voyage (2015)

Live Magnetic Air: The Unlikely Saga of the Superlative Max Webster (2014)

Steal Away the Night: An Ozzy Osbourne Day-by-Day (2014)

The Big Book of Hair Metal (2014)

Sweating Bullets: The Deth and Rebirth of Megadeth (2014)

Smokin' Valves: A Headbanger's Guide to 900 NWOBHM Records (2014)

The Art of Metal (co-edit with Malcolm Dome; 2013)

2 Minutes to Midnight: An Iron Maiden Day-by-Day (2013)

Metallica: The Complete Illustrated History (2013); update and reissue (2016)

Rush: The Illustrated History (2013); update and reissue (2016)

Ye Olde Metal: 1979 (2013)

Scorpions: Top of the Bill (2013); updated and reissued as Wind of Change: The Scorpions Story (2016)

Epic Ted Nugent (2012); updated and reissued as Motor City Madhouse: Going Gonzo with Ted Nugent (2017)

Fade To Black: Hard Rock Cover Art of the Vinyl Age (2012)

It's Getting Dangerous: Thin Lizzy 81-12 (2012)

We Will Be Strong: Thin Lizzy 76-81 (2012)

Fighting My Way Back: Thin Lizzy 69-76 (2011)

The Deep Purple Royal Family: Chain of Events '80 – '11 (2011); reissued as The Deep Purple Family Year by Year Volume Two (1980-2011) (2018)

The Deep Purple Royal Family: Chain of Events Through '79 (2011); reissued as The Deep Purple Family Year by Year (to 1979) (2016)

Black Sabbath FAQ (2011)

The Collector's Guide to Heavy Metal: Volume 4: The '00s (2011; co-authored with David Perri)

Goldmine Standard Catalog of American Records 1948 – 1991, 7th Edition (2010)

Goldmine Record Album Price Guide, 6th Edition (2009)

Goldmine 45 RPM Price Guide, 7th Edition (2009)

A Castle Full of Rascals: Deep Purple '83 – '09 (2009)

Worlds Away: Voivod and the Art of Michel Langevin (2009)

Ye Olde Metal: 1978 (2009)

Gettin' Tighter: Deep Purple '68 – '76 (2008)

All Access: The Art of the Backstage Pass (2008)

Ye Olde Metal: 1977 (2008)

Ye Olde Metal: 1976 (2008)

Judas Priest: Heavy Metal Painkillers (2007)

Ye Olde Metal: 1973 to 1975 (2007)

The Collector's Guide to Heavy Metal: Volume 3: The Nineties (2007)

Ye Olde Metal: 1968 to 1972 (2007)

Run For Cover: The Art of Derek Riggs (2006)

Black Sabbath: Doom Let Loose (2006)

Dio: Light Beyond the Black (2006)

The Collector's Guide to Heavy Metal: Volume 2: The Eighties (2005)

Rainbow: English Castle Magic (2005)

UFO: Shoot Out the Lights (2005)

The New Wave of British Heavy Metal Singles (2005)

Blue Öyster Cult: Secrets Revealed! (2004); update and reissue (2009); updated and reissued as Agents of Fortune: The Blue Öyster Cult Story (2016)

Contents Under Pressure: 30 Years of Rush at Home & Away (2004)

The Top 500 Heavy Metal Albums of All Time (2004)

The Collector's Guide to Heavy Metal: Volume 1: The Seventies (2003)

The Top 500 Heavy Metal Songs of All Time (2003)

Southern Rock Review (2001)

Heavy Metal: 20th Century Rock and Roll (2000)

The Goldmine Price Guide to Heavy Metal Records (2000)

The Collector's Guide to Heavy Metal (1997)

Riff Kills Man! 25 Years of Recorded Hard Rock & Heavy Metal (1993)

See martinpopoff.com for complete details and ordering information.

www.ingramcontent.com/pod-product-compliance
Lightning Source LLC
LaVergne TN
LVHW012113170826
845678LV00001BA/24

* 9 7 8 1 9 1 2 7 8 2 3 1 4 *